Petra Eckhard
Chronotopes of the Uncanny

Lettre

Petra Eckhard (Dr. phil.) teaches American Literature at the University of Graz (Austria). Her research interests include contemporary American prose literature, graphic narratives, and American gothic fiction.

Petra Eckhard
Chronotopes of the Uncanny
Time and Space in Postmodern New York Novels.
Paul Auster's »City of Glass« and Toni Morrison's »Jazz«

[transcript]

The printing of this book was supported by Bundesministerium für Wissenschaft und Forschung in Wien, Österreichische Forschungsgemeinschaft and University of Graz.

**Bibliographic Information published by
the Deutsche Nationalbibliothek**
The Deutsche Nationalbibliothek lists this publication in the Deutsche Nationalbibliografie; detailed bibliographic data are available in the Internet at http://dnb.d-nb.de

© 2011 transcript Verlag, Bielefeld

All rights reserved. No part of this book may be reprinted or reproduced or utilized in any form or by any electronic, mechanical, or other means, now known or hereafter invented, including photocopying and recording, or in any information storage or retrieval system, without permission in writing from the publisher.

Cover concept: Kordula Röckenhaus, Bielefeld
Cover illustration: photocase.com, © cw-design
Proofread & typeset by Petra Eckhard
Graphics (Fig.1 and Fig.2): Roman Klug
Printed and bound in Great Britain by
Marston Book Services Ltd, Oxfordshire
ISBN 978-3-8376-1841-9

Contents

Acknowledgements | 7
Introduction | 9

PART ONE: ORIENTATIONS

The Uncanny: Towards a Definition | 27
Freud | 28
Todorov | 32

Chronotopoetics | 41
Schlosszeit | 45
Stadtzeit | 58

PART TWO: CHRONOTOPES OF THE UNCANNY

Uncanny Architextures: Paul Auster's *City of Glass* | 69
The Labyrinthine Subject | 73
Uncanny Verticality | 83
Ghostly Glass | 91
Rhetoric and Ruins | 105
Quinn's *Camera Obscura* | 114
The Uncanny Comic | 120

Haunted Harlem: Toni Morrison's *Jazz* | 129
Rural Pasts, Urban Presents | 133
Jazz Space | 140
Memory Tracks and Sidewalk Cracks | 150
Black Interiors | 164
The Uncanny Voice | 171

Conclusion | 181
Works Cited | 189

Acknowledgements

This study has benefited from the comments and criticism of many people. First of all, I thank my doctoral supervisors Walter Hölbling and Klaus Rieser for their continuous support of and guidance through the project. I would also like to thank Daniel Gethmann who has been a dedicated reader and critic of earlier drafts and who provided valuable reading material on cultural and urban theory. A very warm thank you goes to Justine Tally for her effective feedback on the Morrison chapter. The graphic design work for the *Stadtzeit* and *Schlosszeit* charts was developed by Roman Klug, to whom I also owe my sincere gratitude.

Most of the research for this study was conducted during a research fellowship at the Graduate Center of The City University of New York, which was funded by the Karl-Franzens-University Graz. I am especially grateful to Joshua Wilner, Professor of English and Comparative Literature at CUNY, from whom I received not only administrative assistance but also generous hospitality during my stay in New York. Finally, I would like to thank my family without whose financial and emotional support this book would not have taken shape.

A version of the chapter 'Uncanny Verticality' was published as: "Getting Up, Down, and Lost: Vertical Mobility in Paul Auster's *City of Glass*. *Exploring Spaces: Practices and Perspectives*. Eds. Dorothea Steiner and Sabine Danner. Wien/Berlin: LIT, 2009. Portions of the chapter on Toni Morrison entitled 'Haunted Harlem: Toni Morrison's *Jazz*' appeared in Michal Peprník's and Matthew Sweney's volume *New York: Cradle of America's Cultural Plurality* (2007) under the title "Haunted Harlem: The Urban Uncanny in Morrison's *Jazz*.

Introduction

Visitors to Rachel Whiteread's sculptures and installations always come across something strange: a village of old, illuminated dollhouses that suggest a living presence inside, a vast concrete rectangle with walls of books and double doors that both face inwards – the latter being the Holocaust Memorial at Vienna's *Judenplatz* constructed in 2000 to commemorate the deaths of about 65.000 Austrian Jews killed by the Nazis between 1938 and 1945. The estrangement that radiates from Whiteread's sculptures is rooted in the tension that is produced when inner spaces are physically turned inside out and thus are made visible to the public eye. Her best known work, entitled "House" (1993) is the concrete cast taken from the inner spaces of an abandoned late-Victorian row house in which Whiteread used to live. For her, the negative double of the house functions as an architectural exposure of the empty 'home' – an inverted intimate inside that materializes personal histories, feelings of memory but also absence, forgetting, and loss. The private and the imaginary, suddenly, become the physical objects of the public gaze.[1]

In "Space-Time and the Politics of Location," Doreen Massey rightly argues that the ghostliness of "House" results from the disruption of our traditional conceptions of time and space:

["House"] worked this disruption, first and most obviously, in a predominantly temporal sense. It set a familiar past in the space-time of today; it made present something which was absent; it was the space of a house no longer there. Secondly, however, it worked spatially: it turned the space inside-out. The

---

1   For a more elaborate discussion of Whiteread's work, see Anthony Vidler, *Warped Space*, 143-149.

private was open to public view [...] the intimate was made monumental and yet retained its intimacy. (49)

The dialogic interactions between the past and the present and the private and the public that are captured in Whiteread's monumental art create in us a feeling of unease or obscurity, not only because the familiar turns into something strange but also because forgotten history takes on physical shape. In "House," Whiteread gives material form to the personal narratives of different people who once inhabited the old Victorian house; with the Holocaust Memorial, she reminds us of the uncountable and inaccessible traumatic memories of death and destruction that the holocaust left behind. Thus, architectural space becomes allegoric for the workings of the human mind and, more specifically, for the unveiling of subconscious processes. Analisa Violich Goodin argues that Whiteread's Holocaust Memorial captures the trauma and the impossibility of its representation in that it "implicitly signals not only that one sculpture is inadequate to the task, but that even an entire library could never tell the story" (49).

Whiteread's works are *uncanny*. They trigger in us uncertainty, disturbance, and doubt as the boundaries between the living and the dead are heavily blurred. They challenge rational modes of knowledge because they confuse the spatial (inner/outer) and temporal (past/present) dimensions of reality. More specifically, they echo the Freudian understanding of the uncanny, according to which "everything that was intended to remain secret, hidden away, [comes] into the open" ("The Uncanny" 132)[2]. In other words, Freud believes that the uncanny manifests itself when the repressed aspects buried in our unconscious suddenly return.[3]

What is even more important, though: Whiteread's sculptures mark the emergence of a postmodern uncanny in the 1990s which is largely

---

2   Throughout this paper the reference entry for Freud's essay "The Uncanny" will be abbreviated with U.
3   While the uncanny has been a dominant motif in Western art and culture ever since the Gothic revival in the eighteenth century, it is not *avant* Freud that it is put into direct relation with the workings of the human unconscious. However, Freud's analysis was not significantly expanded any further until the 1970s, when it reemerged in the post-structuralist studies of Hélène Cixous and Jacques Derrida.

concerned with the collapse of fixed spatial categories and the end of linear temporality. As a visualization of postmodern tropes such as homelessness, restlessness, and memory, Whiteread captures the spirit of the 1990s – an age in which virtual realities, cyberspace, avatars and other products of the new communication technologies start to confuse fixed categories of time and space and thus make the familiar strange. The 1990s have also seen the emergence of trauma studies and the re-emergence of memory discourses, a phenomenon that Andreas Huyssen attributes to the "globalization of Holocaust discourse" (*Present Pasts* 13). For him, "the recurrence of genocidal politics in Rwanda, Bosnia, and Kosovo in the allegedly posthistorical 1990s" (ibid.) signal a repetition of historical trauma on a global scale. Trauma discourses are characterized by a radical destabilization of time, space, and identity, resulting from the mere impossibility of a coherent representation of personal or collective catastrophes. Therefore, representations of trauma are created along the lines of temporal and spatial paradox as they have to rely on the stylistic translation of the involuntary revisiting of past times and spaces.

As a result of the renewed interest in trauma and memory discourses in the 1990s, various academic disciplines devoted their interest and research to the uncanny. Hal Foster's *Compulsive Beauty* (1993), Anthony Vidler's *The Architectural Uncanny* (1994), Jacques Derrida's *Specters of Marx* (1994), Terry Castle's *The Female Thermometer: 18th Century Culture and the Invention of the Uncanny* (1995), or Mladen Dolar's "I Shall be with You on Your Wedding-Night: Lacan and the Uncanny" (1991), are only the most important scholarly works that prove that the uncanny, as Martin Jay has rightly argued, was "the master trope" (20) of the 1990s. Also in American popular culture the uncanny reemerged in the top-selling horror fictions of Stephen King and in the vast number of vampire-themed movies which sprung from this period. Among the most notable examples being Coppola's *Dracula* (1992), Tarantino's *From Dusk Till Dawn* (1996), Carpenter's *John Carpenter's Vampires* (1998) or Norrington's *Blade* (1998).

In *After the End of History*, Samuel S. Cohen classifies the 1990s as "a time between wars" (6), a period that was framed by the end of the Cold War and the beginning of new wars, such as the culture wars, or the war on terror. Although the last decade of the twentieth century saw the demise of Communism, thus soothing the fear of nuclear bomb attacks, in the USA new anxieties were fuelled by the Bush administration and its manipulation of the mainstream media. Social and economical pathologies, acts of home-made terrorism, such as the Oklahoma City Bombing in 1995 and the rise of supremacist hate groups were the main symptoms that led to a growing distrust in the federal government and a deep sense of insecurity towards the nation's global future.

However, the late twentieth century signified not only an era of political and cultural fears but also the era of a more philosophical crisis. When, in the 1980s, Baudrillard noted that Western societies are experiencing "the death of the real," induced by the new media and simulated spaces such as Disneyworld, he already signaled that information technologies producing copies, clones, and cyborgs were to become a major threat not only to empiricism but also to humanity in general. Postmodern subjectivities and realities, indeed, seem to be uncontrollable and indefinable. The postmodern world, as Maria Beville suggests, has become horrific also because "the absolutes of reality and self are not representable but suggestable" (29). The renewed interest in conspiracy theories in the 1990s concerning a 'New World Order' which signified the attempt of anti-globalizers to unveil and expose 'the truth' about the workings of political leadership and the global market also pays tribute to the fact that the threat of unseen forces operating behind the scenes (and screens) was among the key-concerns of late twentieth century culture. Films like *The Truman Show* (1998) or Dan Brown's *The Da Vinci Code* (2000) confirm that the hermeneutics of suspicion also stimulated the discourses in popular culture.

The uncanny, as we have seen, is deeply concerned with all that is unrepresentable. For Freud, it is death or our own mortality that cannot be represented. For Derrida, it is the original presence of an object that cannot be signified. In *Specters of Marx* (1994), Derrida introduces the term *hauntologie*, which he directly relates to his concept of *différence*, denoting the notion that the meaning of signs (or words) is never fixed but always deferred. In other words, the true origin of a sign is always spectral. More broadly speaking, Derrida's *hauntologie* – a combination of the Heideggerian and Freudian uncanny – concerns the notion that living in the present is always affected by (ghosts of) the past. Thus, *hauntologie* also covers the spectral presence of cultural traumas (such as the Holocaust or 9/11) – unpleasant, shocking experiences that we repress and choose not to articulate. Derrida's Gothic idiom also indicates that the uncanny shares many conceptual similarities with postmodern theory. These similarities concern the problematization of a reality in which categories of time and space have become unstable. In "The Contemporary Gothic," Steven Bruhm explains that the reemergence and popularity of the Gothic genre in the late twentieth century can be attributed to the loss and fragmentation of all that which once constituted stable meaning, truth, and identities:

We need [the Gothic] because the twentieth century has so forcefully taken away from us that which we once thought constituted us – a coherent psyche, a social order to which we can pledge allegiance in good faith, a sense of justice in the universe – and that wrenching withdrawal, that traumatic experience, is vividly dramatized in the Gothic. (273)

Ultimately, it is via the Gothic, or its subcategory of the uncanny, that the unrepresentable finds its most accurate representation. And it is postmodern techniques which help us to understand and (mentally) visualize the horrors of postmodernity. Self-reflexivity, pastiche, intertextuality or the blurring of fact and fiction not only can serve the purpose of metafictional play or stylistic radicalization (as exemplified by Charles Moore's *Piazza d'Italia* or the fictions of early post-modernists such as William Gass or John Barth) but can also generate highly uncanny effects. Deconstructed forms are *a priori* disquieting because they do not fulfill our expectations as readers or observers. Los Angeles' Bonaventure Hotel, for example, has become a landmark of postmodern architecture because its visitors are confronted with a collection of signs that mainly serve the purpose of disorientation and spatial estrangement. Most of its guests prefer not to stay but only to witness the confusion for a little while.

In art and architecture, however, making the familiar strange is not a distinctively postmodern phenomenon but has been a *leitmotif* ever since modernism. Brecht's 'alienation effect' or Duchamp's 'ready-mades,' for example, clearly express a negative 'cast' of what once was familiar. Also Jo Collins and John Jervis argue that the uncanny captures the spirit of modernity because "a reflexive 'defamiliarization' [is] central to its programmes for artistic reinvention and renewal" (4). They continue: "'[M]aking the world strange' prepares the way for its inevitable return in disturbing, unrecognized form, in turn a central theme in Surrealism, along with its fascination with the dream, poised uncertainly between sleeping and waking" (ibid.).[4]

Interestingly, it was Freud who also associated the readability of the unconscious mind with the readability of the city. In his lectures on psychoanalysis, he compared monuments in London or the epochal history of Rome's architecture to the trauma history of his patients. Freud often claimed that the work of the psychoanalyst resembles the work of an archeologist and/or detective, because the latter also investigate and reveal all that is inconspicuous and hidden (Zinganel 49). However, it was not before Walter Benjamin's work on modern urbanism that the scholarly work on the uncanny was significantly developed further, since it "extract[ed] the *unheimlich* out of its purely psychological or aesthetic context, and ma[de] it into a category with larger social and cultural implications" (Jay 22). Benjamin's *magnum opus* entitled *The Arcades Project* locates the uncanny in the Parisian arcades of the late nineteenth and early twentieth centuries, a space that for him was populated by ghosts of the past.[5] Also the glass and marble architecture of the arcades were seen by Benjamin as a ghostly new space of inbetweenness – a transitory zone where interior and exterior space merge into one. For Benjamin, modern city life was *a priori* phantasmagoric, because the vast number and juxtaposition of visual signs such as commodity goods displayed in shopping windows, or the anonymous, heterogeneous crowd made the urban experience dreamlike and ghostly. Benjamin generally attributes this ghostliness of the city to the multiplicity and juxtaposition of spatial and temporal markers. In *The Arcades Project*, Benjamin quotes Ferdinand Lion, who vividly illustrates this point:

---

4 For an extensive study on the uncanny in surrealism, see Hal Foster, *Compulsive Beauty*.

5 One of the numerous references to spectral presences can be found in the section entitled "The Streets of Paris" in which he writes: "The name of the 'Chateau d'Eau,' a former fountain that is no longer there, still today haunts several city quarters" (643).

The most heterogeneous temporal elements thus coexist in the city. If we step from an eighteenth-century house into one from the sixteenth century, we tumble down the slope of time. Right next door stands a Gothic church, and we sink to the depths. A few steps farther, we are in a street from out of the early years of Bismarck's rule [...], and once again climbing the mountain of time. Whoever sets foot in a city feels caught up as in a web of dreams, where the most remote past is linked to the events of today. One house allies with another, no matter what period they come from, and a street is born. (M 9.4, 435)

Also in sociological terms, the modern city has always been an expression of class and ethnic heterogeneity which resulted in the formation of social dichotomies, including the private subject and the anonymous mass, or the self and the other. The social reality of the modern city is characterized by a complexity that involves the convergence of social norms and lifestyles and therefore runs counter to objectifiable regularities. In this non-totalizable, unordered space, as Julian Wolfreys asserts, also the subject "remain[s] indefinite, provisional in his or her identity, and thus subject to the uncanny arrival of some other" (172).

In "The Metropolis and Mental Life" (1903), Georg Simmel has noted that the estrangement of the urban subject can also be contributed to the 'lived' sensory experience of the city, i.e., "the intensification of nervous stimulation which results from the swift and uninterrupted change of outer and inner stimuli" (13) that people do not experience when living in rural areas. Simmel goes on:

With each crossing of the street, with the tempo and multiplicity of economic, occupational and social life, the city sets up a deep contrast with small town and rural life with reference to the sensory foundations of psychic life. The metropolis exacts from man as a discriminating creature a different amount of consciousness than does rural life. Here the rhythm of life and sensory mental imagery flows more slowly, more habitually, and more evenly. Precisely in this connection the sophisticated character of metropolitan psychic life becomes understandable - as over against small town life which rests more upon deeply felt and emotional relationships. These latter are rooted in the more unconscious layers of the psyche and grow most readily in the steady rhythm of uninterrupted habituations. (ibid.)

Here, Simmel clearly establishes a connection between urban space and the workings of our psyche that is spatio-temporal. The modern city produces psychic disorders because processes of everyday life take place in an environment that is marked by high density (space) and acceleration (time), or rather, as many spatial theorists (among them Lefebvre, Bachelard, and Sassen) have noted, by a multiplicity of changing temporalities. Urban space becomes temporalized, and thus the city has to be viewed as an entity constantly in motion. Similarly, urbanity provides a multiplicity of ever-changing localities so that the modern subject experiences an overload of spatial possibilities. Richard Lehan rightly states that "the flaneur [sic] is discontented because the city offers more experiences than he can assimilate. He always feels that he is missing out even in the process of experiencing: his state of mind is restless dissatisfaction, aimless desire" (74).

This notion of restlessness and disillusion, engendering estrangement, has been captured by many modernist writers in the USA (such as Fitzgerald, Miller, Dos Passos) and also recurred, in more excessive form, in postmodern urban novels such as McInerney's *Bright Lights, Big City* or DeLillo's *Cosmopolis*. To many urban dwellers, as Benjamin has observed, the overstimulation with urban signs resulted in 'shock' and subsequent trauma, neuroses, or paranoia. Often the damaging effects of 'shock' were coupled with the notion of homelessness since, in the ever-changing and culturally diverse metropolis, a stable conception of 'home' or 'dwelling' was thrown into question.

Interestingly, it was the literary imagination that revealed the uncanny as a specifically urban phenomenon. From the early urban detective fictions of Edgar Allen Poe we know that the uncanny was expressed, as Anthony Vidler rightly notes, through "the contrast between a secure and homely interior and the fearful invasion of an alien presence" (*The Architectural Uncanny* 3). Vidler also quotes Marx, who claims that the urban bourgeois way of life, and in particular the invention of the rent system, rendered traditional notions of domestic security obsolete. The urban subject, Marx argues, "finds himself in someone else's house, in the house of a stranger who always watches him and throws him out if he does not pay his rent" (qtd. in ibid. 5).

Many modernist writers such as T.S. Eliot, James Joyce, Alfred Döblin, F. Scott Fitzgerald or John Dos Passos continued to articulate this uncanny quality of the modern city in their works. Their writings depict the city as an ungraspable, often monstrous, entity that the modern subject has to face and try to comprehend. Most of the literary accounts are dark and nightmarish, because the city emanates a spatio-temporal dynamism that tremendously affects the protagonist's cognition. Dispersed narratives mirror the character's dispersed minds and a reality that is menacing, because space evokes the sudden emergence of the 'other,' and because time no longer follows the laws of nature but those of (invisible) mechanical and industrial forces.[6]

When we move on to the mid-twentieth century, many literary accounts of the uncanny are still built upon modernistic city chronotopes. While the fear of the 'other' and the fragmentation of place, time, and self continue as popular themes in postmodern works, it is the postmodernist acceptance of the unreal that best marks the distinction from its modernist counterparts. Postmodern authors, in general, are no longer interested in solving epistemological dilemmas but accept the fact that illusions, specters, and unconscious forces constitute their reality. According to Jean-Francois Lyotard, post-modernist science "is changing the meaning of the word knowledge, while expressing how such a change can take place. It is producing not the known, but the unknown" (60). This destruction (or deconstruction) of modernist conceptions of reality and knowledge also makes necessary a reappropriation of the urban uncanny in literature.

It was Washington Irving who, in his satirical *Salmagundi Papers* (1807), first applied the word 'Gotham' to Manhattan and its inhabitants, whom he regarded as 'wise fools.' Irving's association is based on a legend according to which the population of a village in Nottinghamshire named 'Gotham' faked madness and stupidity in order to hinder King John from taking up residence there. Accordingly, Gotham was associated with a city of tricksters long before it became associated with *Batman*'s crime-ridden city in which secret evil forces and moral corruption endanger the lives of the citizens. In one of the *Batman* comics, Gotham City is depicted as a dark place "full of lost souls and human garbage which in other cities are hidden in the shadow and never come to light" (Gardner 7).

---

6   See also Jo Collins and John Jervis, *Uncanny Modernity: Cultural Theories, Modern Anxieties*.

Even though Gotham's etymological history proves that there is no direct relation to the Gothic as such, the city's myths of origin, legends, and tales reveal that the people of Gotham seem somehow to be connected to a cultural discourse of the 'hidden.' In *ConspiraCity New York* (2009), Antje Dallmann has found that a considerable amount of contemporary New York City fiction concentrates on tropes and motives that are connected to conspiracies and urban paranoia:

> New York is often imagined as the center of conspiracies but also as the focal point of international networks, which seem to be cosmological in their implications. What is thus invoked is a cultural imaginary, which conceives of [New York] as the (hidden) center of the world – a city that is marked by secret connections. (133, my translation)[7]

In other words, the threat emanates from secret or encrypted forces that reside beneath or behind the city's surfaces. This intensified preoccupation with the hidden dimensions of the urban most likely results from New York's role as a global city, a city which, according to Saskia Sassen, is one of the strategic centers from which international financial markets and global trade flows are controlled. However, the horrific or uncanny nature of these invisible economic and political forces has not only been captured in postmodern literary discourses but also was most forcefully brought to our consciousness with the terrorist attacks on the World Trade Center on September 11.

It is a commonplace that New York is not only a global city in terms of finance and commerce, but also in terms of its influential role as a major immigrant gateway. It is indeed because of its ethnical and cultural heterogeneity that the Gotham uncanny must not be generalized but instead has to be examined along the visible and invisible cultural traces and histories that Europeans, but also Native Americans, Africans, Asians, West Indians and many others, have left on New York City's soil. New York City's uncanny discourses are,

---

7   "New York wird sehr häufig als Zentrum geheimer Verschwörungen, aber auch als Dreh- und Angelpunkt von Weltzusammenhängen vorgestellt, die kosmologisch in ihren Weiterungen zu sein scheinen. Es wird ein kulturelles Imaginäres, ein *urban imaginary*, aufgerufen, das diese Stadt als (verdeckten) Mittelpunkt der Welt sieht, die durch geheime Verbindungen gekennzeichnet ist." (Dallmann 133)

thus, always both global and local. Consisting of various models of urbanity, New York's heterogeneous urban fabric must always be regarded as a product of constantly changing processes of assimilation, acculturation, intercultural translations and thus also of territorial terrors.

Not much criticism has been devoted to the postmodern uncanny and its relation to the urban. Among the most recent works about the uncanny, which also have provided valuable theoretical backup of this study, are Nicholas Royle's book *The Uncanny* (2003), Jo Collins and John Jervis' *Uncanny Modernity: Cultural Theories, Modern Anxieties* (2008), and Maria Beville's *Gothic Postmodernism: Voicing the Terrors of Postmodernity* (2009). However, although they put the uncanny in a postmodern (literary) context, they do not explicitly relate the urban to the uncanny.[8] Still, when dealing with postmodern urban novels one can, amidst (or because of) all metafictional play, detect a conspicuous number of stylistic devices that clearly follow the structural principles of the uncanny. For example, most of the city fictions of Don DeLillo, Thomas Pynchon, Paul Auster, Toni Morrison, or Jay McInerney aim at establishing uncanny effects in that they diffuse spatio-temporal categories and establish ambiguous narrative devices. While most commentaries and analyses have focused on post-structuralist readings of these texts, narratological traces and effects of the uncanny have largely been ignored. Yet, these fictions raise many interesting questions when viewed through the lens of the uncanny: What does the contemporary rhetoric of the urban uncanny reveal about national trauma and collective memory? Why are stylistic devices of the uncanny so appropriate for articulating postmodern fears? Did the transformations of spatio-temporal relations in the age of postmodernity also transform the uncanny as a concept? In what ways does the postmodern uncanny in literary texts affect readerly reception?

Chronotopes of the Uncanny not only demonstrates that the uncanny takes on a prominent role in late twentieth century urban fiction. It also points to the fact that the postmodern affinity with space, signaled by the topographical turn in the humanities, has also

---

8   Here, mention must be made of Julian Wolfreys' article "The Urban Uncanny: The City, the Subject, and Ghostly Modernity," published in Collins and Jervis, *Uncanny Modernity*, which is an exception.

tremendously affected the way in which writers conceive of and articulate the uncanny. More specifically, I seek to put forward a definition of the uncanny along the lines of spatio-temporal relations characteristic of the postmodern period. In a further step, I want to explore how these relations construct feelings of uncanniness and estrangement in the implied reader. The method employed is the close reading of two pertinent novels written at the end of the twentieth century. In particular, this book presents an analysis of the story-oriented as well as the discourse-oriented narratological patterns and investigates how and why these novels exhibit traces of the uncanny. Mostly, the literary analyses are structured along chronotopic motives (the labyrinth, the ruin, etc.) that explicitly reveal the uncanny to the reader. These motives are relevant for two reasons: First, they establish a direct link between New York's postmodern urban fabric and the uncanny. Second, they point to postmodern fears and phenomena that are built around a chronotope that allows the haunting presence of history or a subject's positioning in simulated or illusionary lifeworlds.

Furthermore, I conceive of the uncanny also as a cultural imaginary which has to be read along the most basic parameters of race, class, and gender. Therefore, the uncanny must not be viewed as a mere subcategory of contemporary Gothic, but rather as a literary tool that, more often than not, articulates subjective post-traumatic experiences which, however, can also point to larger, national memory discourses. For example, D. H. Lawrence considered American culture as *a priori* haunted, as David Mogen writes, "by the ghosts of subdued Indian cultures, ghosts which either induce madness or enter into our awareness in ways we cannot comprehend" (qtd. in Lloyd-Smith 86). The uncanny, therefore, is always subjective and culturally specific.

The first part of this study, entitled 'Orientations,' deals with the theoretical and historical framework that is essential for understanding the complexity that shapes the notion of the uncanny. I begin by highlighting the difficulty in defining the uncanny as a concept, arguing that, at its very core, it signals the crisis of binary opposition. This section also juxtaposes Freud's and Todorov's definitions of the literary uncanny and shows why their accounts are highly contradictory and, at times, unconvincing. The intent of this chapter is to develop an understanding of the Freudian implications of the uncanny in literary discourse, but also to point to its limitations and potentialities. Therefore, this book does not advocate a purely psychoanalytic approach but rather makes use of the general idea of 'the return of the repressed' and its spatio-temporal relevance that Freud articulated in his 1919 essay "The Uncanny." In the chapter entitled 'Chronotopoetics,' I apply Bakhtin's concept of the *chronotopos* to the Gothic genre, identifying the timespaces of eighteenth century Gothic fiction (*Schlosszeit*) and tracing their development to the timespaces emerging in Gothic-postmodernist works (*Stadtzeit*). My main argument in this chapter is that whereas the uncanny emerging from *Schlosszeit* is constructed through clearly defined and differentiated notions of time and space, the uncanniness produced by *Stadtzeit* is characterized through the loss of ordered and continuous chronotopic structures.

The second and main part of this study looks at specific literary representations of the postmodern uncanny, showing how two distinguished American novelists writing in the late twentieth century – Paul Auster and Toni Morrison – have effectively translated the postmodern uncanny into their New York fictions. As an example of metafictional Gothic, Paul Auster's *City of Glass* (1985) tells the story of a detective fiction writer-turned-'real' detective who, during his investigation, 'falls' into the state of homelessness and, finally, disappears in the vast urban fabric of New York. From the very beginning we learn that it is the trauma of the death of his son Daniel that has initially triggered the uncanny 'architextures'[9] that the protagonist creates and experiences. In this postmodern anti-detective story, in which the clues do not help to solve the mystery, many of the Freudian motifs of the uncanny, e.g., the *Doppelgänger* or the mechanical doll, are repeated on the story-oriented as well as on the discourse-oriented levels. Also for the reader, the story opens up a bottomless abyss into which all certainties fall, and the search for meaning and significance becomes a never-ending journey into the very depths of the protagonist's subjectivity.

---

9 The neologism 'architexture' can be attributed to Bernd Herzogenrath, who introduced the term in his study *An Art of Desire: Reading Paul Auster* in 1999. Derrida's *archi-écriture* (arch-writing) bears resemblance to the term 'architexture' as applied in this study of the postmodern uncanny. For Derrida, *archi-écriture* denotes the process of original writing or the inscription of the trace that always brings forth *différence* and thus the endless deferral of meaning (*Of Grammatology* 62).

My analysis of Toni Morrison's novel *Jazz* (1992) shows how Morrison's highly disruptive narrative stylistically mirrors the personal hauntings of her main characters. Set during the colorful and culturally productive era of the Harlem Renaissance, the novel establishes an urban aesthetics that is built upon the dialectics of dream and nightmare. Morrison blends the urban spectacle of the Jazz Age with the haunting presence of African American histories of loss and trauma, thus highlighting the importance of cultural memory. The uncanny not only makes itself felt in the city's decaying architecture but also through the processes of musical and verbal storytelling that powerfully conjure up ghosts of the past.

The choice of the two novels was prompted not only by the goose bumps both generated during the initial reading process but, more significantly, by their potential for exploring contrasts. The most obvious dichotomy between the two texts results from the cultural and historical frame of reference which, in Morrison's example, captures the African American experience and an African American genealogical belief system. In contrast, Paul Auster's novel depicts a white, middle-class Jewish American context and world-view. Yet, in both texts the protagonist's dreams and illusions are radically destroyed, and none of the main characters is able to read and make sense of the ambiguous signs of the city. In both novels, it is a criminal act that drives the plot forward. However, the laws of rational logic or empirical truth do not help the protagonists understand and come to terms with their traumatic experiences. Rather, it is an understanding and appreciation of the numinous, of "that which transcends the rational, that which by human definition lies beyond our conception of morality and reason" (Aguirre 3), that enables an understanding of and coming to terms with the wounds the past has left in the character's psyches. The two texts under scrutiny follow the same stylistic principle as applied in Rachel Whiteread's uncanny sculptures. In both texts, the "interior entrop[ies]" (McGrath/Morrow xxi) of the characters are externalized and made visible in public urban space.

Ultimately, the analyses of the two texts show that the uncanny and the postmodern urban experience are inextricably linked and require further attention, also because of the fact that our future will be urban. Approximately half of the world's population is living in cities, and demographic forecasts reveal that urbanization rates will rise considerably in the future. Accordingly, uncanny confrontations between the real and the unreal will more and more find their expression in an urban way of life in which the hidden – in the form of wireless data connections or virtual identities – determines our daily experience. This forecast shows that the uncanny is a timeless phenomenon that we will constantly have to face and need to remystify.

Part One:
Orientations

The Uncanny: Towards a Definition

"If one wants to come closer to the essence of the uncanny," Ernst Jentsch writes, "it is better not to ask what it is" (8). This warning, implying the difficulty of defining the uncanny, however, did not prevent many scholars of the twentieth and twenty-first centuries from beginning to explore this slippery terrain. Freud, Heidegger, Lacan, Todorov, Royle, Kristeva, Vidler, or Punter, to name only the most famous, discarded Jentsch's well-intended piece of advice in order to meet the challenge of defining the indefinable. Yet, after more than a century that has passed since Jentsch's thesis, the mystery of the nature of the uncanny is not solved. "The uncanny *is* uncannily uncanny" (Kunze 5), as a contemporary critic recently remarked. However, there are two academic disciplines that have shed considerable light on the way the uncanny operates. Not surprisingly, psychoanalysis and literary criticism (or should I say "psycho-literary criticism"?) explored the subject most extensively, with both disciplines being concerned with the subject and its representation, or what Paul Ricoeur called "the hermeneutics of suspicion" (32). For example, Freud's essay "The Uncanny" (1919), which is still considered as one of the most influential on the subject, examines Hoffman's tale "The Sandman" in order to exemplify the castration complex and primary narcissism, and Lacan uses Poe's "The Purloined Letter" to further develop Freud's repetition compulsion. *Vice versa*, literary criticism employs psychoanalysis in order to "uncover [the] secret forces" (Freud "The Uncanny" 150) that operate in a character's or author's mind.

The following two concepts on the uncanny, one developed by Sigmund Freud and the other by literary theorist Tzvetan Todorov, are meanwhile classical, if not outmoded, positions. However, they still represent the pivotal theoretical framework for any thorough study of the uncanny and, simultaneously, demonstrate that it is the very elusiveness of the subject that is integral to its understanding.

FREUD

In 1919, Sigmund Freud published an essay on the uncanny aesthetic which also includes an examination of E.T.A. Hoffmann's romantic tale "The Sandman" (1816). The starting-point of Freud's analysis is marked by his argument that the uncanny is most often a sensation of fear or horror that is evoked by "the excessive stress that is laid on psychical reality, as opposed to material reality" (U 151). More specifically, Freud equals the uncanny with 'the return of the repressed,' a process whereby repressed past events or traumata rise to consciousness again.[1] For Freud, the uncanny is first and foremost an intra-psychic phenomenon, a product of the unconscious that fuses the past with the present. Freud therefore claims that the uncanny is "that species of the frightening that goes back to what was once well known and had long been familiar" (U 124). Freud also finds that the aspect of repression is mirrored in the etymology of the German term *unheimlich,* a compound, which brings together the head *heimlich* (denoting 'homely' and 'known') with its modifier prefix *un-* (denoting the negation of 'homely' and 'known'). For Freud, *un-* functions as a lexical indicator of the act of repression because it is due to the prefix that the familiar turns out to be unfamiliar and strange. *Unheimlich* thus always denotes a haunting where the repressed past resurfaces and makes the present strange and frightening.[2] Freud

---

[1] Freud has built up his argument in consideration of Schelling's definition of the uncanny: "[T]he term uncanny (*unheimlich*) applies to everything that was intended to remain secret, hidden away, and has come into the open" (Schelling qtd. in U 132).

[2] Nicholas Royle has extended Freud's lexicographic study by investigating the English term uncanny and came to the conclusion that *unheimlich* is not synonymous with uncanny. However, after consulting various dictionaries, Royle found out that 'canny,' today denoting 'knowing, sagacious' and also 'cunning' and 'artful,' "in its archaic past, [...] has

detects this resurfacing of the past in Nathanael, the suffering protagonist of Hoffmann's tale, who since his early childhood days is haunted by the mythic figure of the Sandman, a nightmarish creature who tears out the eyes of children who refuse to go to bed. But Nathanael is not only haunted by the fictitious character of the children's story but also by a man named Coppelius, with whom he associates the Sandman. Triggered by a gruesome childhood encounter with the grim man, which also brings about the death of Nathanael's father, the protagonist's fear of losing his eyes intensifies, causing fits of terror and finally brings him to commit suicide.

Freud's psychoanalytical reading of the story draws the attention to Nathanael's fear of enucleation, and, metaphorically speaking, to castration anxiety, because, according to Freud, there is a "substitutive relation between the eye and the male member that is manifested in dreams, fantasies and myths" (U 140).[3] Accordingly, it is the Sandman or Coppelius character representing the castrating oedipal father[4] that Freud considers as the main uncanny element in the story. Embodying both, the good and the bad father-figure, representing thus the familiar and the frightening, Coppelius becomes the epitome of the uncanny. On a more general level, the eerie personifications of the Sandman that reemerge later in Nathanael's life, i.e., Coppelius and Coppola, are, according to Freud, nothing but the projections of Nathanael's unconscious, or in other words, manifestations of his neurotic disorder that go back to his traumatic childhood experience.

It has to be noted, however, that Freud, driven by his obsession with the repression (and return) of infantile fears, and thus with the

---

already meant its opposite ('uncanny'): 'having or seeming to have supernatural or occult powers" (11).

3   Whether or not this is a convincing metaphor should be discussed in a medico-psychoanalytic context only. However, castration anxiety here rather refers to the absence of the maternal penis and is thus, according to Samuel Weber, a "restructuring of experience, including the relation of perception, desire and consciousness, in which the narcissistic categories of identity and presence are riven [sic] by a difference they can no longer subdue or command" (qtd. in Bernstein 4).

4   At one point of the story we learn that Nathanael's father "look[s] like Coppelius" and that his mild features change "into a repulsive, diabolical countenance" (E.T.A. Hoffmann 5).

Father/Sandman/Coppelius/Coppola - Nathanael constellation, deliberately fails to take into account other text-immanent features that generate uncanny effects. A case in point is Freud's fundamental rejection of Ernst Jentsch's argument that the literary uncanny emerges out of the Hoffmannesque device of creating intellectual uncertainty. Contrary to Freud, Jentsch does not see the return of the Sandman, or respectively the fear of blindness as the ultimate source of uncanniness but rather concentrates on the effect that emanates from the beautiful and lifelike automaton Olympia, with whom the protagonist falls madly in love in the second half of the story. Jentsch believes that feelings of uncanniness most often arise when the reading subject is confronted with the notion of doubt:

> In storytelling, one of the most reliable artistic devices for producing uncanny effects easily is to leave the reader in uncertainty as to whether he has a human person or rather an automaton before him in the case of a particular character. This is done in such a way that the uncertainty does not appear directly at the focal point of his attention, so that he is not given the occasion to investigate and clarify that matter straight away; for the particular emotional effect, as we said, would hereby be quickly dissipated. In his works of fantasy, E.T.A. Hoffmann has repeatedly made use of this psychological artifice with success. (13)

Freud, however, dismisses this issue, claiming that this "has nothing to do with this effect" (U 138).[5] Surprisingly, Freud later acknowledges that the notion of doubt could play a central role when looking at the hypothetical reader of Hoffmann's story: "It is true that the author initially creates a kind of uncertainty by preventing us – certainly not unintentionally – from guessing whether he is going to take us into the real world or into some fantastic world of his own choosing" (U 139). Freud does, however, quickly proceed with the words: "But in the course of Hoffmann's tale this uncertainty disappears" (ibid.). Freud maintains that by the end of the story every notion of doubt is

---

5   What also might have contributed to Freud's aversion against Jentsch's argument is that Jentsch connected the uncanny to something new, i.e., an automaton, and not to something "long familiar to the psyche" (U 148). One can also read this as a reflection of his "dismissive attitude to modernity" (Mulvey 47).

eliminated, even though he does not provide any textual evidence for his argument. In fact, the story ends with Nathanael lying dead on the ground and Coppelius/The Sandman disappearing in the crowd. Thus no clue or explanation is given as to whether the protagonist's suicide was caused by his neurosis or of the Sandman's 'real' presence in the story.

Later, Freud argues far more convincingly that the feature of involuntary repetition functions as a popular literary device to give rise to the uncanny. Of Hoffmann's *Die Elixiere des Teufels* he writes: "[T]here is the constant recurrence of the same thing, the repetition of the same facial features, the same characters, the same destinies, the same misdeeds, even the same names, through successive generations" (U 142). Due to a "content [...] too rich" (ibid.), Freud, unfortunately, does not present evidence from Hoffmann's writing but instead cites examples of uncanny repetitions as they might occur in everyday reality:

[T]he factor of unintended repetition [...] transforms what would otherwise seem quite harmless into something uncanny and forces us to entertain the idea of the fateful and the inescapable, when we should normally speak of 'chance'. There is certainly nothing remarkable, for instance, about depositing a garment in a cloakroom and being given a ticket with a certain number on it – say 62 – or about finding that the cabin one has been allocated bears this number. But the impression changes if these two events, of no consequence in themselves, come close together, so that one encounters the number 62 several times in one day, and if one then observes that everything involving a number – addresses, hotel rooms, railway carriages, etc. – invariably has the same one, at least as part of the whole. We find this uncanny [...]. (U 144-145)

In another example, Freud mentions the uncanniness that is connected with the unintended returns to the same place when being lost: "One may, for instance, have lost one's way in the woods, perhaps after being overtaken by fog, and despite all one's efforts to find a marked or familiar path, one comes back again and again to the same spot, which one recognizes by a particular physical feature" (U 144). The most uncanny outcome of "the inner compulsion to repeat" (U 145)[6],

---

6 A major concept of psychoanalytical thinking, repulsive repetition is a drive of the unconscious mind that seeks to restore an earlier state of

to use the Freudian idiom, is the double (*Doppelgänger*), which Freud considers as a "disturbance of the ego" (U 143) where "the self may [...] be duplicated, divided and interchanged" (ibid.). Freud thinks that the double invokes a sensation of the uncanny, especially when "a person may identify himself with another and so become unsure of his true self" (U 142).[7] As with the threat of castration, Freud argues, the split of the self is linked with the fear of loss and in a broader sense also with the fear of death. Originally functioning as "an insurance of immortality" (U 142), the double has, according to Freud, developed into "the harbinger of death" (ibid.); as with the *Doppelgänger*, there is always the threat of extinguishing the original self.

TODOROV

With Tzvetan Todorov's *The Fantastic* (1970), the attempt to rationalize the uncanny finds a valuable continuation. Rigorously devoted to the field of literature, Todorov's formalist study approaches the subject from the perspective of literary genres. Strictly speaking, the uncanny is, in Todorov's sense, part of a generic triad which also includes the fantastic and the marvelous. Todorov defines the fantastic as a literary mode that leaves the reader and/or character in doubt whether the supernatural events in the story are 'real' or imagined:

---

things. In "Beyond the Pleasure Principle," Freud explains: "The patient cannot remember the whole of what is repressed in him, and what he cannot remember may be precisely the essential part of it [...] he is obliged to repeat the repressed material as a contemporary experience instead of, as the physician would prefer to see, remembering it as something belonging to past" (18). Freud also refers to traumatic or unpleasant experiences that are repeated unconsciously, for example, in hallucinations or dreams, in order to gain mastery over them. In the context of the uncanny, Freud regards the compulsion to repeat as an outcome of the 'death-drive.'

7   Again, the notion of 'becoming unsure' is considered irrelevant by Freud, although in Hoffmann's story the reader is confronted with the *Doppelgänger* motif and thus with the question whether Coppelius, Coppola, and the Sandmann are one and the same frightening character or not.

In a world which is indeed our world, the one we know, a world without devils, sylphides, or vampires, there occurs an event which cannot be explained by the laws of this same familiar world. The person who experiences the event must opt for one of two possible solutions: either he is the victim of an illusion of the senses, of a product of the imagination – and laws of the world then remain what they are; or else the event has indeed taken place, it is an integral part of reality – but then this reality is controlled by laws unknown to us. Either the devil is an illusion, an imaginary being; or else he really exists, precisely like other living being – with this reservation, that we encounter him infrequently. (25)

With the fantastic, Todorov argues, there is always an ambiguity that forces the reader towards a conclusion: "At the story's end, the reader makes a decision even if the character does not; he opts for one solution or the other, and thereby emerges from the fantastic" (41). As soon as the reader has stopped hesitating between the real and the unreal, he or she has also entered a new genre: The reader has accepted either the uncanny, due to a rational explanation of the phenomenon, or the marvelous, due to "new laws of nature" (ibid.). In the latter case, the supernatural dominates the rational intellect from the very beginning, a literary strategy used for example in Tolkien's *Lord of the Rings*, to name only one of many examples from fantasy (a genre that has become the archetypical application of this concept). The uncanny, in contrast, can be found in many of Radcliffe's or Dostoyevsky's works, in which the seemingly supernatural is nullified with a rational explanation at the story's closure.[8]

As a convincing example for the fantastic, Todorov mentions Henry James's ghost novella *The Turn of the Screw*, which by means of narratological anticlosure leaves the reader with an interpretative dilemma. Do ghosts haunt the old estate, or is it only the hallucinatory perceptions of the governess that gives rise to the uncanny? It is the reader who has to decide. This ambiguity that goes "even beyond the narrative itself" (Todorov 43) is, according to Todorov, one of the three main requirements of a fantastic text: "[T]he text must oblige the

---

8   In Radcliffe's *The Mysteries of Udolpho* (1794), for example, the female protagonist learns by the end of the story that the nightly noises in the castle were not induced by ghosts but by smugglers who hid their treasures in the underground vaults.

reader to consider the world of the characters as a world of living persons and to hesitate between a natural and a supernatural explanation of the events described" (33). As the second requirement for a fantastic text, Todorov mentions that this hesitation can also be generated in a character's mind which, due to the readerly identification with the protagonist, adds to the uncanniness that is experienced by the reader. Finally, Todorov states that the fantastic requires a certain way of reading, as any poetic or allegorical interpretation would kill the notion of doubt. This means that the fantastic must always be read literally, i.e., the reader must not be concerned about hidden or encoded meanings of certain words or expressions.

Although Todorov devotes his study to literary genre, he cannot help but also enter the domain of psychoanalysis when discussing the themes of the fantastic. The themes of self, including, for example, phenomena such as metamorphosis and pan-determinism[9], are a category in which psychical and material reality merge on the semantic level – *"the transformation from mind to matter has become possible"* (Todorov 114). The themes of vision, a subcategory of Todorov's 'themes of self,' are related to the *"perception-consciousness* system" (Todorov 120), especially to visual doubling, and remind one of Freud's theory of compulsive repetition. Second, Todorov discusses the 'themes of the other,' in which fear is aroused through man's relation to his unconscious desires. It becomes obvious that all of Todorov's themes would clearly invite a Freudian reading. However, Todorov does not consider these themes essential for his generic classification. In fact, he concludes with the remark that "psycho-analysis has replaced (and thereby has made useless) the literature of the fantastic" (161).

All of this brings up the question: What are we talking about when we talk about the literary uncanny? On the most basic level, both Freud and Todorov understand the subject as the effect that, operating on the semantic as well as pragmatic level, follows a writer's rhetoric. Far more interesting, however, is that Freud as well as Todorov have

---

9   For Todorov, pan-determinism denotes "a general causality which does not admit the existence of chance and which posits that there are always direct relations among all phenomena, even if these relations generally escape us" (161).

tried to understand and explain the uncanny with the structuralist tool of binary opposition. In fact, both critics argue that it is the destabilization of certain boundaries that accompanies every uncanny experience. Freud, in his lexicographic study of the German term *unheimlich*, proves that even the word itself embodies the blurring of the division between the *heimlich* and the *unheimlich*, the familiar and the strange, the conscious and the unconscious. Similarly, for Jentsch it is the opposition between the living and the artificial that no longer holds when looking at Hoffmann's Olympia. For Todorov, it is the hesitation between truth and illusion that makes it possible to define the fantastic as a literary genre. Still, many contemporary scholars associate the literary uncanny with the notion of ambiguity. Susan Bernstein, for example, convincingly points out that, "[t]he uncanny comes into being as a violation of the law of non-contradiction. Like a ghost it 'is' and 'is not'" (1113). Hélène Cixous has noted that the uncanny "presents itself, first of all, only on the fringe of something else" (528). Indeed, it turns out that the main principle that underlies the uncanny comes closest to that of an oxymoron, a figure of speech uniting two very contradictory ideas (Jackson qtd. in Quéma 86).

Considering what was said earlier in this chapter, the attentive reader will have noticed that Todorov's fantastic bears a striking similarity to Jentsch's uncanny. Both authors, although different in terminology, rigorously center their discussions on the notion of ambiguity. What Jentsch refers to as 'intellectual insecurity' Todorov calls 'hesitation,' what Jentsch names 'uncanny' is for Todorov 'the fantastic.' And Freud, although first seeming to be close to Todorov's approach (regarding the uncanny as a mode in which every notion of doubt is eliminated at the story's closure), by the end of his essay poses the question: "[C]an we completely discount the element of intellectual uncertainty?" (U 153). The answer is obvious: We cannot.

Todorov presents the fantastic as "a frontier between two adjacent realms," (44) which reveals that his idea of the fantastic is in many ways much closer to the idea of the uncanny as Jentsch understood it. Therefore, Todorov's sub-categorization of the uncanny as "the supernatural explained" (41) is misleading and thus far away from the true nature of the uncanny, because the literary uncanny, as one will see shortly, only functions as, "an uncanny double of Todorov's pure fantastic" (Quéma 91). What is most problematic about Todorov's fantastic, now understood as a synonym of Jentsch's uncanny, is that

Todorov expects the reader to eliminate this ambiguity at the narrative's end. If it is the doubt at the very end that brings about the uncanny, then Todorov seems to have forgotten about the ambiguities that manifest themselves during the entire reading process (Bernstein 1125).[10] Even Freud at one point argues in "The Uncanny" that, "[f]or a long time he [the author] may prevent us from guessing the presuppositions that underlie his chosen world" (157).

However, the notion of ambiguity is not only significant to the extent that it is the common denominator of Freud's and Todorov's theories, but also because it initiated the uncanny's very 'invention' in the late eighteenth and early nineteenth centuries. According to the eighteenth century philosopher Marquis de Condorcet, the ambition of the Age of Reason was "to admit only proven truths, to separate these truths from whatever as yet remained doubtful and uncertain, and to ignore whatever is and always will be impossible to know" (qtd. in Leiss, para. 19). Paradoxically, it was the obsession with science and rationalism, enforcing a secular understanding of the world (and thus a rejection of magical belief and superstition), that gave birth to the uncanny. For example, Newton's *Opticks* (1704) or the Lichtenbergian dust figures[11] (1777) seriously challenged the Cartesian principles and thus the prevalent order and understanding of the world. As Michel Baridon explains: "The new paradigms implied not only a more mysterious universe but a universe of plastic forces, of gases and of fluids developing by almost imperceptible motions [...] and none of them reducible to the paradigms of the mechanistic world view" (51).

Furthermore, the Enlightenment's progressivism and, in particular, the mechanical innovations of the late eighteenth and early nineteenth

---

10 Todorov, for example, argues that Poe's "The Fall of the House of Usher" rather belongs to the (sub-)genre of the uncanny, as in his opinion, "the supernatural explanation is merely suggested" (48). Todorov also explicitly states that he does not take into account, for example, the morbid condition of the Usher siblings as an element of ambiguity, and therefore of the fantastic. See Todorov, *The Fantastic*, 48.

11 In 1777, the German physicist Georg Christoph Lichtenberg recognized radial patterns in the dust on his electrophorus. Electricity had manifested itself independently. This phenomenon of self-referentiality could no longer be explained with the truths of mathematics or scientific methods and thus contributed to the fall of the mechanistic world-view.

centuries, radically subverted the distinction between the real and the unreal. For example, the first automatons, like von Kempelen's chess-playing Turk (1770) or Vaucanson's mechanical duck[12] (1742) aroused feelings of insecurity and alienation. As Terry Castle convincingly argues in *The Female Thermometer,* these innovations "also produced, like a toxic side effect, a new human experience of strangeness, anxiety, bafflement, and intellectual impasse" (8). Accordingly, Hoffmann's conceptualization of Olympia was very likely inspired by the Enlightenment's anxieties that arose from the doubtful nature of reality and self. Shelley's *Frankenstein* (1818) or Stevenson's *The Strange Case of Dr. Jekyll and Mr. Hyde* (1885) are obvious examples for the fact that it was the profound insecurity between self/other or real/artificial that tremendously shaped the literary production of the eighteenth and nineteenth centuries and thus also led to the emergence of the literary uncanny.[13]

In addition to being concerned with doubt and ambiguity, Freud's and Todorov's accounts are also bound up with the issue of time. Freud's definition of the uncanny as the *return* of the repressed or the compulsion to *repeat* reveals that it is the fragmentation of linear time that underlies every uncanny effect. In real life as in literature, as Freud has shown, the uncanny confuses temporality, breaks down the boundary between the 'then' and the 'now.' In case of repetition, as James Phillips explains, the disruptive effect can be compared to "a spiral in which the moving present is constantly sweeping backward and forward at the same time" (11). With Freud's repetition compulsion, then, it is the very act of repetition that creates the uncanny effect. As Neil Hertz notes: "The feeling of the uncanny would seem to be generated by being reminded of the repetition compulsion, not by being reminded of whatever it is that is repeated"

---

12 One of the first animal-automatons, Vaucanson's *Canard Digérateur,* flapped its wings, ate, and digested grain.
13 The production and consumption of Gothic fiction in Europe was, of course, also a way of re-establishing old patterns of perpetuity. Fred Botting argues that many gothic works of the romantic era "are also attempts to explain what the Enlightenment left unexplained, efforts to reconstruct the divine mysteries that reason had begun to dismantle, to recuperate pasts and histories that offered permanence and unity in excess of the limits of rational and moral order" (23).

(qtd. in Royle 90). For example, in Vonnegut's *Slaughterhouse-Five* (1968), the uncanny emerges together with the constant recurrence of the scent of mustard gas and roses, illustrating the involuntary reenactment of the war experience in Billy Pilgrim's mind.

Looking at the temporal dimension of Todorov's fantastic, it is the act of hesitation that disrupts temporal chronology and continuity. As an interruption of interpretational progress, hesitation entails a temporization of the character and/or reader. While hesitating between two different ontological possibilities, the character or reader momentarily leaves the pane of linear time, thus retreating into a state of timelessness. Similar to Freud's timeless unconscious, this state of timelessness causes a sudden break, a *caesura* in the continuity of time. Contrary to Todorov's theory, however, this momentary hesitation is not a singular phenomenon but occurs several times in a narrative, thus resembling a process of zigzagging in which the character/reader constantly moves to and fro between a temporal and a non-temporal level. Like repetition, hesitation makes linear time stammer. Based on the principle of transgression, hesitation prompts the reader to constantly alternate between two worlds, one 'real,' one imaginary.

Both Freud and Todorov regard reality as a pivotal frame of reference that determines whether a story is considered as uncanny or not. They assume that the precondition for the uncanny is the mimetic act of constructing a reality that comes as closely as possible to a fixed or empirical reality.[14] Only within this world, both argue, is it for the

---

14 Todorov postulates a 'common' empirical reality in which supernatural phenomena do not occur. However, he does not consider that what is considered as 'reality' is always determined by time and culture. In the Native American tradition, for example, it is still common to communicate with dead ancestors, and in the early days of colonialization the devil was part of the Puritan's reality. Today, in the Western hemisphere, it is astrology, ufology, or virtuality that shatters the notion of a 'common' idea of reality. This might also be the reason for Todorov's concluding remark that the fantastic as a genre is no longer possible in a world of postmodernity.

uncanny possible to (re-)surface.¹⁵ Thus, one can see that the uncanny cannot only emerge out of the fissure in the linearity of time but also out of the chasm that lies between two (mental) spaces.

Interestingly, Ernst Jentsch was the first theorist who hinted at the uncanny's spatial dimension: "Without a doubt, this word [i.e., *unheimlich*] appears to express that someone to whom something 'uncanny' happens is not quite 'at home' [...]. In brief, the word suggests that a *lack of orientation* is bound up with the impression of the uncanniness of a thing or incident" (8)¹⁶. Contrary to Jentsch, Freud and Todorov, obviously driven by the modernist urge to explore literature along the lines of internal time, however, have refrained from taking into account spatial categories that, as the next chapter will show, are fundamental to every manifestation of the literary uncanny.

Only with the advent of postmodernity and the *spatial turn* in the humanities did issues of uncanny space enter the academic literary discourse.¹⁷ Foucault's 1967 remark that "the anxiety of our era has to do fundamentally with space a great deal more than with time" ("Of Other Spaces" para. 7), has early articulated the accumulated needs of discussed forms of uncanniness along the lines of spatial concepts. Contemporary scholars, such as Mladen Dolar, Anthony Vidler, Donald Kunze or David Punter have pointed to the uncanny's topological importance for literary studies. Vidler, for example, claims that the uncanny "has, not unnaturally, found its metaphorical home in architecture" (*The Architectural Uncanny* 11), and David Punter introduces the "uncanny of virtual locality" (133), denoting the eeriness that readers or characters experience when human beings can no longer be located at a single place at a single time. Donald Kunze

---

15 Indeed, the uncanny effect of Kafka's *Verwandlung* relies on the fact that the story is not set in an enchanted fairy-tale world but in the home of a working-class family around 1900.

16 See also Vidler, *The Architectural Uncanny*, 23.

17 It has to be noted that the analysis of space, or spatial settings, is a well-established field in literary studies and that, for example, Gothic fiction has always been analyzed according to parameters of space. However, this study's point of departure regards the uncanny as something primarily characterized by a certain inexplicability and a temporal dimension in the sense of a "disquieting return" (Vidler, *The Architectural Uncanny* 25), the latter clearly reflecting the modernist dominance of time over space.

even argues that the uncanny as a fuzzy concept itself is rooted in the spatial dimension, claiming that the uncanny "transcends categories because it goes to the heart of space, which it converts through its reciprocal action of isolation and contamination, constructing distance then collapsing it" (5).

In fact, Kunze's remark does not only hint at the necessity to approach the uncanny from the perspective of space-time, but simultaneously provides an explanation for the question why Freud's and Todorov's definitions of the uncanny are, at times, slightly problematic. Although providing valuable insights into the manifold ways of how the uncanny can manifest itself, their studies also show that matters become complicated when attempting to force the literary uncanny into generic classification or a medico-scientific context. Todorov's study, for example, becomes unconvincing as soon as he pins down the uncanny to "the supernatural explained" (41). In this way, Todorov does not only deprive the uncanny of its inherent magic but also reduces it to a conceptual result that only *follows* the act of reading. Likewise, Freud's obsession with psychoanalytical interpretations leads to his failure to recognize the many layers of uncanniness that characterize Hoffmann's writings. The literary uncanny, therefore, is neither a genre, nor a fictional neurosis. Rather, it has to be approached as an atmospheric value of threat that is created by the multiple ways of how fictional time *and* space interact. Uncannily, what comes to mind again is Freud's lexicographic study, which proved that the German *un*heim*lich*, in fact, has, at its very heart, incorporated this spatial dimension all along.

Chronotopoetics

In his classical work *The Poetics of Space* (1958), Gaston Bachelard develops a phenomenology which draws a vital connection between psychoanalysis and topological space, arguing that through memory time is always securely fixed in space:

In the theater of the past that is constituted by memory, the stage setting maintains the characters in their dominant rôles [*sic*]. At times we think we know ourselves in time, when all we know is a sequence of fixations in the spaces of the being's stability – a being who does not want to melt away, and who, even in the past, when he sets out in search of things past, wants time to 'suspend' its flight. In its countless alveoli space contains compressed time. That is what space is for. (8)

Bachelard's assumption that the products of our psyches, i.e., memories, traumata, imaginations, emotion, or thoughts can be localized in space also implies that every resurfacing of the past, be it fictional or not, correlates with certain spatial categories or objects. Uncanny space, thus, is constructed by that which is subjectively repressed. Accordingly, the expressionist paradigm that the experience or perception of physical space is always determined by mental activities or, respectively, the workings of the individual psyche, is one of the fundamental principles around which the uncanny is constructed. Also Anthony Vidler argues that "[t]he 'uncanny' is not a property of a space itself; it is a representation of a mental state of projection that precisely elides the boundaries of the real and the unreal in order to provoke a disturbing ambiguity, a slippage between waking and dreaming" (*The Architectural Uncanny* 11).

Although a space is, according to Vidler, not *a priori* endowed with uncanniness, it can evoke an aura that is created and maintained by culturally conditioned knowledge or cultural narratives. Which space is invested with uncanny qualities is not only dependent on the workings of the subjective mind alone but also on the collective Weltanschauung of a certain culture. In a lecture on "The Hybridity of Culture," delivered in Vienna in 2007, Homi Bhabha recounts a personal uncanny experience he had when visiting Nürnberg. Standing at the Zeppelinfeld, a former military parade ground where, during the days of National Socialism, Hitler used to deliver his public speeches, he was struck by a moment of horror when suddenly shouts of joy resounded from the nearby Frankenstadion, in which a football-game was going on. Even though long dispossessed from its former function, the place suddenly shed its dark light of the past onto the present. Bhabha's experience of the uncanny resulted from the localization of the past in space, thus transforming the Zeppelinfeld into a momentary icon of cultural memory. History, as Bhabha's story shows, cannot be "dead" or "over," as involuntary memory brings it back to light.

In an often quoted passage of "Theses on the Philosophy of History," Walter Benjamin states that we are living in a present that is constantly interrupted by images of the past: Benjamin's understanding of history radically departs from historicism or traditional historiography in the sense that it does not regard history as a chronological chain of events.[1] For Benjamin, it is not the continuous flow of time that signifies history, but rather a *caesura*, a sudden moment of standstill, in which the 'Then' merges with the 'Now:'

The true picture of the past flits by. The past can be seized only as an image which flashes up at the instant when it can be recognized and is never seen again. "The truth will not run away from us": in the historical outlook of historicism these words of Gottfried Keller mark the exact point where historical materialism cuts through historicism. For every image of the past that is not recognized by the present as one of its own concerns threatens to disappear irretrievably. [...] To articulate the past historically does not mean to

---

1 Historiography assumes a clear dividing line between the past and the present. For the historicist, the past is over and hermetically sealed behind the doors of museums, archives and libraries (Mulvey 124).

recognize it "the way it really was" (Ranke). It means to seize hold of a memory as it flashes up at a moment of danger. ("Theses" 255)

In other words, repressed (cultural) content that involuntarily returns in the form of an image is unrepeatable and manifests itself, just like the apparition of a ghost, only in a moment of threat that entails the awareness of loss or forgetting[2] (Hamacher 66). This image, as Benjamin argues elsewhere, capturing the collision of past and present, is always ambiguous. The image is also the sphere in which the uncanny manifests itself as an absent presence or present absence. In *Camera Lucida*, Roland Barthes points out that the process of photography captures the past as it becomes significant in the present. Taking a picture, thus, becomes a metaphor of the uncanny moment which he calls, "the terrible thing which is there in every photograph: the return of the dead" (9).

Since the late twentieth century, scholars from various fields of the humanities have further developed the notion of cultural memory[3] along the lines of timespace. Inspired by the topological turn in cultural studies in the 1990s, which brought forth a privileging of the spatial over the temporal, history was no longer seen solely through the lens of time, but rather through the lens of space. With Pierre Nora's notion of the *lieu de memoire,* for example, space becomes not only a crucial component of remembering but the medium through which cultural memory is conceptualized. For Nora, a *lieu de memoire*

---

2   Benjamin's historical materialism has been used extensively to explain phenomena in our culture of postmodernity, in which new media, virtual realities, and consumer capitalism have rendered a traditional conception of history or reality obsolete. In a postmodern world, the past can no longer be distinguished from the present; the old can no longer be distinguished from the new. Everything that is produced immediately becomes a relic of the past (Hartoonian 185).

3   In *Present Pasts*, Andreas Huyssen talks about the recent emergence of a memory culture in North Atlantic societies that he regards as a reaction to new media technologies and the subsequent loss of lived tradition. Huyssen believes that "in this prominence of academic 'mnemo-history,' memory and musealization together are enlisted as bulwarks against obsolescence and disappearance, to counter our deep anxiety about the speed of change and the ever shrinking horizons of time and space" (71).

has the same purpose as Benjamin's image, namely "to stop time, to block the work of forgetting [...] to immortalize death, to materialize the immaterial" (19). Drawing on France's national identity, Nora highlights the significance of sites of memory (e.g., cemeteries, museums, libraries and monuments), as in Western postmodern societies they have come to replace "milieux de memoire, real environments of memory" (7). Paradoxically, however, these spaces, being more than appropriate for triggering uncanny experiences, do not necessarily have to be real in order to conceptualize or obtain cultural memory. Looking at many examples of Romantic fiction, it is the imagined haunted house or castle that has continued to be the most vivid memory space in which the past comes to life again. Fictional timespaces can, as Anthony Vidler argues, also develop into "cultural signs of estrangement for particular periods" (*The Architectural Uncanny* 11).

The most influential scholar who developed a theory on literary timespaces was Mikhail Bakhtin, who in his 1981 essay collection *The Dialogic Imagination* claims that meaning and cognition can only be the result of dialogic relationships. Inspired by Einsteinean physics[4], Bakhtin introduces the term chronotope (which translates into 'time space') to refer to "the intrinsic connectedness of temporal and spatial relationships that are artistically expressed in literature" (84). Bakhtin applies his dialogics of space and time to the generic class of the novel, a genre which since the Greek romance has developed a multiplicity of chronotopes, reflecting different ideologies and world-views.[5] For Bakhtin, the chronotope is not simply "a generic signifier" (Smethurst 67) but rather "an optic for reading texts as x-rays of the

---

4 Bakhtin does not use the term chronotope in its strict physical or mathematical sense but rather makes use of the term's figurativeness: "The special meaning it has in relativity theory is not important for our purposes; we are borrowing it for literary criticism almost as a metaphor (almost, but not entirely). What counts for us is the fact that it expresses the inseparability of space and time (time as the fourth dimension of space)" (Bakhtin 84).

5 In *The Dialogic Imagination*, Bakhtin aims at a "historical poetics" (85) and thus investigates and compares the chronotopic relations as they are developed in early forms of the novel, such as the Greek Romance, the Adventure Novel of Everyday Life, and the Chivalric Romance.

forces at work in the culture system from which they spring" (Holquist 425-426). Looking at the literary uncanny from the perspective of timespace, therefore, reveals not only how the uncanny, as an atmospheric value, is established in a work of narrative fiction but also, and even more importantly, provides the essential socio-cultural framework in which the uncanny, as a cultural construct, operates at a certain point in history.

SCHLOSSZEIT

While focusing on classical examples of the novel, Bakhtin, in his "Concluding Remarks," briefly mentions the chronotopic motif of the Gothic castle, which he labels *Schlosszeit*, thus hinting at an early relationship between the chronotope and the uncanny. The castle in eighteenth century Gothic fiction, Bakhtin argues, "is saturated through and through with a time that is historical in the narrow sense of the world, that is, the time of a historical past" (245-246). Indeed, in many Gothic settings, time and space merge through the fictional conception of an antiquated space. Bakhtin emphasizes that these architectural spaces, often depicted as decaying or in ruin, have a fundamental relationship to time as they represent a materialization of the past that indicates permanence and continuity:

The castle is the place where the lords of the feudal era lived (and consequently also the place of historical figures of the past); the traces of centuries and generations are arranged in it in visible form as various parts of its architecture, in furnishings, weapons, the ancestral portrait gallery, the family archives and in the particular human relationships involving dynasty primacy and the transfer of hereditary rights. And finally legends and traditions animate every corner of the castle and its environs through their constant reminders of past events. (246)

In fact, the fictional return to bygone times and places is a defining and fundamental feature of the Gothic genre. As commonly known, the dark ages have always strongly been associated with barbarous practices, superstition, and mysteries. Supernatural phenomena were, in fact, part of a medieval perception of reality, as Addison writes in *The Spectator* (1712):

Our Forefathers looked upon Nature with more Reverence and Horrour [*sic*], before the World was enlightened by Learning and Philosophy, and loved to astonish themselves with the Apprehensions of Witchcraft, Prodigies, Charms and Enchantments. There was not a village in England that had not a Ghost in it, the Church-yards were all haunted, every large Common had a Circle of Fairies belonging to it, and there was scarce a Shepherd to be met with who had not seen a Spirit. (419)

Especially from an enlightened perspective, feelings of horror and terror were more likely to be experienced in the dark periods of history than in the light of reason and thus belong to the "not-here, not-now, an Other place, an Other time" (Aguirre 92). Or as Mighall puts it: "The Gothic dwells in the historical past, or identifies 'pastness' in the present, to reinforce a distance between the enlightened now and the repressive or misguided then" (xviii).

Despite, or maybe because of, the fact that the Age of Reason was keen to substitute the existence of supernatural forces with systematic knowledge, the irrational was always an integral part of cultural imagination and production. Fred Botting claims that this duality of eighteenth century aesthetics served to establish limits and boundaries: "Good was affirmed in the contrast of evil; light and reason won out over darkness and superstition" (8). Botting also argues that the transgression of moral limits was clearly aimed at strengthening the social ideologies of the Enlightenment. However, with the advent of romanticism, cultural manifestations of the irrational became more and more dominating, gradually losing their function of mere antithesis. Thus, the irrational changed from a manipulative social tool into a strong antagonistic force that highly questioned the values of the enlightened age. The production of Gothic fiction was also a way of re-establishing old patterns of perpetuity: "They [Gothic works] are also attempts to explain what the Enlightenment left unexplained, efforts to reconstruct the divine mysteries that reason had begun to dismantle, to recuperate pasts and histories that offered permanence and unity in excess of the limits of rational and moral order" (Botting 23).

In fiction, this longing for perpetuity and irrationality was expressed through the establishing of spatial settings that epitomized the desolation of time. For example, in Radcliffe's Gothic classic *The Romance of the Forest* the depiction of the ruined abbey of St. Clair provides the atmospheric framework and foreshadows the heroine's later encounter with the uncanny:

It [the Abbey] stood on a kind of rude lawn, over shadowed by high and spreading trees which seemed coeval with the building and diffused a romantic gloom around. The greater part of the pile appeared to be sinking into ruins, and that which had withstood the ravages of time showed the remaining features of the fabric more awful in decay. The lofty battlements, thickly enwreathed with ivy, were half demolished, and become the residence of birds of prey. Huge fragments of the eastern tower, which was almost demolished, lay scattered amid the high grass, that waved slowly to the breeze. (15)

Here, the romantic aesthetic of decay relates to the uncanny in the sense that something familiar has become strange through the process of deterioration. Furthermore, the setting radiates a sense of mortality, as relicts of the past lie buried under the collapsed structures. Motivating the notions of disorientation, chaos, and ambiguity, spaces of decay not only represented the antipode to the civilized and progressive, but also a classical chronotope of the uncanny. Dylan Trigg notes that spaces of decay "evoke a peculiar disunity between the continuity of the present and the stagnation of the past [so that] we find ourselves at once in a space of both presence and absence" ("The Uncanny Space of Decay", para. 2).

It also has to be noted, however, that the romantic aesthetic of the primeval and incomprehensible was also inherent in the irrational structures of medieval architecture. Pinnacles, skeleton vaults, and gargoyles evoked a mysterious aliveness that not only radically antagonized any sense of formal order or clarity (as advocated by the Greeks) but that proved to be an essential tool in Gothic writing to indicate a space that is haunted and in which the past returns in the form of the supernatural.

Most of the early Gothic novels, however, are not only historical in the sense that they are set in medieval spaces, and thus in a fictional past (FPa), but also in the sense that they themselves embed stories of an earlier fictional past. Also on the level of discourse, the Gothic novel applies an anachronistic mode in which the past also haunts the fictional present (FPr) through the return of the dead, ancestral curses, or legacies. In *The Castle of Otranto*, for example, it is an ancient prophecy which makes the gigantic helmet kill Manfred, the prince of

Otranto, and which makes a statue bleed. What is most relevant in terms of time-space relations is that in the traditional Gothic novel, supernatural forces or dark powers always return within the thick stone walls of the antiquated space, or that the haunting 'other' always lurks behind a closed door. As illustrated in Figure 1, the chronotope of the Gothic novel clearly localizes the uncanny within a closed or walled-off space.

Figure 1. Schlosszeit: The uncanny as localized in closed space.

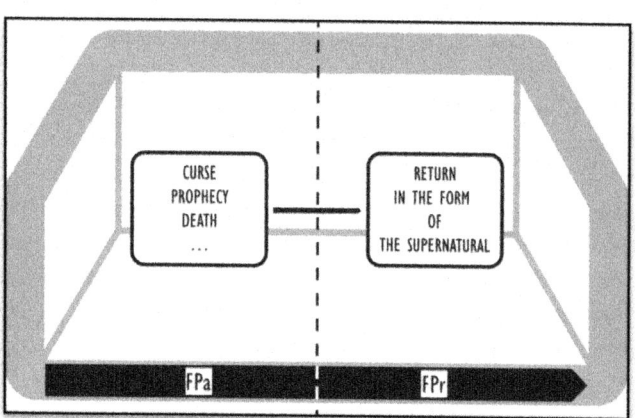

The inside, representing always a space of menacing enclosure, fulfills the function of a prison from which it seems impossible to escape. Often, the hidden underground structures that are almost always part of the closed space of a medieval building expand the closed space on a vertical level. Secret passages, underground vaults, and dark labyrinths are always associated with danger and significantly enforce the secrecy and obscurity associated with medieval settings. In *The Castle of Otranto*, when Isabella flees from Manfred, the castle's subterranean space is depicted as follows:

The lower part of the castle was hollowed into several intricate cloisters; and it was not easy for one under so much anxiety to find the door that opened into the cavern. An awful silence reigned throughout those subterraneous regions, except now and then some blasts of wind that shook the doors she had passed, and which, grating on the rusty hinges, were re-echoed through that long labyrinth of darkness. Every murmur struck her with new terror; (25-26)

However, Isabella's flight through the dark labyrinth does not lead her to the outside but to the contiguous convent of St. Nicolas, another walled-off space.[6] The feature of seclusion is inevitably linked with a literary device that Mark S. Madoff labeled the "locked-room mystery" (49). Madoff connects the feature of seclusion with the dialectics of inside and outside of Gothic space. He writes: "Outside contains those actions and attitudes proudly called modern, civilized, enlightened. Inside is the ancient, barbaric, disorderly, passionate, indecorous place where the Gothic protagonist, like the reader, arrives only through apparently accidental transgression" (51).

Although this contrasting point of view might work for a generalized approach, it does not work when incorporating the geographical dimension of Gothic space. The outside might be open and the terrain of the victim rather than that of the source of evil, however, the proximate outside does not necessarily antagonize the scary inside. Many works of early Romantic fiction prove that the feature of enclosure, implying an impossibility to escape the evil powers, often transcends the thick stone walls of the castle or the abbey. In most of the early accounts of Gothic fiction the terror of space is not limited to the premises of dark and old castles but also includes its geographical surroundings, which also serves the function to continue the imprisonment of the protagonists and the forlornness to escape.

Many medieval settings of the uncanny are remote and usually only surrounded by untamed nature. In the eighteenth century natural landscape was considered inferior and thus represented something that

---

6 Audrone Raskauskiene argues that especially women writers of the eighteenth century regarded the closed space of the castle symbolic of patriarchal authority (9). The power and threat from which the sentimental heroines flee goes most of the time back to a male arch villain – a tyrannical father figure, a demonic lord of the castle, or a villainous monk. Even in the 'enlightened age', aristocratic family orders and religious doctrines continued the male's absolute power in society. Hogle has noted that the eighteenth and early nineteenth centuries can be seen as "a still-antiquated and male-dominated world full of terrors for every female" (10). Raskauskiene has also dealt with the semantically charged space in Gothic fiction and argues that in many early examples, "[t]he man, the castle and the landscape are unified into one" (9).

had to be tamed by human intellect. Consequently, many works of early Gothic fiction embrace a geographical setting that is as mysterious and menacing as the castles and specters themselves. Radcliffe's castle of Dunbayne, for example is, "built [...] upon a high and dangerous rock" (*The Castles of Athlin and Dunbayne*, para. 18). The medieval edifice described in the preface of *A Sicilian Romance* (1790), "stands in the centre of a small bay, and upon a gently acclivity, which, on one side, slopes towards the sea, and on the other rises into an eminence crowned by dark woods" (para.1). In Shelley's *Frankenstein*, the monster is found on a "tremendous and ever-moving glacier" (Chapter 10, para. 2), and in Radcliffe's *The Castles of Athlin and Dunbayne* the narrator wanders in the rugged wilderness of the Scottish Highlands, a landscape characterized by "uncultivated nature, [...] cataracts and vast moors unmarked by the foot of a traveler" (para.7). The reader is confronted with a natural vastness that can also be seen as a continuation of the closed space of oppression. Nature becomes insuperable and hostile.[7]

It has to be noted, however, that these bizarre environments, where human existence is challenged to the highest degree, mainly served the literary purpose of distancing. Only by setting the uncanny tales in unfamiliar and grotesque locales[8] was it possible to make ancestral curses and ghostly presences imaginable (Grein 10-11). Also Gerhard Hoffmann observes that the fictional construction of uncanny space always requires a radical departure from organized, rational, or homely models of space:

As far as the motives of the uncanny and the conception of uncanny space are concerned, they are often established through the lack of normal conditions and

---

7   The Romantics located sublime terror in magnificent and awe-inspiring works of nature, such as the solitary grandeur of mountains, the dark summits of forests, or the roaring water of the ocean. On the concept of the sublime see Edmund Burke, *Philosophical Enquiry into the Origins of our Ideas of the Sublime and Beautiful* (1757).

8   Early Gothic novels were preferably set in Mediterranean regions, such as Italy or Southern France, in order to detach the inexplicable from eighteenth century England. Furthermore, Southern Europe functions as a prototypical Gothic setting, "continuing the association of Catholicism with superstition, arbitrary power and passionate extremes" (Botting 64).

are notably evoked through the withdrawal of possibilities of orientation and communication; most often through solitude, darkness, and silence. (164, my translation)

Although Gerhard Hoffmann's essential parameters in the construction of Gothic settings continue to be dominating up to the twentieth and even twenty-first centuries, it has to be noted that from the nineteenth century onwards the chronotopic motives of the literary uncanny have changed. For example, the advent of Gothic fiction in America entailed a fundamental shift that brought the uncanny much closer to the reader's domestic reality. Even though many American Romantic writers, most notably Poe[9] and Hawthorne, continued to use many chronotopic features invented by their English predecessors (i.e., set their stories in 'far-away' lands)[10], the *mise-en-scènes* of American Gothic were considerably shaped by the geographical, cultural, and ideological context of the new nation. Charles Brockden Brown, as one of the first professional writers of America, set all of his Gothic romances on national terrain. In his foreword to *Edgar Huntley* (1799), Brown states that his works have to move beyond the Victorian model of Gothic space:

Puerile superstition and exploded manners, Gothic castles and chimeras, are the materials usually employed for this end. The incidents of Indian hostility and the perils of the Western wilderness are far more suitable; and for a native of America to overlook these would admit of no apology. (7)

Apart from the fact that Gothic writing in the New World was ahistorical in the sense that it could not romanticize a medieval past, authors were mostly drawing on the cultural 'here and now' that was,

---

9   For Poe, the theme of monstrosity could be found in all kinds of the human experience and thus manifested itself in the natural, the supernatural, and the numinous, which also explains his broad range of uncanny settings and situations.

10 For example, the Edenic garden depicted in Hawthorne's "Rappaccini's Daughter" (1844) is located in Padua, Italy. Clearly separated from the outside world by a thick stone wall, the garden is a space of enclosure and isolation in which the evil power in the form of (the science of) Doctor Giacomo Rappaccini manifests itself.

from the early days of colonialization onwards, intrinsically connected with the fear of the unknown 'other.' For example, from a Puritan point of view, the demonic was either located in the unexplored deep forests or the "uncivilized" natives.[11] Hawthorne's *The Scarlet Letter* (1850) brings back the horrors of the Puritan witch trials of the seventeenth century in Massachusetts, thus giving an account of the religious fanaticism of a Puritan ideology in which "the devil [was] lurking in the wilderness" (Caroll qtd. in Mogen/Sanders/Karpinski 20).

Furthermore, the fictional landscapes of American Gothic writers also aimed at challenging the naïve optimism and faith in progress and individual freedom proclaimed by Jefferson, thus pointing to the dangers and the downside of the American Dream. Gothic writing in America expressed skepticism towards the perfectibility of the American nation and an idealized American subject and therefore was, as Eric Savoy remarks, "a negation of the Enlightenment's national narratives" (9). In fact, the distinctiveness of the genre lies in literary devices that express, as Eric Savoy puts it in "The Rise of American Gothic," "anxieties about the individual's capacity for common sense and self-control within the unstable social order of the new American republic" (172).

Especially Edgar Allen Poe's images of individuals suffering in dark and confined spaces stood in stark contrast to the poetic landscapes painted by his contemporaries. As Kenneth Silverman remarks:

[A]t a time when James Fenimore Cooper, Ralph Waldo Emerson [and others] were creating a feeling of space and self-reliant freedom, he [Poe] was creating in his many accounts of persons bricked up in walls, hidden under floorboards, or jammed in chimneys a mythology of enclosure, constriction, and victimization. (qtd. in Savoy 181)

In Poe's "The Fall of the House of Usher," (1839) for example, it is the architectural ruin of the Usher estate that the narrator approaches

---

11 In "Wilderness, Metamorphosis, and Millenium," David Mogen asserts: "But for most of the first two centuries of colonization Satan's influence was to Puritan settlers as much a fact of life as the New England winter; and to Puritan eyes Indian religion was clearly a form of witchcraft [...]" (95).

on a "dull, dark, and soundless day in the autumn of the year" (1461) that, from the very beginning, sets the scene for the uncanny climax of the story, i.e., the return of Roderick's deceased sister from the dead. In the tale, the reader encounters an imagery of burial and enclosure, i.e., the coffin, the tomb, the subterranean tunnel, and finally the collapse of the Usher estate. Also in his classic "The Pit and the Pendulum," (1842) which is set during the time of the Spanish Inquisition, Poe's nameless protagonist suffers in an irrational and dark space of enclosure, reminiscent of Prianesi's *Carceri*:

In its size I had been greatly mistaken. The whole circuit of its walls did not exceed twenty-five yards. For some minutes this fact occasioned me a world of vain trouble; vain indeed -- for what could be of less importance, under the terrible circumstances which environed me than the mere dimensions of my dungeon? But my soul took a wild interest in trifles, and I busied myself in endeavours to account for the error I had committed in my measurement. The truth at length flashed upon me. In my first attempt at exploration I had counted fifty-two paces up to the period when I fell; I must then have been within a pace or two of the fragment of serge; in fact I had nearly performed the circuit of the vault. I then slept, and upon awaking, I must have returned upon my steps, thus supposing the circuit nearly double what it actually was. My confusion of mind prevented me from observing that I began my tour with the wall to the left, and ended it with the wall to the right. (439)

Still, Poe's accounts of imprisonment and of symbolic blackness are not simply a continuation of the Victorian Gothic aesthetic but rather a comment on the difficulty of coming to terms with the formulation of a national identity. Critical discourse has it that Poe's ubiquitous "darkness" is a subliminal response to slavery[12] from a white supremacist perspective (Goddu 81). Poe has often been labeled a proslavery Southerner whose "literary practice and criticism support the racist stereotypes of plantation fiction" (Lee 752). Taking into account his obsession with the workings of the unconscious mind, however, one could argue that the "Poe chronotope" does not

---

12 Teresa A. Goddu explains: "Whereas the blackness of Melville's and Hawthorne's gothic romances is equated with Calvinistic depravity, the proper subject for the southern writer and the southern gothic [...] is slavery" (75).

primarily promote a racist anti-abolitionist ideology but represents an architectural metaphor for the prison of the mind whose darkness, as Savoy puts it, represents "the abject underside of a national 'normality' (182). Poe's claustrophobic settings are what Aldous Huxley once called "metaphysical prisons," (para. 7) meaning spaces "whose seat is within the mind, whose walls are made of nightmare and incomprehension, whose chains are anxiety and their racks a sense of personal and even generic guilt" (ibid.). Poe's "metaphysics of race" (Lee 771) are reflected in a self-determining chronotope in which the actual parameters of time and space become irrelevant as they extend endlessly. The irrational dark prison of Poe's fiction could be located anywhere and at any time, but in fact only gains significance as a *mise-en-abyme*, endlessly reflecting how complex the 'dark unknown other' must have been to the American psyche.

The idea of 'wholeness' and 'unity' that is alluded to through the imagery of closed space (as well as expressed through Poe's poetic diction and hidden messages) can also be seen as a response to what Mitsuo Kamio has termed the "locked-in consciousness" (53). Kamio explains:

In the age of Romanticism the absence of God has eliminated even its proper features of transcendency and omnipresence, so that human beings are obliged to seek unity within their inner world. [...] The abysmal inner-world where time and space extend limitlessly in any dimension is also the world which makes the self dissolve centrifugally into any direction. The center vanishes, the eternal wandering begins. Wandering itself formulates true existence. Abysses swallow up abysses. Selves absorb selves. How can human beings escape from the self as a labyrinth without having Ariadne's thread? The autistic incarceration of mind, that is, the locked-in consciousness is the final phase of Romanticism. (53)

On a larger scale, Kamio rephrases Pascal's notion of the *misére de l'homme*,[13] a crisis of the human condition that in the seventeenth century was attributed to a man-made universe whose power structures were no longer comprehensible.

---

13 In his *Pensées*, Pascal laments on the decline of Christian faith, bringing forth a psychological instability in humankind.

It is also with Poe and Brown that the literary uncanny enters urban and industrial terrain, and in this way also the immediate world of the reader. With *Arthur Mervyn or Memoirs of the Year 1793* (1800) and its gloomy descriptions of eighteenth century Philadelphia, Brown initiates the urban uncanny in Anglo-American literary history.[14] The evil force that transforms the city streets into a terrifying underworld, however, does not spring from sorcery or an ancestral curse but from a historical fact: the outbreak of the yellow-fever in Philadelphia in 1793. When Arthur, the protagonist of Brown's novel, returns to the city, it has tremendously changed. Instead of a "spectacle enchanting and new" (Brown, *Arthur Mervyn*, chapter III, para.16) he finds a deserted and morbid cityscape, only populated by ghosts-like creatures:

The market-place, and each side of this magnificent avenue, were illuminated, as before, by lamps; but between the verge of Schuylkill and the heart of the city I met not more than a dozen figures; and these were ghost-like, wrapped in cloaks, from behind which they cast upon me glances of wonder and suspicion, and, as I approached, changed their course, to avoid touching me. [...] I cast a look upon the houses, which I recollected to have formerly been, at this hour, brilliant with lights, resounding with lively voices, and thronged with busy faces. Now they were closed, above and below; dark, and without tokens of being inhabited. From the upper windows of some, a gleam sometimes fell upon the pavement I was traversing, and showed that their tenants had not fled, but were secluded or disabled. (Brown, *Arthur Mervyn*, chapter XV, para. 6)

Often read as an allegory of America's post-revolutionary economical illness, Brown's novel points to the political insecurities and instabilities apparent in the newly established nation. As Teresa A. Goddu remarks, "America in the 1790s was both buoyed by a liberal ideology that believed in the benefits of commerce and troubled by the vestiges of a civic republicanism that feared commerce was an infection" (32). The themes of (moral) devastation and illness are depicted through the spatial trope of confinement that is projected onto the closed space of the quarantined city. Of the streets of Philadelphia

---

14 Charles Brockden Brown's gothic novel *Wieland; or the Transformation* (1798) is considered the pioneer work which triggered the Gothic literary tradition in America, inspiring other famous Gothicists such as Edgar Allan Poe.

the protagonist of Brown's novel remarks: "Never in the depths of forests or caverns was I equally conscious of loneliness" (Brown, *Arthur Mervyn*, chapter XV, para. 19). The author's configuration of space also establishes a stark contrast between the city as the locus of contamination and evil and the idyllic countryside that is associated with salvation and pureness. Thus, the uncanniness of the story arises from the spatial topography of urban closed space, here a space that is constantly mirrored or repeated. Although the threat of the yellow fever is also projected onto the city streets of Philadelphia, its main source can be located within confined space. In the city Arthur Mervyn enters dark prisons, closets, and narrow passages, claustrophobic microcosms that mirror, or repeat, the larger urban space of seclusion.

Also some of E.A. Poe's urban detective stories locate the mystery in closed spaces, the most famous example being "The Murders of the Rue Morgue" (1841), in which a homicide is committed within the walls of a room locked. The task of the detective, therefore, lies in the investigation of how the murderer entered and escaped the locked room.[15] This 'locked room mystery' creates an obscurity that is reduced to the spatial configuration of inside and outside:

> In the detective's realm, 'inside' is a place of unexpected, inexplicable peril, of chaos which seems to sweep aside even the usual laws of physics. In the detective's realm, 'outside' is a place of banal order and reason, of hopeful safety from the rage whose results stay locked inside a room. (Madoff 50)

As with Brown's clear dichotomy of country and city as spatial equivalents for good and evil, also Poe's stories heavily rely on a clear division of inside and outside. The characters the reader encounters in these closed spaces, Poe's Roderick Usher, the nameless prisoner of "The Pit and the Pendulum," or Brown's contaminated citizens, are all depicted as passive, static, or lifeless – either literally dead as victims or heavily paralyzed from physical or psychological distress, again bearing a striking similarity to Piranesi's faceless prisoners, identities "reduced to a diaphanous state of suffering" (Kindermann 7). The radical abstraction of the individual, as apparent in many works of

---

[15] It has to be noted at this point that the uncanniness apparent in traditional detective novels can, to a large extend, be attributed to the action, i.e., the mysterious act of murder itself (G. Hoffmann 169).

early American Gothic, mirrors the anonymity of a societal apparatus that, in the late eighteenth and early nineteenth century blindly followed materialism and ratio.

Also with later writers of American Gothic, such as Henry James or Charlotte Perkins Gilman, fictional threats and horrors continue to be constructed through the chronotopic configuration of confinement and stasis. For example, in Gilman's "The Yellow Wallpaper" (1892) the nameless female protagonist suffers in complete isolation while undergoing a rest-cure. The locked room of the colonial mansion in which the story is set, figuring as a symbol of nineteenth century patriarchal hierarchies, is furnished with a wallpaper that suddenly comes to life:

The front pattern does move—and no wonder! The woman behind shakes it! Sometimes I think there are a great many women behind, and sometimes only one, and she crawls around fast, and her crawling shakes it all over. Then in the very bright spot she keeps still, and in the very shady spots she just takes hold of the bars and shakes them hard. (Gilman 809)

Here, the theme of isolation is reinforced through the pattern of the wallpaper, resembling another prison within the prison from which a crawling woman wants to free herself. It is this mirroring or reduplication of semantically charged space as well as the woman's encounter with her imprisoned double that produces the uncanny effect of the story.

Similarly, in Henry James' "The Jolly Corner" (1908), 65-year old Spencer Brydon encounters his ghostly alter-ego, the man he could have been had he not left New York, in the hermetic space of his childhood home (G. Hoffmann 170). In both Gilman's and James' narratives, the uncanny manifests itself in its truest Freudian sense, because both protagonists encounter their schizoid selves or, rather, the anthropomorphizations of the repressed, as "nothing new or strange, but [as] something that was long familiar to the psyche" (U 148). The fact that the characters meet their uncanny doubles in closed and confined spaces is no coincidence when considering that Freud also conceptualized the workings of the human psyche along the lines of spatiality. As Ross C. Murfin explains:

Freud [...] powerfully developed an old idea: that the human mind is essentially dual in nature. He called the predominantly passional, irrational, unknown, and unconscious part of the psyche the *id,* or "it." The *ego,* or "I," was his term for the predominantly rational, logical, orderly, conscious part. Another aspect of the psyche, which he called the *superego,* is really a projection of the ego. The superego almost seems to be outside of the self, making moral judgments, telling us to make sacrifices for good causes even though self-sacrifice may not be quite logical or rational. And, in a sense, the superego *is* "outside," since much of what it tells us to do or think we have learned from our parents, our schools, or our religious institutions. (503)

Thus, closed and dark space, representing the unconscious or the repressed aspects of our mind, becomes the most appropriate setting for the sudden emergence of the *id*. Interestingly, what happens within these closed spaces is that binary oppositions, such as the real and the illusionary or the objective and the subjective, are rendered obsolete (Murfin 508). But it is not until the advent of the postmodern age that this transgression of boundaries which, as noted earlier, lies at the very heart of the uncanny, will fully be translated into the Gothic chronotopes of urban America.

STADTZEIT

Whereas up to the twentieth century the uncanny remained clearly localizable as emanating from a spatial "inside," i.e., the medieval castle, the locked room, or the dark cabinet of the mind, it was the rise of the big cities that brought forth a fundamental transformation of its chronotopic features. In *The Arcade Project*, Walter Benjamin claims that the uncanny is mainly a product of modern[16] life and, in particular, of the urban experience (Vidler, *The Architectural Uncanny* 4). In the metropolis, as Georg Simmel has noted in "The Metropolis and Mental Life," (1903) the subject is exposed to spatial disturbances and

---

16 In most general terms, 'modern' always implies the idea of man's mastery over nature and is used to describe a wide range of periods. In this paper, 'modernity' refers to the historical period from 1870-1950, which was marked by socioeconomic phenomena such as industrialization, rapid urbanization, and consumerism.

ambiguities that result from an "intensification of nervous stimulation" (13) brought forth by "the rapid crowding of changing images" (ibid.) and "the unexpectedness of onrushing impressions" (ibid.). It is this very overload with all different kinds of stimuli which also furthers the emergence of encounters with the uncanny. In *Myth and Metropolis*, Graeme Gilloch echoes Benjamin's concept of 'shock' which, "engender[ing] forgetfulness and a distinctive form of memory, the mémoire involontaire," (8) exhibits a striking similarity to the *modus operandi* of the Freudian uncanny.

One of the horrors felt by many newcomers to the big city was certainly the confrontation with the crowd, a gathering of anonymous neighbors, paradoxically embodying both "[the] nearness and remoteness of every human relation" (Simmel qtd. in Vidler *Warped Space* 70). Therefore, the urban subject as the familiar 'other' is uncanny per se as it epitomizes the ambiguity between the same and the other, the strange and the familiar, the sociable and the solitary. Also Walter Benjamin ascribes the threat and unease that emanates from the modern city mainly to the heterogeneous mass, arousing fear and estrangement. This horror has already been captured in Edgar Allen Poe's 1845 story "The Man of the Crowd," where a narrator first observes and then follows a mysterious man within "the tumultuous sea of human heads" (1600) until he grows "wearied unto death," (1605) realizing that the stranger, like all the other people in the crowd, including himself, "cannot be read" (ibid.). In the crowd, the source of evil, the murderer, or the mystery itself, disseminates and consequently can no longer be located. Similarly, in "Les sept vieillards" (1861), Charles Baudelaire compares the Parisian urban subject to a ghost that, in being both, visible and invisible, manifests itself as part of modern urban mobility.

In both of these early fictional accounts of the urban uncanny, ghostly encounters are no longer limited to spaces of enclosure but take place outside, in the open and public sphere of the street. Furthermore, Baudelaire's ghost and Poe's man of the crowd are both "phantom figure[s] of the city's pulse" (Wolfreys 173), epitomizing a certain mechanized 'flow' fueled by the spirit of progress that, at the beginning of the twentieth century, is to become the master trope of high modernism.[17] With the emergence of industrial capitalism as a new political economy, transformations in the social, cultural, and literary sphere were very often interpreted along the lines of mechanized flux.[18] As Gilloch explains: "[T]he accelerated tempo and new machine-based rhythms of metropolitan life led to a distinctively modern temporal sensibility rooted in the commodification of time (equation of time and money) and repetition (fetishism and fashion)" (8).

In literature, stylistic responses to modernity's embrace of temporal flow were the "stream-of-consciousness" technique, the Bergsonian notion of *durée* as a recurring theme or strategy, or the use of literary symbols that signify modern temporality. In Dos Passos' *Manhattan Transfer* (1925), for example, it is the sense of mechanized motion that gives the novel its uncanny touch. By applying cinematic techniques, such as the radical skipping of transitions or the sudden alternation between different locales and perspectives, Dos Passos does not only capture the fast pace of the metropolis but also the immediateness of the uncanny moment. Accordingly, we do not get a very detailed view into the character's minds, which results from the fact that the snapshots of the character's lives are taken by an "objective" third-person narrator who, through his seeming role as an unbiased observer of events, is resembling the mechanical eye of a camera. The subway, whose monotonous rattling sound vocalizes like "Man-hattan Tran-sfer. Man-hattan Tran-sfer," (Dos Passos 116) further underlines the image of the city as an energetic and directive force. According to Heather M. Crickenberger, the title of Dos Passos' novel "is seemingly insignificant to the work as a whole, but in reality serves as a metaphor for the novel's underlying theme: people pause and move on and matter very little in the long run" (para. 20). In the novel, train cars are filled with "jiggling corpses, nodding and swaying as the express roared shrilly towards Ninty-sixth Street" (Dos Passos

---

17 As one of the prime examples of modernist literature, Eliot's "The Waste Land" (1922) also depicts urbanity using the imagery of death and decay.
18 Walter Benjamin has even equated the social behavior of people in the crowd with the monotony and repetitiveness of assembly-line work: "Dem Chockerlebnis [sic], das der Passant in der Menge hat, entspricht das 'Erlebnis' des Arbeiters an der Maschinerie" (*Charles Baudelaire* 128).

293-294), suggesting paralyzed and alienated urban subjects trapped in the veins of an overpowering machine-city.

As in many modernist chronotopes, the dimension of space only plays a subsidiary role. All characters seem to be lost in a nowhere-city in which there is only the illusion of a "center of things" (Dos Passos 4) or, rather, a spatial order. The highly fragmented narrative presents New York as the epitome of disorder, a spatial condition which does not allow the characters to fully develop. In this sense, the modernist chronotope of Dos Passos' novel bears a striking similarity to the timespaces depicted in the so called "city symphonies," a subgenre of documentary film which emerged out of the avant-garde movement of the 1920s. Similar to Dos Passos' novel, city symphonies such as Alberto Cavalcanti's *Rien que les heures* (1926) or Paul Strand and Charles Sheeler's *Manhatta* (1921) apply the technique of montage in order to visually capture the pulsating rhythm of the metropolis. In *Documenting the Documentary*, William Guyn argues that through the random accumulation of city scenes "symphonic documentaries abandon continuity of action and with it the notion of the central protagonist" (91). The characters are thus defined through the temporal coordinates of the chronotope, hence symbolizing the modern subject's need to establish a sense of order and orientation.

The modernist timespace displays a favoritism of (chronological) time over space. In *The Postmodern Chronotope*, Paul Smethurst argues that until the mid-twentieth century this privileging of time over space was a defining feature of Western ideology: "In modernist culture, it seems that social space was sidelined by more pressing problems of time, and place was regarded as an historical and possibly regressive construct, and therefore a hindrance to progress" (37). Indeed, modernism's goal, as apparent in the utopian architecture of Le Corbusier, was to break with the past in the sense of "replac[ing] the historical by the sleek" (Sennett 170-171). As Foucault contends, it was not until the topographical turn in the humanities in the latter half of the twentieth century that spatial categories were no longer treated as "the dead, the fixed, the undialectical, the immobile" ("Questions on Geography" 70).

In postmodernism, by contrast, the (literary) uncanny is no longer the product of a "temporal master-narrative" (ibid.) but rather that of spatial practice. With Foucault proclaiming that "the anxiety of our era has to do fundamentally with space, no doubt a great deal more than time" ("Of Other Spaces" para.7), also the uncanny experiences a reconceptualization of its spatial and temporal features. The major reason for this shift towards (open and fractured) space can be attributed to processes of globalization and the emergence of new media and communication systems, which have tremendously altered our sense of perception and reality. Especially the shift from analogous to digital techniques of representation has transformed the notions of time and space into highly variable categories. If the category of space in postmodernism is replacing that of time in modernism, time then will be degraded in the sense that it only becomes a supporting tool to understand the larger category of space. In her study *Gegenwartskonzepte*, Katrin Stephart, echoing Bergson, explains how the concept of temporality is altered when viewed in relation to the dominant referent of space:

From a spatial perspective we consider time as a sequence of simultaneities; from a temporal perspective, as a sequence of successions. Hence, we can only recognize simultaneous states, while our consciousness changes continually. There is a parallel existence of the flow of our consciousness and external states so that we can compare and relate our inner states with those of the outside world. (71, my translation)[19]

In the world of postmodernity, as Fredric Jameson pointed out in an interview, "[t]ime has become a perpetual present" (qtd. in Stephanson 6) in which past, present, and future operate on the same level. This simultaneous existence of temporalities deprives space of depth and thus reduces it to mere surface. Consequently, it is only through the spatialization of time that multidimensional space, or "hyperspace," to use the Baudrillardian idiom, comes into existence. In a further step, one can also argue that in a postmodern world, space and time dissolve

---

[19] "Bei einer räumlichen Sichtweise betrachten wir Zeit als Folge von Simultaneitäten, bei einer zeitlichen als Folge von Sukzessionen. Im Raum können wir nach dieser Definition nur gleichzeitige (also simultane) Zustände erkennen, während sich unser Bewußtsein kontinuierlich (also sukzessive) wandelt. Parallel zum Fluß unseres Bewußtseins existieren die Zustände der Außenwelt, sodass wir unsere inneren Vorgänge mit äußeren Zuständen vergleichen und in Beziehung setzen können" (Stephart 71).

into factual illusoriness, or in other words, into an illusion that really exists and cannot be avoided.

The postmodern American city has often been interpreted as the locus of factual illusoriness, finding its most visible expression in New York's Times Square, a space of pure virtuality, in which everything, as Derrida argues, "is at the same time profound and superficial, opaque and transparent, a secret that is all the more a secret in that no substance hides behind it" (*Specters of Marx* 154). The postmetropolis is indeed a space of illusionary perception, of doubling and fracture. As such, it is an environment in which categories between the real and the unreal or the animate and the inanimate, the inside and the outside, the private and the public, and the now and the then, constantly blur, thus revealing "the uncanny presence of a disturbing otherness" (Collins/Jervis 1). The Gothic chronotope of the postmodern city, therefore, is one that, according to Botting, "involves a pervasive cultural concern – characterized as postmodernist – that things are not what they seem" (171).

Furthermore, the postmodern city plays a crucial role as a cultural contact-zone, a site "where postmodern and postcolonial transnational culture developed in a continuous and contentious dialogue between a multiplicity of cultural groups, critical positions, heterogeneous voices" (Lenz 13). Viewed in this light, the uncanny as constructed through the transgression of ethnic and cultural boundaries gains further significance in the sense of Kristeva's "spectral identity" which she defines as "[a] massive and sudden emergence of uncanniness, which, familiar as it might have been in an opaque and forgotten life, now harries me radically as separate, loathsome" (qtd. in Quéma 102). The alienation the urban immigrant or, more generally, the 'other,' experiences must be understood in terms of cultural memory discourses – a category that is inextricably connected with space and time. Through processes of memory, the subjective home or past is constantly revisited which entails the recognition of 'otherness' in the subject's present social reality.

In *The Location of Culture*, Homi Bhabha uses the term "unhomely" in order to denote "a paradigmatic colonial and post-colonial condition," (9) thus pointing to the notions of alienation, displacement, and haunting as seen from a multiethnic urban perspective. David Punter's recent formulation of a "diasporic uncanny" (133) also suggests that in contemporary literary discourses topoi such as postcolonial displacements or the loss of an ancestral homeland are more and more being articulated through the Gothic tropes of haunting or spectrality.[20]

No matter whether the encounter with the uncanny is triggered by the ambiguities of factual illusoriness or cross-cultural encounters with the 'other,' in postmodern urban fiction, the Gothic chronotope most often takes its form by means of repetition and/or reduplication. As Heinz Ickstadt argues:

> Repetition (or the variation of the ever same) is the principle of composition in narrative space that is constructed like a surface. It is addressed and broken up by stylistic alienation of the every-day – the recognition of that which is frequently encountered, the overlap of a recognized thing with its photographic double, the *double-take* or the *déjà-vu*. That which manifests itself before our eyes as memory-content becomes unfamiliar, and reality, in the self-referential problematizing of its appearance, uncanny. (218, my translation)[21]

In the postmodern urban fabric, a space that is characterized by openness, heterogeneity, and fragmentation, the fictional past (FPa) and fictional present (FPr) intermingle in the uncanny moment as the subject moves through urban space. Thus, the uncanny can be experienced in any place and at any time, depending on the subject's individual frames of reference. A traumatic event (a) that had occurred in the fictional past and which was being repressed can suddenly resurface at any location in the fictional present (c) or in present reality (R).

---

20 According to Punter, the "diasporic uncanny" is exemplarily portrayed in the works of Derek Walcott, Salman Rushdie, Pauline Melville, Chitra Banerjee Divakaruni or Jamaica Kincaid (133).

21 "Wiederholung (oder auch die Variation des Immergleichen) ist das Kompositionsprinzip einer als Oberfläche konstruierten Erzählwelt. Sie wird in stilistischen Verfremdungen des Alltäglichen – im Wiedererkennen des Oft-Gesehenen, im Überlappen von wahrgenommenem Gegenstand mit seiner photographischen Duplikation, im double-take oder im déja-vu – zugleich thematisiert und aufgebrochen. Denn das Vor-Augen-Kommende wird als scheinbar Erinnertes unvertraut und Realität in der selbstreferentiellen Problematisierung ihres vertrauten Erscheinens unheimlich." (Ickstadt 218)

Figure 2. Stadtzeit: The dissemination of the uncanny

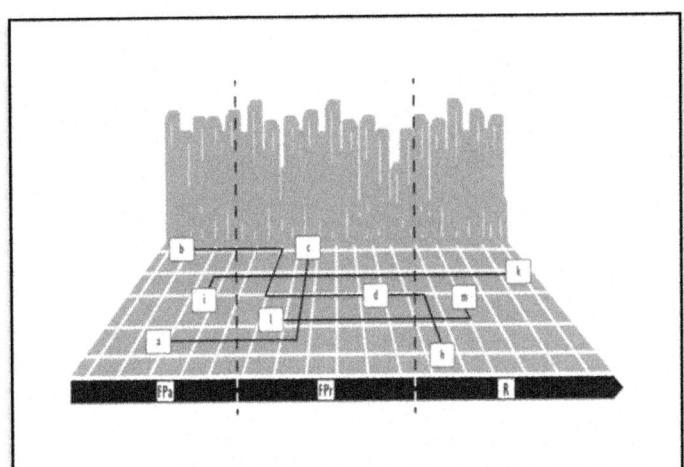

As not restricted to a determined place, encounters with the uncanny can multiply and turn into a communal experience. With *Stadtzeit* the uncanny itself is radically displaced as it transgresses the old established boundaries of confined space with the effect that in our age, as David Spurr has poignantly stated, "[a] city street and a ruined wall wield potentially as much terrifying power as once held the ghost of Hamlet's father" (25).

Part Two:
Chronotopes of the Uncanny

Uncanny Architextures:
Paul Auster's *City of Glass*

"What better portrait of a writer than to show a man who has been bewitched by books?" (*City of Glass* 98)[1] asks Daniel Quinn, the protagonist of Auster's *City of Glass*, at a revealing point of the story. Even if this rhetorical question is an allusion to Cervantes and, more precisely, to his skill with playing with intertexts, authorial personae, and language, the portrait Quinn is sketching is nothing but a mirror image of Paul Auster. Paul Auster is indeed bewitched by books, as much as he is bewitched by language. The author of *The New York Trilogy*, from which *City of Glass* forms the first of three novels, has been described by previous scholars as "the epitome of the postmodern" (Barone 6), a label that can be mainly attributed to his literary practice, brimming with metafictional puns, ironic doublings, and ontological uncertainties. Representing a radical counter-discourse to realist fiction and the positivist attitude, Auster's anti-detective novel playfully points to the virtuality and arbitrariness of language and, in a further step, also to the impossibility of arriving at absolute truth or knowledge. This shift away from epistemological issues towards ontological issues characterizes the postmodern aesthetic and, in particular, Auster's oeuvre. In *The Art of Hunger*, he remarks: "Mystery novels always give answers; my work is about asking questions" (295).

In Auster's *City of Glass*, it is primarily the complex interaction between the heterogeneous city, discontinuous time, and representation that estranges the reader from rational models of reality

---

[1] Throughout this book the reference entry for *City of Glass* will be abbreviated with *COG*.

and knowledge. As a deconstructed version of a traditional detective story, *City of Glass*'s narrative trajectories do not result in a rational explanation or a final uncovering of the mystery. Rather, all the clues that detective-protagonist Daniel Quinn collects seem to point back to themselves, thus producing a complex web of uncanny dissociations.

Already at the very beginning of the story does the uncanny reveal itself to the protagonist and the reader: Daniel Quinn picks up the ringing phone in the middle of the night and hears "a voice unlike any he had ever heard [...] at once mechanical and filled with feeling, hardly more than a whisper and yet perfectly audible, and so even in tone that he was unable to tell if it belonged to a man or a woman" (*COG* 7), asking for the detective Paul Auster. Whereas Quinn experiences the uncanny moment solely through the ghostliness of the unknown voice, the uncanniness the reader experiences manifests itself through the aesthetics of metafiction. As soon as the ontological author's name is mentioned on the intradiegetic plane, the reader is left in a state of alienation, as usually, echoing Foucault, "the author's name is not ... *fictional*" ("What is an Author?" 123). As stated above, the uncanny emerges out of the ambiguity produced by the sudden lack of boundaries between the 'real' and the fictional world, or more specifically, from the unexpected return of the non-mimetic, i.e., all that which should have remained hidden in order to maintain the mimetic illusion. The fact that Paul Auster, now referring to the actual flesh-and-blood author, also received two nightly phone calls in which a person asked for a detective agency (and which served as the major inspiration for the novel's beginning) further nourishes the unstable relationship between fact and fiction.

Similar to the fluid narratological frame of *City of Glass*, which renders impossible a clear localization of the author, also the spatial setting of the novel is marked by the lack of clearly marked boundaries. Daniel Quinn perceives his urban environment as a vast space without borderlines or clear points of reference, so that, consequently, his walks through the city become journeys of disorientation and de-differentiation:

New York was an inexhaustible space, a labyrinth of endless steps, and no matter how far he walked, no matter how well he came to know its neighbourhoods and streets, it always left him with the feeling of being lost. Lost, not only in the city, but within himself as well. [...] By wandering aimlessly, all places became equal and it no longer mattered where he was. (*COG* 4)

In *The Architectural Uncanny*, Anthony Vidler notes that manifestations of uncanniness are mainly dependent on the relationship between a subject and his or her spatial surroundings. Vidler draws his line of argumentation from a key passage of Jentsch's analysis of the uncanny, which he, as previously noted in this book, relates to the notion of intellectual uncertainty. In Freud's "The Uncanny," Jentsch's argument is summarized as follows: "The better oriented in his environment a person is, the less readily will he get the impression of something uncanny in regard to the objects and events in it" (125). Freud exemplifies Jentsch's hypothesis by recounting a personal story in which he experienced the uncanny as a result of disorientation:

Strolling one hot summer afternoon through the empty and to me unfamiliar streets of a small Italian town, I found myself in a district about whose character I could not long remain in doubt. Only heavily made-up women were to be seen at the windows of the little houses, and I hastily left the narrow street at the next turning. However, after wandering about for some time without asking the way, I suddenly found myself back in the same street, where my presence began to attract attention. Once more I hurried away, only to return there again by a different route. I was now seized by a feeling that I can only describe as uncanny, and I was glad to find my way back to the piazza that I had recently left and refrain from any further voyages of discovery. Other situations that share this feature of the unintentional return with the one I have just described, but differ from it in other respects, may nevertheless produce the same feeling of helplessness, the same sense of the uncanny. (U 144)

Similar to Freud's experience, Quinn's New York constantly radiates an "uncanny presence of disturbing otherness" (Collins/Jervis 1) because his spatial lostness makes him prone to "the uncanny of real experience" (U 154). Quinn's fundamental disorientation, as the reader learns at the beginning of the story, is generated by the trauma that the death of his son Peter has left behind. Hence, Quinn is from the very beginning a victim of the uncanny in the classical Freudian sense, experiencing the involuntary return of the repressed:

Every once in a while, he would suddenly feel what it had been like to hold the three-year-old boy in his arms – but that was not exactly thinking, nor was it even remembering. It was a physical sensation, an imprint of the past that had been left in his body, and he had no control over it. (*COG* 5)

New York, therefore, is Quinn's psycho-city. According to Paul Schindler's phenomenology, space is *a priori* anthropological: "[It] is not an independent entity (as Kant has wrongly stated) but is in close relation to instincts, drives, emotions and actions" (qtd. in Burgin 151). More precisely, the city of Auster's trilogy can be read in analogy with Merleau-Ponty's space of schizophrenic experience:

A schizophrenic patient [...] stops before a landscape. After a short time he feels a threat hanging over him. There arises within him a special interest in everything surrounding him, as if a question were being put to him from outside to which he could find no answer. Suddenly the landscape is snatched away from him by some alien force. It is as if a second sky, black and boundless, were penetrating the blue sky of evening. This new sky is empty, 'subtle, invisible, terrifying'. [...] The schizophrenic no longer inhabits the common property world, but a private world, and no longer gets as far as geographical space. (334-335)

Quinn's New York is this private world, "the nowhere he had built around himself" (*COG* 4). As a space of psychological introspection,[2] the city also becomes "an area of free space in which what does not naturally exist may take on a semblance of existing" (Merleau-Ponty 128). When Merleau-Ponty further argues that lived space[3] is always mediated through the body, he also indicates that the perception of space and the formation of identity are mutually dependent.

---

2 'Intraspection' is a neologism frequently used in academic discourses on behaviourism. While extraspection denotes the reflections about objects belonging to the outside world, intraspection concerns reflections about the self and the look 'within.'

3 Merleau-Ponty makes a distinction between 'lived' (or 'subjective') space and 'objective' space, the latter denoting geometrical or Euclidian space, i.e., space that can be mathematically measured. 'Lived space,' in contrast, is constructed through lived existential experiences and is always related to a particular subject.

In the following, and in consideration of the main character's cognitive mappings, a variety of chronotopic motives and heterotopic text strategies will be identified and analyzed in order to show how Auster's uncanny 'architextures' process the manifold uncertainties of time and space that the postmodern world has generated.

THE LABYRINTHINE SUBJECT

Bearing the name of a sacred weapon –*labyrinthos* literally meaning "the palace of the double axe" – the architectural structure of the labyrinth is etymologically infused with the connotation of something threatening. Ever since ancient and medieval times, the labyrinth has represented a site of great mystery and deadly adventure. From Greek mythology we know, for example, that Daedalus' labyrinth imprisoned the monstrous Minotaur; in ancient Egypt it was the preferred architectural form used for funerary temples that, by cleverly hiding the pharaohs' bodies and treasures[4] behind trap doors or dead ends, often brought forth the mysterious death of grave robbers. In medieval Europe, cathedral labyrinths marked out on the floor of Christian churches functioned as the site of prayer rituals, symbolizing the torturous path to spiritual salvation.[5] Regardless of the labyrinth's differing mythological or cultural connotations, its function is always, as Kim Förster has argued, to indicate spatial confusion and the threat of confinement:

In common linguistic usage, the term [labyrinth] refers to a perplexing situation in which the subject finds him- or herself trapped. At the same time, a labyrinth implicates a space which is designed only for the purpose to deliberately bewilder its walker. In this respect, the labyrinth also entails an

---

4   In his extensive study entitled *Labyrinths and Mazes*, W.H. Matthews claims that the Labyrinth of Egypt situated above Lake Moeris can be considered the first labyrinthine structure recorded in the history of humankind.
5   In the romantic period, labyrinths and mazes were inflicted with more positive connotations. Especially hedge-mazes were used as playgrounds or were the preferred site for lovers' *rendez-vous*. (Matthews 1)

experience of imprisonment that precludes an unequivocal route or way out. (248, my translation)[6]

Many scholars dealing with the subject of labyrinths (W.H. Matthews, Herman Kern, Kim Förster or Paul Basu) further mention the necessity of distinguishing between two basic designs that also determine the way in which a subject walks through a labyrinthine space. The unicursal structure, as exemplified by the Cretan type and the Chartres type, only consists of one single twisted path, leading the walker to the center and then back to the exit.[7] In contrast, the multicursal structure is characterized by a multiplicity of different paths and junctions from which the walker has to choose from. This structural difference entails that the act of moving through a unicursal labyrinth is always direct and continuous. The multicursal structure, by contrast, does not allow a continuous movement through space since junctions or dead ends heavily disturb the flow of walking. As Eugenia Virginia Ellis remarks: "The characteristic quality of movement through the multicursal maze is halting and episodic, which each fork or alternative requiring a pause for thought and decision, and emphasizes an individual's own responsibility for his or her own fate" (374). It is the multicursal form that fundamentally breaks with the linearity of time and the homogeneity of space, thus being the physical representation

---

[6] "Allein im populären Sprachgebrauch verweist der Begriff schon auf eine unübersichtliche und daher verwirrende Situation, in der das Subjekt gefangen ist. Ein Labyrinth wird aber auch mit einem Ort in Verbindung gebracht, der derart geplant und angelegt ist, dass sich das Individuum, das sich dort aufhält und fortbewegt, leicht verirrt. In dieser Hinsicht bringt das Labyrinth für den räumlich Handelnden bzw. für den Benutzer des Ortes dann häufig auch eine Gefängniserfahrung mit sich – scheinbar gibt es keinen eindeutigen Weg und keinen Ausweg" (Förster 248).

[7] Obviously there is a contradiction between the literal and visual depictions of the Greek labyrinth, because within a single-path structure Ariadne's yarn would be useless. However, as Joanna S. Stein remarks, the ancient Greeks seemed to be aware of this contradiction and regarded it as a more general metaphor, for example, to express the state of being 'lost' psychologically. Stein concludes: "[T]he form of a labyrinth may be significant in its symbolic connotations within texts, but the definition of a labyrinth has little to do with its possession of one or many paths" (24).

of *Stadtzeit*, a timespace that evokes the postmodern paradigms of disorientation and de-differentiation.

Throughout Auster's work, the architectural translation of *Stadtzeit* forms a major discursive and structural element which expresses the complexity and uncanny contingency of the postmodern urban experience. For example, in Auster's *In the Country of Last Things*, the female protagonist Anna Blume remarks: "Bit by bit the city robs you of certainty. There can never be any fixed path, and you can survive only if nothing is necessary to you. Without warning, you must be able to change, to drop what you are doing, to reverse" (6). Similarly, Quinn's New York is a space of fallacious reasoning so that his urban spatial practice can only be that of aberration. Quinn is fundamentally lost or directionless, aimlessly drifting in urban space, asking himself at some point of the story: "But if I'm going out, where exactly am I going?" (*COG* 12) In the process of investigation, Quinn constantly finds himself at many crossroads, intersections, and dead ends, and all the things that happen to him are driven by chance alone.

But also other characters are lost in the urban maze: Peter Stillman Sr., the old man Quinn investigates, "never seem[s] to be going anywhere" (*COG* 58). He walks the street of New York as being trapped in a labyrinthine structure, constantly looking for clues that might guide him to the center:

As he walked, Stillman did not look up. His eyes were permanently fixed on the pavement, as though he were searching for something. Indeed, every now and then he would stoop down, pick some object off the ground, and examine it closely, turning it over and over in his hand. It made Quinn think of an archaeologist inspecting a shard at some prehistoric ruin. (*COG* 59)

When trying to make sense of Stillman's arbitrary wanderings through Manhattan, Quinn transcribes Stillman's daily routes in the city map and, in an uncanny moment, realizes that his walks form letters:

The next day gave him a lopsided 'O', a doughnut crushed on one side with three or four jagged lines sticking out the other. Then came a tidy 'F', with the customary rococo swirls to the side. After that there was a 'B' that looked like two boxes haphazardly placed on top of one another [...]. Next there was a tottering 'A' that somewhat resembled a letter [...]. And finally there was a second 'B' [...]. Quinn then copied out the letters in order: OWEROFBAB.

[...] Making due allowances for the fact that he had missed the first four days and that Stillman had not finished yet, the answer seemed inescapable: THE TOWER OF BABEL. [...] But the letters continued to horrify Quinn. The whole thing was so oblique, so fiendish in its circumlocutions, that he did not want to accept it. Then doubts came [...]. He had imagined the whole thing. [...] It was all an accident, a hoax he had perpetrated on himself. (*COG* 70-71)

Figure 3. Quinn's transcriptions of Stillman's walks

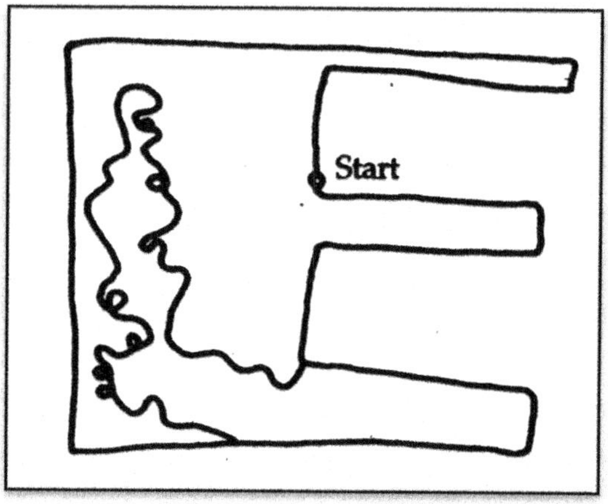

Source: Auster, Paul. *City of Glass*. In: *The New York Trilogy*. London/Boston: Faber and Faber, 2004. 69.

The horror Quinn experiences is grounded in the realization that the letters bring back to mind the subject of Stillman's research project, which aims at reconstructing the Tower of Babel. In other words, the uncanny is manifested through "the recurrence of the 'premodern' in the modern" (Brooker 157). What enforces his disquieting experience is the intellectual insecurity of whether the letters will point to any outside reality, i.e., his detective case. Of course, Stillman's transcribed walks only lead into an epistemological dead end as, in fact, the letters, or respectively the clues Quinn thinks he has gathered, refer only back to themselves. Quinn, realizing that his transcriptions do not lead to a climatic discovery, finds himself stuck in the process of investigation:

Quinn was deeply disillusioned. He had always imagined that the key to good detective work was a close observation of details. The more accurate the scrutiny the more successful the results. But after struggling these surface effects, Quinn felt no closer to Stillman than when he first started following him. (*COG* 67)

The tower (built of letters) is not only conceived as a *pars pro toto* for New York's ambitious skyscraper architecture, but also hints at the linguistic confusion that is caused by the arbitrariness between signifier and signified. As Derrida writes in *Psyche: The Invention of the Other:* "The Tower of Babel does not merely figure the irreducible multiplicity of tongues; it exhibits an incompletion, the impossibility of finishing, of totalizing, of saturating, of completing something on the order of edification, architectural construction, system and architectonics" (104). Derrida, drawing on Voltaire's analysis of the entry 'Babel' in the *Dictionaire Philosophique*, also claims that 'Babel' does not only denote God's name (as in Oriental tongues *ba* stands for father and *bel* for God) but also "the confusion of tongues [and] the state of confusion in which the architects find themselves with the structure interrupted" (ibid. 192).

The metaphor of the city as labyrinth epitomizes "the art of losing one's way" (Vidler *Warped Space* 84) and shows that the uncanny, as Auster himself has pointed out, has become the new 'order' of our postmodern urban reality:

We are continually shaped by the forces of coincidence, the unexpected occurs with almost numbing regularity [...] the world is a place beyond our understanding. We brush up against these mysteries all the time. The result can be truly terrifying – but it can also be comical. [...] The unknown is rushing on top of us at every moment. ("Interview with Larry McCaffery" 277)

In Auster's novel the labyrinthine city literally becomes a text, as Roland Barthes proclaimed in *Semiology and Urbanism*, or rather a hypertext, a vast assemblage of different (narratorial) paths wherein the reader and/or detective has to orientate him/herself (Ellis 374). Pedestrian movement, as de Certeau suggests, turns into an act of enunciation. Hence, Stillman's walks (producing letters) can be compared to a speech act that is untranslatable, therefore leading into a blind alley. Neither Quinn nor Stillman are able to decipher the semiotic matrix the city lays out for them. Accordingly, they never arrive at the center of things: At the end, Quinn simply disappears into the city's nothingness, just as his clients do, and Stillman Sr., jumping off the Brooklyn Bridge, dies "in mid-air, before he even hit[s] the water" (*COG* 123). Instead of finding Ariadne's thread, Quinn remains trapped in New York's urban fabric as much as he remains trapped within the impossibility of translations and also within the network of his multiple identities.

Evoking the Nietzschean notion of the labyrinth as self, Quinn's aimless wandering can be read as an attempt to find and explore his true self. His multiple identities, that of the detective Paul Auster, the fictional detective Max Work, Stillman's son Peter, a homeless, etc., are chronotopically translated into the multiple pathways of the labyrinth that Quinn decides to take. On one of the first pages of the graphic adaptation of *City of Glass* by Karasik and Mazzuchelli (2004), the image of the labyrinth forms the visual *tertium comparationis* linking the confusing bric(k)olage of urban signs and the protagonist's identity (translated into his fingerprint).

Auster's application of labyrinthine narrative strategies also irritates and frustrates the reader because arriving at a neat conclusive ending is taken *ad absurdum*. The resolution, the reader realizes, lies in the process of walking itself and not in the arrival at a final truth, a center. The maze comes to life only through a subject who wanders through it, and the final destination is always dependent on the wanderer. "A labyrinth human being," writes Nietzsche, "never seeks the truth, but – whatever he may try to tell us – always and only his Ariadne" (55, my translation)[8]. This means that the saving thread is yarned out of a complexity of truth(s) that also takes into account the dimension of the subjective unconscious.

Quinn is a labyrinthine subject, since his pedestrian rhetoric does not follow a logic or causal pattern. Rather, his spatial practices are relevant in ontological terms. When Quinn recites a line by Baudelaire, he equals spatial disorientation with the depersonalization of the subject, the loss of self: "Il me semble que je serais toujours bien là où je ne suis pas. In other words: It seems to me that I will always be happy in the place where I am not. Or, more bluntly: Wherever I am

---

8 "Ein labyrinthischer Mensch, sucht niemals die Wahrheit, sondern einzig seine Adriane – was immer er uns auch sagen möge" (Nietzsche 55).

not is the place where I am myself" (*COG* 110-111). Baudelaire's paradoxon echoes Quinn's fundamental displacement and, simultaneously, comes to signify a city that has turned into a heterotopia[9] in the Foucauldian sense, a place of the unhomely, representing the spatialized 'other,' a realm that lies between the real and the unreal.

But what does 'other' exactly mean for Foucault? Heterotopic spaces are 'other' in the sense that they are real but at the same time also illusionary or virtual. In "Of Other Spaces" (1967), Foucault compares the concept of heterotopia to a mirror which through the process of reflection makes it possible for the subject to locate him/herself in a place where he/she is not:

> In the mirror, I see myself there where I am not, in an unreal, virtual space that opens up behind the surface; I am over there, there where I am not, a sort of shadow that gives my own visibility to myself, that enables me to see myself there where I am absent: such is the utopia of the mirror. But it is also a heterotopia in so far as the mirror does exist in reality, where it exerts a sort of counteraction on the position that I occupy. [...]. It makes this place that I occupy at the moment when I look at myself in the glass at once absolutely real, connected with all the space that surrounds it, and absolutely unreal, since in order to be perceived it has to pass through this virtual point which is over there. (para. 13)

In other words, heterotopias are real spaces that simulate reality. Just like multicursal labyrinths, with their multiple pathways, halls, and rooms, heterotopias confuse the subject's sense of orientation. Foucault's metaphor of the mirror also indicates that heterotopias simulate spatially constructed identities. This characteristic feature links the concept of heterotopia to the concept of the uncanny, as both

---

9   In the preface to *The Order of Things*, Foucault first applied the term 'heterotopia' (literally 'the other space') to language: "Heterotopias are disturbing, probably because they secretly undermine language, because they make it impossible to name this and that [...] utopia permits fable and discourse: they run with the very grain of language and are part of the fundamental formulation of the fabula; heterotopias [...] desiccate speech [...] they dissolve our myths and sterilize the lyricism of our sentences" (xix)

presuppose a connection to reality but at the same time render this reality strange.

In addition to the feature of alterity, all heterotopias share the feature of structural heterogeneity. Foucault, therefore, refers to heterotopic spaces as sites "that have the curious property of being in relation with all the other sites, but in such a way as to suspect, neutralize or invert the set of relations that they happen to designate, mirror or reflect" ("Of Other Spaces" para.11). David Harvey helps to shed light onto Foucault's fuzzy concept when he defines it as "the coexistence in 'an impossible space' of 'a large number of fragmentary possible worlds', or more simply, incommensurable spaces that are juxtaposed or superimposed upon each other" (48). Quinn's New York is indeed a landscape of difference, "a neverland of fragments" (*COG* 72). The city that is depicted resembles a chaotic space full of "broken people, [...] broken things, [...] broken thoughts" (*COG* 78), a space in which a multitude of social worlds and subjectivities collide and whose institutional order has been considerably shattered. As Helmut Wilke claims, the idea of brokenness or fragmentation is central to the conception of heterotopia: "A heterotopia addresses a horrifying uncertainty: the decomposition of order" (7, my translation).[10] Through the simultaneous presence of spatial fragments, heterotopias are always ambiguous spaces that are constantly changing, thus making the subject more prone to experience intellectual uncertainties, or, respectively, the uncanny. Auster's New York is indeed a city in which, above all, uncertainty reigns. New York is an *ultima thule*, a place that cannot be mapped and, as such, is responsible for the fact that Quinn's attempt to unveil the detective case is *a priori* doomed to failure.

However, heterotopias do not only disrupt the continuity of space but also the continuity of time. For Foucault, heterotopias are heterochronic, i.e., "begin to function at full capacity when men arrive at a sort of absolute break with their traditional time." ("Of Other Spaces" para. 22) For example, in museums or cemeteries, two heterotopic spaces that Foucault mentions in his study, different time periods of the past are interconnected with the present in one single 'real' space. In the same vein, Stillman's wanderings have the purpose to restore

---

10 "Heterotopia wendet sich einer erschreckenden Verunsicherung zu: der Auflösung der Ordnung" (Wilke 7).

the ultimate past, to return to the Edenic state. It is not a coincidence that the old man's walks are limited to the area of the Manhattan Valley and the Upper West Side, the only part of Manhattan that is bordered by two parks, Riverside Park on the West and Central Park on the East. Quinn records Stillman's movements through the city as follows:

And yet, as if by conscious design, he kept to a narrowly circumscribed area, bounded on the north by 110th Street, on the south by 72th Street, on the west by Riverside Park, and on the east by Amsterdam Avenue. No matter how haphazard his journeys seemed to be – and each day his itinerary was different – Stillman never crossed these borders. Such precision baffled Quinn, for in all other respects Stillman seemed to be aimless. (*COG* 58)

The 'gardens' bordering Stillman's mobility zone on the East and the West are a spatialized reminder of a paradise lost and of the fact that Eden has changed its parameters of inside and outside. What once used to be the green center symbolizing (linguistic) harmony and divine order now represents the outer walls of a fallen world. What once used to be the primordial home now signifies the essence of the unhomely.

Stillman is haunted by the ambiguities that postlapsarian language generates. Unable to repress the free-floating signifiers, Stillman experiences this part of New York as the locus of linguistic confusion. By trying to rebuild the fallen language system, Stillman perceives the city from the temporal perspective of the past. However, this past that constantly intermingles with Stillman's present is not limited to prelapsarian times but also stands in close connection to the age of modernism. His philosophy of life follows strategies characteristic of a modernist aesthetic in that he is obsessed with the idea of re-establishing order to a world that for him lies in fragments. Stillman's specter of the past is therefore both, premodern and modern, signifying both order *and* chaos.

This philosophical oxymoron is also symbolized by New York's grid, an artificial framework of roads produced by rectangular blocks that was introduced to Manhattan with the Commissioner's Plan in 1811. Structurally following the Cartesian coordinate system, the implementation of the grid not only radically eliminated the island's former topography of hills and streams but also the histories of place that had once been established by the indigenous population. As

Zygmunt Bauman explains: "Grids substituted faceless, anonymous, 'nodes' for self-imposing and meaning-enforcing, dictatorial centres – with a hope to impose an artificially and artfully designed homogenous uniform space upon the chaos of nature and historical contingencies" (209). This rationalization of 'wilderness' was literally 'smoothing the way' for a city that was soon to become the most visual representation of the nation's striving for progress.

In "The Grid as City Plan," Peter Marcuse points out that the grid's major function was to accelerate economic growth through the real estate industry and that the systematic parceling of the landscape had the advantage to render the urban fabric more coherent and transparent for government authorities (421). Placing utilitarianism over aesthetic qualities, the grid was also foreshadowing the modernist architectural paradigm that form should follow function. Taking its name from "a medieval instrument of torture" (ibid. 290), the gridiron form evokes not only the ruthlessness of utilitarianism (for the sake of aesthetic qualities) but also the notion of being trapped in anguish of body or mind. In the graphic adaptation of Auster's novel, Peter Stillman Jr.'s confusing monologue strictly follows the stylistic device of a nine-panel grid division resembling prison-bars that uncannily bring to mind the professor's son nine-year captivity in a dark room, i.e., a space in which disorientation is induced by darkness.

Just like the Tower of Babel, symbolizing both the unity and the confusion of languages, the grid also comes to stand for the strange synchronicity of order and disorder. In fact, as Bauman argues, "[t]he grid did not make urban space uniform, easy to read and safe to move through. It soon turned into a matrix for heterogeneity, a canvas onto which a variety of city dwellers was yet to embroider its own, unplanned and erratic designs" (129). For the walking subject, New York's network of streets is seldom perceived as an orderly structure, but rather as a chaotic assemblage of heterogeneous blocks, or a multiplicity of little different worlds. As Rem Koolhaas remarks in *Delirious New York*: "The Grid defines a new balance between control and de-control in which the city can be at the same time ordered and fluid, a metropolis of rigid chaos" (20). Accordingly, the grid shares the same conceptual features with the labyrinth that, as Paul Basu argues, are grounded on structural paradox:

The labyrinth [...] simultaneously represents order and disorder, clarity and confusion, integration and disintegration, unity and multiplicity, artistry and chaos. This duplicity is deeply perspectival; to the "maze-walker" immersed in the structure's passages, the labyrinth is constricted, fragmented, and confusing, whereas to the "maze-viewer," able to rise above the convoluted chaos and perceive its pattern, the dazzling artistry of the labyrinth is made apparent in all its admirable complexity. (49)

UNCANNY VERTICALITY

In *Metafiction: The Theory and Practice of Self-Conscious Fiction*, Patricia Waugh proclaims that "in the post-modern period, the detective plot is being used to express not order but the irrationality of both the surface of the world and its deep structures" (82-3). Yet, in *City of Glass* this irrationality has a certain vertical logic which is conveyed through characters that are constantly ascending and descending, literally as well as metaphorically. Auster's use of vertical imagery is an effective literary strategy which, in a very postmodern fashion, challenges linear and rationalistic constructions of meaning and, at the same time, points to socio-political hierarchies that are apparent in the postmodern metropolis.

"Wer die Stadt lesen kann, kann nicht gleichzeitig in ihr gehen," writes Dorothea Löbbermann, alluding to Michel de Certeau's famous essay "Walking the City" which came out one year prior to the publication of *City of Glass*. In the essay, de Certeau comments on a line displayed on a poster he noticed on the 110th floor of the World Trade Center: "*It's hard to be down when you're up*" ("Walking the City" 180). Indeed, positioning oneself in urban space along the vertical axis entails an often confusing change of perspective and agency, so that, for example, with the act of ascending a tower or skyscraper, the pedestrian leaves social space to become inflicted with "the pleasure of 'seeing the whole'" (ibid. 152) and thus with authority. Michel de Certeau writes:

To be lifted to the summit of the World Trade Center is to be lifted out of the city's grasp. One's body is no longer clasped by the streets that turn and return it according to an anonymous law; nor is it possessed, whether as player or played, by the rumble of so many differences and by the nervousness of New

York traffic. When one goes up there, he leaves behind the mass that carries off and mixes up in itself any identity of authors or spectators. An Icarus flying above these waters, he can ignore the devices of Daedalus in mobile and endless labyrinths far below. (ibid. 180)

However, even if the panoramic view from above temporarily frees the viewer from the chaotic space of lived urban experience on the streets below and transforms the city into a 'readable' and coherent whole, the notion of an ordered and graspable city will, in reality, always turn out to be an illusion. Trapped in a hyperreality, or rather, a vertical labyrinth in which all points of reference have been lost, Quinn wonders: "Was it possible to be at the top and at the bottom at the same time?" (*COG* 118), thus echoing a paradoxon similar to the one articulated by Michel de Certeau. His state of fundamental disorientation (and homelessness) is an indication for the fact that he has lost his stable economic position.

In a similar fashion, the reader looking down onto the novel is in a god-like position and thus inflicted with a certain authority. This authority lies in the individual reader's ability to participate in the process of resolving the mystery, to symbolically yarn Ariadne's thread in order to find his/her way out of the textual maze. This postmodern paradigm that makes the reader as important as the protagonist, the narrator, or the author suggests a collapse of hierarchy and a disruption of linear succession. Accordingly, all instances involved in the literary work exist simultaneously and are denied a fixed position in the communication process.

"God, Heaven, and life are *up*, the Devil, Hell and Death are *down*" (Fiske 199-200). This ultimate spatial metaphor, as articulated by John Fiske in *Reading the Popular*, is often seen as the very starting point for a vertical concept of order determining social status and class differences. Especially in an urban context, this socio-spatial construction is most visibly expressed in the skyscraper, the architectural celebration of modern capitalism, reflecting the ideology of the dominant class. Height symbolizes power and, as noted earlier, gives the viewer the illusion of mastering what lies below. This implies that the poor and powerless, living down below, are denied a holistic sense of the city. In "Weg(be)schreibungen, Ortserkundungen: *Transients* in der amerikanischen Stadt," Dorothea Löbbermann argues that this unprivileged position in urban space, in fact, is not only disadvantageous but enables those living 'below' to 'master' a city that, lying remote from tourist attractions and shopping paths, is pure and authentic:

Although the homeless are denied a total view of the city, they are granted a look behind its smooth surface. In the cultural imaginary, they are positioned within the city's bowels, within its raw streets and subterranean tunnels. Even if their world does not evidently make sense and even if – or because of – this world is marked by lack, trauma, addiction, and madness, their world seems to be the last realm of truth. (266, my translation)[11]

Towards the latter half of *City of Glass*, Quinn suddenly finds himself among a crowd of homeless wanderers. In a passage neatly structured and graphically set off by indention, Quinn gives a detailed account of the fallen people surrounding him:

Hulks of despair, clothed in rags, their faces bruised and bleeding, they shuffle through the streets as though in chains. Asleep in doorway, staggering insanely through traffic, collapsing on sidewalks – they seem to be everywhere the moment you look for them. Some will starve to death, others will die of exposure, still others will be beaten or burned or tortured. [...]

There are women with their shopping bags and the men with their cardboard boxes hauling their possessions from one place to the next, forever on the move, as if it mattered where they were. There is a man wrapped in the American flag. There is the woman with a Hallowe'en mask on her face. There is the man in a ravaged overcoat, his shoes wrapped in rags, carrying a perfectly pressed white shirt on a hanger – still sheathed in the dry-cleaner's plastic. There is a man in a business suit with bare feet and a football helmet on his head. There is the woman whose clothes are covered from head to toe with Presidential campaign buttons. There is the man who walks with his face in his

---

11 "Den homeless entgeht [...] der Blick auf die Stadt als Ganzes, aber dafür sehen sie 'hinter die Oberfläche', denn sie befinden sich – in der kulturellen Imagination – im Inneren der Stadt, in ihren Eingeweiden, den nackten Straßen, den unterirdischen Tunneln. Selbst wenn ihre Welt keinen augenfälligen Sinn macht, selbst wenn – oder gerade weil – sie von Mangel, Trauma, Sucht und Wahnsinn geprägt ist, so erscheint ihre Welt gewissermaßen als die letzte ‚wahre' Welt." (266)

hands, weeping hysterically and saying over and over again: 'No, no, no. He's dead. He's not dead. No, no, no. He's dead. He's not dead. (*COG* 108-110)

Auster's use of a 'direct quote' graphically illustrates a more direct and trustful view behind the city's neat façade. After Quinn has lost his case and has recognized the social decay and impoverishment that surrounds him, he also opts for a more 'truthful' life on the streets. By transforming into a homeless phantom and hiding in the city's "darkest recesses and forgotten margins" (ibid.), Quinn enters a level of the city in which "no one ever noticed [him]" (*COG* 117), because he almost "melted into the walls of the city" (ibid.). This 'melting' indicates that Quinn has the need to overcome the very tension between the city's great heights and abyss-like depths. His melting into a brick wall does not just hint at a dissolving of spatial boundaries – above/below, inside/outside, private/public – but also at Quinn's dilemma of being displaced in a city in which he is neither at home nor away, neither present nor absent.

Just as New York, which can be seen as a "neither here nor there" (Turner 95), its homeless subjects can likewise be seen as neither present nor absent, since they cannot be mapped or recorded but are still 'out there.' Wandering the city like phantoms, suddenly vanishing from and reemerging onto the city surface, the homeless construct a space of verticality that, according to Anthony Vidler, is "assumed to hide, in its darkest recesses and forgotten margins, all the objects of fear and phobia that have returned [...] to haunt the imaginations of those who have tried to stake out spaces to protect their health and happiness" (167).

The real world down below, we also learn from Löbbermann, is not restricted to the horizontal plane of the city. In fact, it extends into the "subterranean tunnels" (Löbbermann 266), space that is literally invisible. Jennifer Toth's study *The Mole People: Life in the Tunnels Beneath New York City* (1993) or Marc Singer's award-winning documentary *Dark Days* (2000) show that the retreat of the homeless into the very depths of the city is not only an urban legend. Rather, underground communities are a reality and the tragic consequence of what Derrida once postulated as one of the ten major evils of the new world order: the massive exclusion of homeless people from the political (and public) sphere. New York City has always played an outstanding role as far as the number of homeless people are concerned. Most notably, the number of homeless was rising in the 1980s – a consequence of high unemployment, a rise in housing prices and 'deinstitutionalization,' a national regulation implemented in the 1970s that excluded most of mentally ill people from receiving stationary hospitalization. Left without continuous medical support, many people with mental disorders were unable to socially (re-)integrate into their communities and ended on the street. When former New York Mayor, Rudi Giuliani, started cracking down on the homeless population of New York in the early 1990s, many of the drifters and beggars who were evicted refused to move into shelters, preferring instead to retreat into the city's underground. As Jennifer Toth writes: "Those evicted from Grand Central went mainly to the tunnels under Penn Station on the West Side, and into tunnels under the Port Authority bus terminal. Some went deeper under Grand Central, down below the levels of subways and trains" (47).

Literally unmapped and unseen, the 'mole people' have inspired many writers to use the underground as an urban setting that is not exclusively charged with negative connotations. Very often in contemporary fiction, the dark underground serves as an antithesis to the 'civilized' world above, allowing for the individual to be free from the bondage of social norms and cultural stereotypes. Hence, *heimlich* and *unheimlich* change their connotations. As we can see from Ralph Ellison's *Invisible Man* (1952), whose African American male protagonist submerges into a secret coal cellar because people above ground refuse see him, the retreat underground symbolizes not only a radical critique of the hierarchical social system but also a journey into the mythical depths of subjectivity and selfhood. Just like the nameless narrator of Ellison's novel, the homeless subjects described by Toth and Singer similarly opt for a life in the dark because the constant eviction from private and public spaces nullifies their existence and identity. However, in the real world, surviving underground also makes it necessary to surface periodically, which results in an oscillation between the upper and lower levels of the city. This also signals that the homeless people down below, as Sharon Zukin argues, are "professionally committed to liminality" (242).[12] The perpetual

---

12 'Liminality' is a fairly young term that has not found its entry into many dictionaries. Deriving from Latin *limen*, it literally means 'threshold.' In "Liminality and Communitas," Victor Turner defines the liminal as an in-

movement upwards and downwards entails a constant change of perspective, though, which makes it even more difficult for the tunnel dwellers to locate or place themselves in urban space.

On the day Stillman is released from prison, Quinn starts his surveillance at Grand Central Station, where the old man is expected to arrive. Quinn arrives at the station early because he "wanted time to study the geography of the place" (*COG* 50) and soon becomes aware that in this subterranean labyrinth of "numbered gates [...], hidden staircases, unmarked exits [and] dark alcoves," (ibid.) a man like Stillman could easily vanish. The reader is then suddenly confronted with the emergence of two Stillmans from this complex underground world. One man is "dressed in an expensive blue suit" (ibid. 56), the other is "a shabby creature, [...] broken down and disconnected from his surroundings" (ibid.). Knowing, as we do, that the underground system of Grand Central Station has always been inhabited by a large number of homeless people, Stillman's shabby double could be regarded as representing those innumerable homeless people evicted from the tunnels, ever entering the world above ground.

Quinn's quest for meaning constantly confronts him with the notion of 'the fall,' which turns out to function as a recurrent narratological motif throughout the novel. For example, Stillman's dissertation, entitled "*The Garden and the Tower: Early Visions of the New World*" (*COG* 41), includes a critical reading of Milton's *Paradise Lost*, claiming that,

Adam's one task in the Garden [of Eden] had been to invent language, to give each creature and thing its name. In that state of innocence, his tongue had gone straight to the quick of the world. [*sic*] His words had not been merely appended to the things he saw, they had revealed their essences, had literally brought them to life. A thing and its name were interchangeable. After the fall this was no longer true. Names became detached from things; words devolved into a collection of arbitrary signs; language had been severed from God. The story of the Garden records not only the fall of man, but the fall of language. (*COG* 43)

---

between state or being, a person or thing "neither here nor there; [...] betwixt and between the positions assigned and arrayed by law, custom, convention, and ceremony" (95).

In this Adamic theory of language, it is due to the fall that the signifier can no longer be seen to correspond with the signified; the sign therefore becomes arbitrary. Accordingly, for Stillman the city resembles a wasteland of empty, or rather, free-floating signifiers and is thus "the most forlorn of places, the most abject" (*COG* 78).

Quinn, in the course of his investigations, gradually 'falls' from his middle-class bourgeois status into a state of homelessness. Hiding in the container opposite the Stillman apartment, he realizes that his change of identity is inevitably linked to a dramatic reconceptualization of space: "And all of the things he discovered during the days he was there, this was the one he did not doubt: that he was *falling*. What he did not understand, however, was this: in that he was *falling*, how could he be expected to catch himself as well?" (*COG* 118, my emphasis) In the novel, the notion of descent also reverses the spatial imagery of the American Dream, which is strongly associated with a vertical movement up the economic latter of success. When at one point in the story, the yo-yo becomes dysfunctional in Quinn's hand, "dangling at the end of its line" (ibid. 101), Auster metaphorically foreshadows Quinn's decent into homelessness.

Reading Auster's New York along the lines of a vertical axis, one also needs to consider the notion of phallic power structures that are at work in the novel. It is vital to mention that Virginia Stillman is the only notable female character in the story and the only notable female character in a city whose architecture is often associated with a white phallocentric ideology. With the characterization of Virginia Stillman as a devoted wife restricted to the domestic sphere, Auster might allude to the lack of alternative discourses that characterized the literary canon up to the postmodern period. Just like Stillman's dissertation "present[ing] a largely westernized, colonialist, masculinist view of the development of America, in which America is globally central and Christianity is the supreme religion" (Smith 44), Virginia[13], therefore, functions as a symbol of exclusion. However, the spatial practice of walking the city's grid opens up a counter discourse that works against the vertical dimension and thus also against the female as the 'uncanny' other in the story. Also Stillman's dream of re-erecting the Tower of Babel is a symbolic attempt to continue the

---

13 Etymologically deriving from Latin *virgo*, the name Virginia also evokes the notions of purity and (linguistic) innocence.

tradition of the grand narratives, historiographic accounts that present America's past in a neat, homogenous, and exclusivist way.

The notion of the urban labyrinth as applied in Auster's novel, be it vertically or horizontally structured, suggests the transcendence of architectural categories such as outside or inside, above or below, fiction or reality. New York has often been described as the quintessential city in which the striving for power has almost exterminated the history, legends, and identities that are so vital for creating a 'sense of place.' Indeed, de Certeau has noted that "New York has never learned the art of growing old by playing on all its pasts. Its present invents itself, from hour to hour, in the act of throwing away its previous accomplishments and challenging the future" ("Walking the City" 152). De Certeau's words also refer to processes of *tabula rasa* in the architectural sense, signifying the erasure of 'old' structures and the radical return to a 'blank canvas' onto which new structures can be built. In New York, as Justin Davidson has pointed out in the *New York Magazine*, "towers are merely placeholders, temporary arrangements of future debris" (1). Since 1993 the urban topography of New York has changed considerably, as more than 76.000 new buildings have been constructed and 44.000 have been demolished to make way for the new. The grandeur of New York is thus grounded in the process of destruction, as "growth through trauma" (2), as Davidson puts it.[14]

In his 1962 poem "An Urban Convalescence," James Merrill verbalizes this constant urge to return to an innocent architectural state: "As usual in New York, everything is torn down/ Before you have had time to care for it./ Head bowed, at the shrine of noise,/ let me try to recall/ What building stood here./ Was there a building at all?" (901). Reading New York City as a space which, because of its constant removal of historical structures, is "as empty and as spectral as the subjects inhabiting it" (Beville 104) also makes necessary a

---

14 As Davidson states, many great cities have grown out of havoc: "Paris, gutted by Baron Haussmann in the mid-nineteenth century, Chicago and London, leveled by fire; Rome, radically reorganized by Pope Sixtus V in the late 1580s; San Francisco, flattened by an earthquake in 1906" (2). In 1857, Emperor Francis-Joseph decided to demolish the city wall of Vienna, thus clearing the space for the Ringstrasse, the city's historistic splendor.

consideration of the manifold mysteries generated by the glass surfaces that constitute the fragile pillars upon which Auster's uncanny city is built.

GHOSTLY GLASS

From the perspective of structural chemistry, glass is an amorphous substance, meaning that its atoms do not exhibit an orderly pattern, but rather a random, irregular structure. Due to the unordered conglomeration of molecules, glass is brittle and can break into pieces. It is also the feature of amorphousness, literally meaning 'a state without form,' that is responsible for the phenomenon that glass is transparent and that light waves can be reflected or absorbed. The basics of thermodynamics teach us that when exposed to extreme heat, glass can change its state of aggregation from solid to liquid – again, the result of the gradual loosening of its atomic structure.

In Auster's novel, all these physical features of glass are translated into motifs, metaphors, and other rhetorical devices that stand in close relation with the uncanny. Furthermore, the novel's overall composition is one that is fundamentally amorphous, lacking a clear organization. At many times, the reader is tricked by the novel's overall illusoriness. Just like a glassy surface, the text only pretends to let the reader through (so that s/he can establish meaning that relates to an external reality) but in fact represents a solid wall that only reflects and confuses the structures it surrounds. The postmodern device of self-referentiality, therefore, finds its most notable expression through the metaphor of (reflective) glass. Looking at story-related aspects of the novel, Quinn's detective case gradually loses its atomic structure and finally dissolves into mere nothingness. Similarly, as Quinn becomes obsessed with the case, his social status and identity gradually 'melt' (when he turns into a homeless) until he finally 'vaporizes,' simply leaving behind his red notebook in the empty room.

Also Stillman Jr.'s use of language is fundamentally 'without form.' When Quinn initially pays his client a visit to learn more about his case, he becomes witness of Stillman Jr.'s linguistic behavior that at times seems nothing but an unordered accumulation of sounds: "Wimble click crumblechaw beloo. Clack clack bedrack. Numb noise, flacklemuch, chewmann. Ya, ya. Ya. Excuse me. I am the only one who understands these words" (*COG* 17). The young man's speech which, in Bernd Herzogenrath's words, "oscillate[s] between manic volubility and wordless stupor" (31), represents the notion of disorientation on a linguistic level. Stillman's disability to articulate himself in a coherent way is the result of a language experiment conducted by his father when he was a child. Being obsessed with the idea to restore the pure language of god, Stillman Sr. isolated his son in a dark room for nine years, hoping that he would achieve the pure language that was once spoken in paradise. The professor's study draws on two biblical episodes that he considers the origin of linguistic amorphousness. According to Stillman, it was the Fall of Man, which initiated the end of the Edenic language:

Adam's task in the garden had been to invent language, to give each creature and thing its name. In that state of innocence, his tongue had gone straight to the quick of the world. His words had not been merely appended to the things he saw, they had revealed their essences, had literally brought them to life. A thing and its name were interchangeable. After the fall this was no longer true. Names became detached from things; world devolved into a collection of arbitrary signs; language had been severed from God. The story of the Garden, therefore, not only records the fall of man but the fall of language. (*COG* 43)

Second, Stillman's theory draws on the story of the fall of the Tower of Babel that brought about the confusion of languages. Stillman regards the myth of Babel as an expansion of the story of the Fall of Man. For the old professor, these two biblical episodes have shattered not only the 'original unity' between God and Man but also the perfectibility and absoluteness of God's language that once unified both a sensual as well as an intellectual meaning. (Herzogenrath 38) For Stillman, postlapsarian language is like shattered glass, bits and pieces that once belonged together but have now lost their stable connection – "words devolved into a collection of arbitrary signs" (*COG* 43). Obviously, the untranslatable language produced by Stillman's son is the articulation of trauma, a linguistic return of the repressed. At the same time, however, Stillman's uncanny language points to the ambiguity of the literary sign and the function of modern (literary) art to make the familiar strange. As exemplified by modernist and, in particular, futurist writers[15] and Russian formalists, the poetic function relies on the principle of linguistic alienation, of widening the gap between the signifier and the signified. Therefore, it is no coincidence that Stillman's son repeatedly compares his diction to "beautiful poems" (*COG* 19).

Stillman's urge to create a new Babel in which prelapsarian language is restored is often read by literary critics as an analogy to the modernist attempt to restore order to a world that, after WWI and new means of transportation, communication, and living, has become highly fragmented. Stillman's language, as many other symbols in the novel, clearly points to the shatteredness of a once intact universe. In many ways, Stillman's attempt to reconstruct the fallen Tower of Babel echoes the poetic glass utopias of the modernist German writer Paul Scheerbart, for whom glass was the material out of which an Edenic city could be rebuilt. In *Glass Architecture* (1914), a series of aphorisms composed to be inscribed onto Bruno Taut's *Glasspavillion*, he writes:

The surface of the Earth would change greatly if brick architecture were everywhere displaced by glass architecture. It would be as though the Earth clad itself in jewellery of brilliants and enamel. The splendor is absolutely unimaginable. And we should then have on the Earth more exquisite things than the gardens of the Arabian Nights. Then we should have a paradise on Earth and would not need to gaze longingly at the paradise in the sky. (32)

It was Scheerbart's architectural mysticism that also articulated the visionary ideas of a collective of German expressionist architects and artists that after World War I formed under the name of "The Glass Chain" (*Die Gläserne Kette*). Their name, deriving from their secret epistolary exchange of theories and visions, soon became a synonym for an expressionist architectural style that advocated glass as the unifying material link between the world and the cosmos. With its characteristic features of boundlessness, weightlessness, and clarity, glass was the material most apt to fulfill avant-garde mind exper-

---

15 Filippo Tommaso Marinetti's "Technisches Manifest der futuristischen Literatur" (1912) demands a poetics in which the discursive unity and grammatical order is radically destroyed for the sake of abstraction and alienation.

imentations, such as that of Bruno Taut, who in *Alpine Architektur* (1920) imagined a city of glass on the summit of a mountain. Especially for Taut, the glass crystal became the "leitmotif of modernity" (Vidler "New Skins" 25) and renewal in the sense that it could give birth to an architecture that could make the individual overcome the crisis of the modern world and could make it return to a more stable, unified, and primitive state. Needless to say, the fantastic conceptions of Taut and his followers have never been realized, and Taut himself admitted that his models are fundamentally unpractical. Nevertheless, Taut's glass ideology was gradually applied to more pragmatic projects. Even though un-built, Mies van der Rohe's "Glass Skyscraper" (1922) foreshadows much of New York's contemporary glass and steel high rises, among them Foster's Hearst Tower, the Museum of Modern Art, the Millenium Hilton, or Fox and Fowle's glass tower on Times Square.

As exemplified by Mies van der Rohe's "Glass Skyscraper," glass architecture becomes the material manifestation of the (post)modern uncanny as it produces intellectual ambiguity in many ways. Depending on certain light conditions, the glassy curtain enables the building to do both hide and reveal. Hence, when the light is switched on at night in a room, the building can uncannily bring to light what is supposed to be hidden. If illuminated from the outside, however, it reflects its outer surroundings, functioning like a mirror, thus making invisible the inner structures of the building. As Justin Davidson argues, glass is the materialization of paradox:

> But the chief allure of glass in this era of deceptive exhibitionism is its usefulness in crafting illusion. A glass wall carries with it the suggestion of obviousness; it is the architectural equivalent of a magician's rolled-up sleeve. Glass looks insubstantial and yet it keeps the weather out. It's brittle yet remarkably immune to age; weightless yet able to carry a load; revealing as it keeps secrets. (4)

In "Nothing to Go on: Paul Auster's *City of Glass,*" William G. Little refers to the novel as "an incarnation of minimalist modernism" (149) because it embodies the desire for abstraction, purity, and wholeness. At the same time, however, the book ridicules and decomposes these very ideas. Buildings and rooms made of glass create optical illusions that echo the transit from one level of consciousness to the other, thus symbolizing the Freudian return of the repressed. For Quinn, New York functions as a hall of mirrors in which he perceives himself and his environment as real and unreal at the same time. Just like the glassy surface of a skyscraper constantly alters and alienates its 'content' due to light conditions and perspective, so does *City of Glass* reflect and deform conventional strategies of narration. Shaped by the painful memories of the loss of his wife and son, but also by the postmodern city's factual illusoriness, Quinn's reality becomes highly distorted and constantly gives birth to uncanny mirror-images and situations of explicit doubling that indicate the postmodern confusion with time, space, and identity.

Mirror Moments, Bric(k)olage Identities

In Western societies, mirrors have functioned as symbols of mimetic representation and self-consciousness from ancient or even prehistoric times onwards. Plato used the mirror metaphor to explain that a work of art is nothing but a (poor) copy of the real world, and the myth about Narcissus falling in love with his own reflection indicates the mirror's function as a tool of simulation *and* deception. A mirror can play tricks on us. It can change our perception of space, for example, by making a room appear much bigger than it actually is. It can distort our spatial position, as we can find ourselves in and outside the mirror at the same time. Mirrors are tools of illusion and magic not only because they confuse categories such as external and internal, but also because they signify both sameness and difference. The mirror repeats, doubles, but at the same time produces something distinct or 'other.' Paradoxically, the mirror enables us to become both subject and object.

With the advent of psychoanalysis, the mirror image became primarily associated with the process of identity formation and, in particular, with fundamental psychological distinctions such as the self and the other, or the conscious and the unconscious. Among the most notable examples in psychoanalytic theory is Lacan's mirror stage, describing the process whereby the child recognizes his/her body image in the mirror, thus developing a sense of self and ideal wholeness but also, when looking back at its flesh-and-blood self, a crisis of imperfection and fragmentation. For Freud, a mirror image forming a double always conjures up the notion of death, which is why we experience the sight of our double uncanny. Through doubling, the subject perceives him/herself as decomposed and sees his/her counterpart as a threat. "There is nothing more uncanny," writes Heinrich Heine, "than seeing one's face accidentally in a mirror by moonlight" (qtd. in Rank 43).

As noted earlier in this study, Freud conceives of the double not only in symbolic terms but also as a psychological phenomenon. For him, a double can also emerge through the division of the self which is caused by an intra-psychic conflict or disturbance of the ego. Drawing on Otto Rank's psychoanalytical observations, Freud also reads the manifestation of a second consciousness as "an energetic denial of the power of death" (Rank qtd. in U 142).[16] In this vein, Freud mentions a tradition in ancient Egypt in which artists created doubles of the dead out of durable materials in order to avoid the "extinction of the self" (ibid.).[17]

In *City of Glass*, Auster applies a great number of different doublings, most of which can be read along the lines of psychoanalytical theory and, in particular, in relation to the Freudian uncanny as the return of the repressed. The uncanny mirrorings Quinn experiences indicate that his process of investigation, in fact, concerns nothing but his own self. Quinn (just like all the main characters in the novel) is literally in his mirror stage, which "undermines the very logic of identity" (Bennett/Royle 39).

The protagonist's first encounter with the phenomenon of doubling is of anthropological nature and occurs at Grand Central Station, the place where Quinn's investigation of Peter Stillman Sr. starts. Looking for the old man in the crowd, he is suddenly confronted with two Stillmans, one clothed in rags, the other in an expensive suit:

Directly behind Stillman, heaving into view just inches behind his right shoulder, another man stopped, took a lighter out of his pocket, and lit a cigarette. His face was the exact twin of Stillman's. For a second Quinn

---

16 For Freud, the notion of the double is grounded in primary narcissism, the self-love an infant experiences in early childhood in which the individual self is not yet defined.

17 Also the body-soul dualisms in Christian thought or the dichotomy established by the Chinese yin and yang philosophy can be read along the lines of anthropological manifestations of the double (Rogers 6).

thought it was an illusion, a kind of aura thrown off by the electromagnetic currents in Stillman's body. But no, this other Stillman moved, breathed, blinked his eyes; his actions were clearly independent of the first Stillman. [...] Quinn froze. There was nothing he could do now that would not be a mistake. Whatever choice he made – and he had to make a choice would be arbitrary, a submission to chance. Uncertainty would haunt him to the end. (*COG* 55-56)

The ambiguity that Quinn's encounter with Stillman's anthropological composite provokes lies in the antagonism between the 'good' and the 'dangerous' Stillman. The old man's shabby double must be read along the lines of subordination and, more precisely, along the lines of repression. Stillman's identity is split visually, now also bringing to light the repressed or unconscious part of his self, represented in the form of a homeless person. Stillman's shabby double anthropomorphizes the failure of his own linguistic experiment and, in a wider sense, also the loss of temporal continuity (historicism), spatial totality, and, finally, the lack of absolute meaning and coherence. The doubling of Stillman Sr., therefore, is an expression of a postmodern aesthetic which uses the double as an "ironic literary device that undermines suggestions of universal harmony, essential duality, psychological wholeness, or stable signification" (Slethaug 30).

According to Quinn, Stillman's double may also be the result of the radiation of aura, a term that Walter Benjamin defines in "Little History and Photography" as "a strange tissue of space and time; the unique appearance of a distance however near it may be" (515) that is attached to a work of art. For Benjamin, this distance has faded in the age of mechanical reproduction, as the process of reprography destroys an artwork's temporal and spatial authenticity. Benjamin claims that the mass publication of books or the advent of photography and film has rendered the original and its aesthetic distance absent. Thus, the aura of an object of art is destroyed, as the viewer can no longer communicate with its tradition and historical context.

Benjamin adds that the modern city enforces "the disintegration of aura through the experience of shock" (*Charles Baudelaire* 154). In the urban environment the observer's gaze translates into a hectic perception of a flood of images in which distance is reduced to a minimum. In *City of Glass*, Quinn points out that "[t]he world was outside of him, around him, before him, and the speed with which it kept changing made it impossible for him to dwell on any one thing for very long" (*COG* 4). This point of view, however, would assume that in modern or postmodern times any reproduced work of art is *a priori* empty of auratic quality and therefore useless. The Stillman that Quinn decides to follow is clothed in rags, and his spatial practice is limited to collecting worthless objects from the street. Accordingly, the Stillman-as-bum is the personified equivalent of an object of art which, in the process of modernization, has lost its historical authenticity and therefore its aura. Stillman Sr. is a fictional construct, a *l'object art* that at times may appear useless to the reader: neither is he a developed character, nor does he commit a crime, nor does he contribute to the mere possibility of advancing the detective plot. He represents the gaze destroyed and, as follows, the very essence of anti-detective fiction. Stillman's neat double, in contrast, represents our longing for making sense of the world, of being presented the original story, the perfect image. However, the perfect image or, in our case, the well-made-detective-story is only an illusion, just like the god-like view onto the city that makes us believe that we can 'read' or fully grasp its logic.

However, knowing that Paul Auster applies the chronotope of *Stadtzeit* in which the past constantly returns through spatial simultaneities, history and tradition cannot be totally lost. In fact, the aura uncannily returns in the process of mirroring, pointing back to its original source(s). Through the literary device of intertextuality, Auster brings to life fictions of the past to reestablish an aura that was once lost. Cervantes' *Don Quixote*, Poe's "William Wilson," Carroll's *Alice in Wonderland* or Milton's *Paradise Lost* clearly function as ghost texts that haunt Auster's novel in the sense that they indicate the return of realist modes of narration. Through these intertextual references or textual phantoms, the uncanny manifests itself as an absent presence of previous texts that constantly intermingle with Auster's story. The uncanny, therefore, is the illusion of aura.

The variety of intertexts also mirror the themes and motives established in *City of Glass* and *vice versa*. Auster's novel not only echoes Don Quixote's obsession with adventurous fiction and the taking on of heroic identities but also the *Doppelgänger* motif of Poe's "William Wilson," the semantic theories established by Carroll's egg-character Humpty Dumpty, or the pointlessness of following a man through an urban labyrinth, as illustrated in Poe's "The Man in the Crowd." The attentive reader suddenly realizes that *City of Glass*, in fact, is a story reflecting many stories already told. However, as Robert Nye writes in *Faust*, the act of repetition is not meaningless but, paradoxically, induces variation in the sense that it renders the familiar unfamiliar: "Es gibt immer noch eine andere Version [...] nachdem man alles, was man zu wissen glaubt, auf so unterschiedliche Weise erzählt hat, wie man nur kann, gibt es immer noch etwas, was man nicht erzählt hat und noch eine andere Art, es zu erzählen" (qtd. in Grabes 113). In this vein, also the other novels of the trilogy, *Ghosts* and *The Locked Room*, are nothing but a distorted mirror image of *City of Glass*. Karasik and Mazzuchelli's graphic adaptation of *City of Glass* is yet again another variation of the same story in the seemingly endless universe of narrative possibilities.

In Wayne Wang's 1990 cinematic masterpiece *Smoke*, for which Paul Auster wrote the screenplay, a character named Auggie takes more than 4.000 pictures of the same street corner at the same time of day, claiming that "sometimes the different [pictures] become the same, and the same ones disappear." Auggie goes on: "The earth revolves around the sun, and every day the light from the sun hits the earth at a different angle" (Auster *Smoke* 44). Collecting his photographs in different albums, Auggie captures the temporality of alterity and variation by means of spatial repetition. Although the familiar street corner stays the same, it is rendered strange through the differing rhythms and histories that spatial practices have inflicted on it. Variation and alterity, as Roland Barthes argues in *The Rustle of Language*, is an aesthetic element of (the postmodern) literary text which functions as a "multidimensional space in which are married and contested several writings none of which is original" (53). When Quinn is unable to make out the Stillman he is supposed to follow, he has to rely on the principle of chance alone. Quinn is stuck in an urban world in which the copy or reflected image comes to substitute the real.

The second example of anthropological doubling occurs towards the end of the story, when Quinn notices his reflection in a shop window, "not recogniz[ing] the person [...] as himself" (*COG* 142-43). This uncanny mirror moment in which Quinn realizes that he has transformed into a bum comes to stand for the instability of the protagonist's identity. Unconsciously taking on the social role of the man he first investigated, Quinn also becomes a mirror image of the old Stillman. Having lost his apartment because of his obsession with the case, Quinn has literally become homeless. Without a domestic place to return to or to identify with, his subjectivity disseminates into the complexity of New York's urban space. In the graphic adaptation of Auster's novel, the protagonist's mirror moment in which he perceives his new shabby persona in a variety of differently framed mirrors indicates that the postmodern self is nothing but "a pastiche of styles glued to a surface" (Ellis 126). The alterity of frames and mirrors displaying different details of Quinn's corpus signifies the essence of repetition itself: It opposes generality. As Deleuze points out in *Difference and Repetition*:

To repeat is to behave in a certain manner, but in relation to something unique or singular which has no equal or equivalent. And perhaps this repetition at the level of external conduct echoes, for its own part, a more secret vibration which animates it, a more profound, internal repetition within the singular. (1)

The visual *mise en abyme* that splits Quinn's persona into a variety of fragments (of the same) also alludes to Quinn's internal crisis of the self that follows the act of repression and manifests itself via the process of autoscopy[18].

In linguistic terms, Quinn's bric(k)olage identity is expressed through the abyss structures created by the doubling of names, initials, or numbers, a form of repetition which I call semantic doubling. The various instances of semantic doubling serve the purpose to point to our language's potential to play mirror tricks on us. Also Bernd Herzogenrath suggests that language deceives in that the linguistic sign represents "a surface (signifier) promising depth (signified)" (67). For example, Daniel Quinn shares the first name with Auster's fictional (and also actual) son, and at the same time his name mirrors the initials of Don Quixote, the hero of Cervantes' story. Quinn's pen name is that of William Wilson, which is also the name of Edgar Allen Poe's protagonist in his famous story about *Doppelgänger*. Strangely, it is Quinn's fictional alter ego named Max Work that he perceives more real than his true self as a writer. As a result of the process of repression, Quinn "becomes increasingly haunted by the ghosts of his

---

18 Psychologically speaking, Quinn may also suffer from negative autoscopy, a psychological disorder in which the patient does not recognize his/her mirror image as him/herself.

characters, of other writers who precede him, and of his own 'other' selves" (Rubinstein 252-253). Identifying much more with his self-constructed private eye, Quinn explains his distorted perception of identity through the homonymic doubling of 'I,' 'i,' and eye':

> The term [private eye] held a triple meaning for Quinn. Not only was it the letter 'i,' standing for 'investigator,' it was 'I' in the upper case, the tiny life-bud buried in the body of the breathing self. At the same time, it was also the physical eye of the writer, the eye of the man who looks out from himself into the world and demands that the world reveal itself to him. For five years now, Quinn had been living in the grip of this pun. (*COG* 8)

Once again, repetition occurs on the phonological sameness of 'I' and 'eye,' but still Quinn's detective persona ('eye') is fundamentally different to his repressed self ('I'), shaped by painful memories, loneliness, and displacement.

Another example of semantic doubling concerns the repetition of numbers. In "The Uncanny," Freud claims that this phenomenon gives rise to uncanniness as it suggests the eerie presence of an unseen force that undermines or manipulates the subject's sanity and/or sense of reality:

> There is certainly nothing remarkable, for instance, about depositing a garment in a cloakroom and being given a ticket with a certain number on it – say 62 – or about finding that the cabin one has been allocated bears this number. But the impression changes if these two events, of no consequence in themselves, come close together, so that one encounters the number 62 several times in one day, and if one then observes that everything involving a number – addresses, hotel rooms, railway carriages, etc. invariably has the same one, at least as part of the whole. (144-145)

In other words, simply by means of spontaneous recurrence something ordinary will turn into something uncanny.

In *City of Glass*, letters and numbers are strangely mirrored, thus indicating a mystery that can never be solved. For example, in the novel the number 69 is a recurring element that contributes to the story's uncanniness. Quinn's process of investigation starts when he visits Peter and Virginia Stillman in their apartment located on 69th Street. Shortly after Quinn sees his mirror image in a display window and realizes that he has become a homeless, he heads towards 96th Street where he enters Central Park in order to take a break from his investigation. Stillman Sr. was arrested in 1969, and Quinn at one point wonders whether "the moon landing of that same year had been connected in any way with what had happened [and] why Christopher, the patron saint of travel, had been decanonized by the Pope in 1969, just at the time of the trip to the moon" (130). When Quinn reads Stillman's thesis on a new Babel, which the professor wrote under the pen name Henry Dark, Quinn comes across two dates, both of which contain the (mirrored) number 69:

So ended Stillman's synopsis of Henry Dark's pamphlet, dated 20 December 1690, the seventieth anniversary of the landing of the Mayflower. Quinn let out a little sigh and closed the book. The reading room was empty. He leaned forward, put his hand in his hands, and closed his eyes. '1960,' he said aloud. He tried to conjure up an image of Henry Dark, but nothing came to him. In his mind he saw only fire, a blaze of burning books. Then, losing track of his thoughts and where they had been leading him, he suddenly remembered that 1960 was the year that Stillman had locked up his son. (*COG* 49)

Quinn firmly believes that the mirrorings and doublings of 69 point to another clue that will help him to learn more about Stillman and his murderous intentions. Assuming that the birth of New England is related to Stillman's motivation to imprison his son also triggers the uncanny in the implied reader, who is supposed to start wondering whether the sudden return of the number 69 is in any way significant for Quinn's case. In fact, however, the reader is once again lured onto a hermeneutic path that leads to a dead end, as the number 69, being symbolic for the perfect pair or the (inverted) double, only signifies back to the stylistic device of doubling itself. However, this does not prevent the characters or readers from experiencing an uncanny moment because unintended repetition, be it of semantic, phonological, or anthropologic nature always, as Freud has pointed out, "forces us to entertain the idea of the fateful and the inescapable, when we should normally speak of chance" (U 144).

Similarly, the number 3 occurs repeatedly on various narratological levels. The *New York Trilogy* consists of three stories that are in a way the same, but still different, as Auster employs different names of characters and different settings. Before Quinn picks up the phone it rings three times, and in total he receives three calls. Quinn meets (and introduces himself to) Stillman Sr. three times. Finally, the 'real' Paul Auster was born on February, the 3rd. Numerologically speaking, the number three is related to alchemy, multiplicity, and creative power, but also self-centeredness, all of which are major themes in the novel.

As part of his 1914 study on *Doppelgänger*, Otto Rank also discusses the double as a mimetic form that is applied to the multiple selves of the author that the reader encounters through characters or narrators. F. Scott Fitzgerald once remarked that "[t]here never was [...] a good biography of a good novelist. There couldn't be. He's too many people if he's any good" (qtd. in Rogers 3). Also in *City of Glass*, Auster's strategies of decomposition point to the fragmentation of authorial identity and authorial presence. In an extradiegetic loop, Paul Auster, the flesh-and-blood author of *City of Glass*, gives birth to two fictional doubles of himself. First, the detective named Paul Auster that Virginia Stillman seeks to contact and, second, the replica of the 'actual' writer Paul Auster whom Quinn consults towards the end of the story. Hoping that he would find the real detective whose identity he had taken on at the beginning, Quinn runs over the pages of the phonebook, finds an entry named Paul Auster and decides to pay him a visit. However, when Quinn encounters Auster face-to-face, he has to learn that, once again, the linguistic clue is useless for his investigation:

"I have a feeling there's been a terrible mistake. I came here looking for Paul Auster, the private detective." [...].
"The what?" Auster laughed, and in that laugh everything was suddenly blown to bits. Quinn realized that he was talking nonsense. He might just as well have asked for Chief Sitting Bull – the effect would have been no different.
"The private detective," he repeated softly.
"I'm afraid you've got the wrong Paul Auster."
"You are the only one in the book."
"That might be," said Auster. "But I'm not a detective."
"Who are you then? What do you do?"
"I'm a writer." (*COG* 94)

In *The Art of Hunger*, Paul Auster explains that his fictional presence reflects a process of border-crossing that brings to light a secret part of his identity that, in the realist tradition, is supposed to be hidden or masked:

> I don't mean my autobiographical self, I mean my author self, that mysterious other who lives inside me and puts my name on the covers of books. What I was hoping to do, in effect, was to take my name off the cover and put it inside the story. I wanted to open up the process, to break down walls, to expose the plumbing [...] The self that exists in the world – the self whose name appears on the covers of books – is finally not the same self who writes the book. (293)

The exposure of Auster's different identities that are usually summarized under one umbrella term, i.e., 'Paul Auster,' are in itself a mirroring of Quinn's different authorial identities: Quinn writes under a pen name, i.e., that of Max Work. At the same time, he takes notes in the red notebook when pretending to be the detective Paul Auster. Is Quinn then nothing but a mirror image of the 'true' Paul Auster?

While all this logically points to the postmodern paradigm of self-referentiality, the doubling of names is a strategy that clearly evokes the uncanny. As Freud himself recounts: "One cannot help feeling slightly uncomfortable on discovering that a stranger has the same name, as I realized very clearly, not long ago when a Herr S. Freud called during my consulting hours" (*The Psychopathology of Everyday Life* 28). The uncanniness that is attached to the repetition of names results from the paradox that, as Derrida points out, "a proper name does not name anything which is human, which belongs to a human body, a human spirit, an essence of man" ("Aphorism" 427). In other words, a name is nothing but a sign whose signifier can never point to a stable signified. This then means that the double or the 'other' in one's self is *a priori* part of one's name and thus of one's (authorial) identity, which is a quite frightening idea. In *City of Glass*, the uncanny is mainly related to existential questions such as: Who is the author? Who is the narrator? Who is the reader? These questions, however, are again not intended to be answered but rather point to the fact that in a postmodern world hermeneutic processes are always multilayered, interactive, and non-exhaustive.

Another relevant aspect about the author's name concerns the notion of immortality. As Nicholas Royle has argued, a name is uncanny *per se* because it "is capable of outliving its bearer" and thus "itself becomes an uncanny harbinger" (191). Through the act of writing the author gives birth to an immortal copy of himself that 'outlives his/her bearer' as soon as his work is published and consumed. In being both fictional and real and thus mortal and immortal, Paul Auster impersonates a ghost writer in its very literal sense.

RHETORIC AND RUINS

Not only is New York City a confusing maze of mirrors, it is also a "junk heap" (*COG* 78) constructed of "broken people, [...] broken things, [...] broken thoughts" (ibid.). Peter Stillman describes the city as "the most forlorn of places, the most abject," which is an obvious nod to Julia Kristeva's concept of abjection[19] which she relates to "the place where meaning collapses" (2). For Kristeva, the abject is caused by a radical disturbance of system and order, as it "[d]oes not respect borders, positions, rules" (ibid 4). Quinn perceives New York City as the architectural translation of the domestic destroyed; as a non-place where the notion of home, along with all its connotations of security, family, and identity, has become irrelevant. We have seen in a previous chapter that homelessness is a dominant motif in the story, signaling the alienation that the (post)modern urban condition invokes. Needless to say, however, Auster's decision to depict New York as a material wasteland goes far beyond a critique of the social decay of the 1980s. Rather, it suggests the mysterious interrelation of (repressed) memory, reality, and the production of art.

Ever since the Gothic novel we know that it is the decaying, crumbling castle that most effectively evokes the ghostly presence of bygone times and the lack of order, reason, and rationality. Even if the ruin we encounter in *City of Glass* is post-industrial, it nonetheless continues to epitomize the nostalgic and the uncanny. In *The Aesthetics of Decay*, Dylan Trigg notes that the city as ruin "proves its epistemological value as it undermines the residue of certainty" (7). Ruins are spaces of obscurity because they confound and ridicule temporal linearity and spatial totality and constitute a condition of

---

19 Kristeva's notion of the abject shares a structural similarity to Freud's uncanny in that it also connects two temporalities that resurface in a moment of recollection. Therefore, the time of the abject is both "of veiled infinity and the moment when revelation bursts forth" (Kristeva 9).

temporal dislocation. It is the ruin's incompleteness or fragmentariness that stimulates the observer's memory or imagination. For Gevork Hartoonian, however, the ruin is more than just an inscription of a temporal or chronotopic phenomenon, because "it involves the decay of material and of course a sense of aesthetic appreciation that is bound with that sense of transitoriness that is essential to modernity" (183).

In "Nostalgia for Ruins," Andreas Huyssen argues that the ruin is an essential topos and expression of the modern age:

Real ruins of different kinds function as projective screens for modernity's articulation of asynchronous temporalities and for its fear of and obsession with the passing of time. […] The architectural ruin seems to hover in the background of an aesthetic imagination that privileges fragment and aphorism, collage and montage, freedom from ornament and reduction of the material. (11)

In *City of Glass*, the fear of and disillusionment with asynchrony and the passing of time is exemplified in the character of Stillman Sr., who is obsessed with collecting broken objects – "from the chipped to the smashed, from the dented to the squashed, from the pulverized to the putrid" (78) – that he wants to rename. The broken object serves as a *pars pro toto* that indicates that the crisis of the (post)modern city is first and foremost a crisis of representation. As Hartoonian writes: "[I]n modern times, all production immediately falls into ruin, thereafter to be set in stone without revealing what it had once signified, since the inscriptions are illegible or written in the dead language" (185).

The ephemeral quality that characterizes modernity and modernism is firmly attached to the commodified object which in a process of constant renewal makes the status of ruin permanent. Through the increased speed of production cycles, the new is constantly reinvented and almost simultaneously falls into ruination. Through trends and (retro-)fashions, the old can no longer be distinguished from the new. What further complicates this synchronism of production and dereliction is that the commodified object is abstracted from its origin or, more precisely, from the social processes that we once associated with products in pre-industrial times. Objects under capitalism do no longer carry associations of social relations, for example, a family history, but rather radiate, as Benjamin claims, a *phantasmagoria*[20], a certain 'magic' that derives from the object's hidden traces of origin or production. By using *phantasmagoria* as a metaphor for commodity fetishism, Benjamin hints at the obscure relationships between consumer and producer, consumer (subject) and object but also, most importantly, for our discussion of the uncanny, between the external and internal (psychological) world.

The fetishized object destroyed is relevant for the construction of uncanniness in more than one sense. For Stillman, it represents Lacan's[21] *object petit a*, the unattainable object of desire that materializes his phantasm: to return to the language spoken in Eden. Stillman uses a broken umbrella to exemplify his dilemma of 'want' that also concerns unambiguous representation:

> Because it can no longer perform its function, the umbrella has ceased to be an umbrella. It might resemble an umbrella, but now it has changed into something else. The word, however, has remained the same. Therefore, it can no longer express the thing. It is imprecise; it is false; it hides the thing it is supposed to reveal. [...] Unless we can begin to embody the notion of change in the words we use, we will continue to be lost. (*COG* 77-78)

Even if he renames the broken umbrella, will he not be able to reverse the fall of language and cut through the arbitrary bond between the signified and the signifier. The useless umbrella, therefore, signifies, as Donald Kunze points out, "a materialization of the fact of a lack" (10).

Like the *objet petit a*, Stillman's objects are non-functional remnants that only serve the purpose to stimulate Stillman's desire to return to an archaic state, to a better and simpler linguistic past. Solely focusing on collecting his objects of desire, Stillman loses himself in the Lacanian order of the symbolic, in a world in which there is no

---

20 The term *phantasmagoria* generally denotes exhibitions of optical illusions produced by apparatuses such as a magic lantern or *camera obscura* in the late eighteenth and early nineteenth centuries. See also Adorno's definition of phantasmagoria in *Versuch über Wagner*.

21 For Lacan, the unconscious operates just like a language system in which the relation between the signifier and the signified is arbitrary. Also the subject defines him/herself via language.

essential 'meaning,' an order that always lacks something. When committing suicide, Stillman is already aware of the fact that his objects of desire are indeed objects that are forever lost, objects whose names will never reveal their true essence and thus will never be 'whole' again. As "prelapsarian language is revealed as a phantasmatic illusion" (Herzogenrath 8), Stillman has to accept that the (linguistic) state of ruination is permanent and that he would be haunted forever.

How does all this relate to the uncanny? For Lacan, the uncanny pertains to an outside object that signifies lack. More specifically, for Lacan, the 'other' (A) is uncanny *per se*: "[It is] something *entfremdet*, something strange to me, although it is at the heart of me, something that on the level of unconscious only a representation can represent" (71). What follows is that the uncanny, as Dagmar von Hoff and Marianne Leutzinger-Bohleber rightly argue, always entails a crisis of linguistic representation:

Both Sigmund Freud and Jacques Lacan understand the uncanny as a threat to proper language, as an anxiety that concerns the loss of its function to symbolize. This positions the uncanny not only in close proximity to the threat of a psychosis but also to processes of de-realization that follow severe traumatizations. (103, my translation)[22]

In chronotopic terms, Stillman Sr.'s world is that of *extimité* (a portmanteau word fusing exterior and intimate), a city that is both foreign and familiar at once because the urban landscape is considerably shaped by the character's projections of trauma. Stillman's trauma is that of the fall of language, and the ruinous city is its architectural realization, constantly reminding him of 'lack.' Similarly, Quinn's loss of his wife and son is the intimate aspect that manifests itself in the city's exterior space in the sense that the subject's psychological condition is literally inscribed into the city's 'architexture.' On a larger scale, the notion of lack or incompleteness

---

22 "Sowohl Sigmund Freud als auch Jacques Lacan verstehen das Unheimliche als eine Bedrohung der vernünftigen Sprache, als eine Angst um die Symbolisierungsleistung, was das Unheimliche nicht nur in die unmittelbare Nachbarschaft Nachbarschaft einer Bedrohung einer Psychose sondern auch von Derealisierungsverfahren nach Extremtraumatisierungen stellt." (103)

is also manifest in the novel's overall composition that, at least on its surface, presents white male hegemony as a natural condition in the American city. By deliberately neglecting the (repressed) histories of America, such as those of African Americans or Native Americans, *City of Glass* becomes a materialization of 'lack' in the sense that it is both a discourse of radical exclusion but, at the same time, also a discourse of national trauma (implying the notions of 'forgetting' and 'repression').

Second, the narratological space of *City of Glass* – Quinn's *extimité* – is also the realm where the distinction between the subject and the object (of desire) collapses. According to Lacan, it is the unattainability of the desired object that generates a fragmentation of the self as well as a confusion about subject and object, as *object petit a* is always an expression of the subject's self. For Quinn, Stillman represents the object of investigative desire. The graphic novel depicts Stillman as a mechanical puppet, deriving its energy from an outside source. Similarly, Quinn, in a moment of inquisitive obsession, literally turns into a piece of trash when he crawls into the metal garbage bin to escape the rain. As an anthropomorphization of the abject, both men turn into the fragments out of which their own dystopia is built. As Wolfgang Werth explains, the significance of the subject as trash relies on the repressive power-relationships of a capitalist and post-Fordist society that brought forth the (post-)modern crisis (or death) of the subject as such:

The 'modernity' of this post-apocalyptic urban scenario lies in the [...] reevaluation of trash, which becomes the master-trope for a social existence, that is unaware of terms such as subjectivity, ethics, or morals. It is through the fetishization of material that 'modernity' emerges. In the end, trash triumphs over its producers and beneficiaries, so that the human being becomes almost indistinguable from it. (144, my translation)[23]

---

23 "Die 'Modernität' dieses post-apokalyptischen urbanen Szenarios besteht in der Fokussierung und Neubewertung des Mülls, der zur Schlüsselmetapher einer Wirtschafts- und Existenzweise wird, die weder Begriffe wie Subjektivität, Ethik und Moral kennt, sondern in der Fetischisierung des Materials zu sich selbst kommt. [...] Am Ende triumphiert der Müll über seine Verursacher und Nutznießer – der Mensch ist von ihm prinzipiell nicht mehr zu unterscheiden." (144)

However, looking more closely into the old professor's project, his fictional existence, even if it may be worthless at first sight, might have a bigger relevance than just being an indication for a society being fundamentally dystopian or miserable. Selecting trash from the city's pavements, Stillman follows in the footsteps of the historic figure of the ragpicker[24] introduced in Baudelaire's "On Wine and Hashish" (1851):

[The ragpicker] is responsible for gathering up the daily debris of the capital. All that the city has rejected, all it has lost, shunned, disdained, broken, this man catalogs and stores. He sifts through the archives of debauch, the junkyards of scrap. He creates order, makes an intelligent choice; like a miser hoarding treasure, he gathers the refuse that has been spit out by the god of Industry, to make of it objects of delight or utility. (7)

For Walter Benjamin, Baudelaire's description of the ragpicker is "an extended metaphor for the procedure of the [modernist] poet" (*Charles Baudelaire* 80). Both acts, writing and collecting, ensure the preservation of cultural history, express a nostalgia for the past and thus also the necessity to regard the past as an important feature of the present. For Stillman, the broken objects signify "a dominant past now absent" (Trigg, *The Aesthetics of Decay* 8), but at the same time the potential for recreation. Echoing the surrealist aesthetic of the ready-made, Stillman finds "the streets an endless source of material, an inexhaustible storehouse of shattered things" (78), which via the processes of selection and renaming can restore a system of representation that denotes realism in its very essence.

Even if Stillman's utopian project is doomed to failure, his broken items functions as *souvenirs* in the most literal sense (*sou* = underneath + *venir* = to come) not only because they are the materialization of memory but also because they illuminate the insignificant, that which for others might have lost its value and is therefore supposed to lie buried under a surface (Wolfreys 170). Stillman is on an archeological mission that seeks to extract the hidden or lost 'truths' about humankind, the grand narratives that in a postmodern conception of reality are becoming more and more obsolete. As Gilloch explains:

---

24 For the literary image of the ragpicker in the American tradition also see Dos Passos' play *The Garbage Man* (1923).

"[T]he truth content of a thing is released only when the context in which it originally existed has disappeared, when the surfaces of the object have crumbled away and it lingers precariously on the brink of extinction" (14). What Stillman fails to recognize at the beginning of his quest is that his prowl for shattered objects cannot restore a past or language once lost, but that it rather sheds light onto all the alternative discourses neglected or oppressed by traditional storytelling or art history. In his essay "Tradition and Injunction," Phillipe Simay comments on Benjamin's (and Baudelaire's) conception of the ragpicker as both revolutionary social critic and avant-garde artist: "Beside the official art history, which conserves from the past only the masterpieces, [the ragpicker's] collection lets a subterranean history appear; it gives a right of inclusion to those anonymous objects never considered by the dominant class; it does justice to the ignored objects" (147).

For Stillman, the 'ignored objects' only serve as the carriers of a new vocabulary. As objects of waste are equated with empty signifiers, the process of selecting and renaming comes to symbolize the literary practices of composition and deconstruction. Also the language of Stillman's traumatized son Peter consists of incomprehensible and thus valueless, random speech which is again an expression of the radical foreign- or otherness that is often seen as the essence of the modernist aesthetic. Whereas the estrangement from the ordinary can be seen as an element of modernism, it is dematerialization, composting, and contingency that constitute the postmodern twist of Stillman's role as a ragpicker. From conceptual art we know that the *l'objet d'art* does not necessarily need materialization but that the creative act can also be reduced to the processes of selection and contextualization. Stillman's spatial practice, therefore, echoes Lawrence Weiner's aphorism that "without language, there is no art" (qtd. in Grabes 97, my translation), but also that language as one of the most radical forms of pictorial abstractions is a powerful tool to make the familiar appear radically strange.

Also Stillman Sr. and Quinn dematerialize in that they, being isolated and homeless subjects, disseminate into the trash-city. In *City of Glass*, the self turns out to be many things at once: subject, object, projection, phantom. Hence, it is not only the city as ruin which, in its essence, is fragmentary and incomplete, but the urban subject as well: "[T]he subject to be open to the city must also remain indefinite, provisional in his or her identity, and thus subject to the uncanny arrival of some other" (Wolfreys 172). In many ways, the chronotopic motif of the ruin, be it architectural or ontological, enforces encounters with the uncanny, as, according to Auster, it always signals "the presence of the unpredictable, the powers of contingency, the utterly bewildering nature of human experience" (*The Art of Hunger* 270-271).

Peter Stillman Jr.

Peter Stillman Jr.'s physical description alone leads to the assumption that he is 'other' and belongs, as Hazel Smith points out, "to a different order of reality" (36). The uncanniness that is attached to his persona relies mostly upon the revocation of the opposition between the human and non-human:

> The body acted almost exactly as the voice had: machine-like, fitful, alternating between slow and rapid gestures, rigid and yet expressive, as if the operation were out of control, not quite corresponding to the will that lay behind it. It seemed to Quinn that Stillman's body had not been used for a long time and that all its functions had been relearned, so that motion had become a conscious process, each movement broken down into its component submovements, with the result that all flow and spontaneity had been lost. It was like watching a marionette trying to walk without strings. (*COG* 15)

Similar to Hoffmann's Olympia, who turns out to be a humanoid doll, Stillman Jr. can be literally read as a 'still man,' a lifeless object. Due to the experiment of his father, Stillman Jr. turns into an 'object of linguistic investigation,' forced to be 'still' and 'quiet' in order to learn God's language. To Quinn, the young man's movements appear artificial and resemble those of a humanoid robot.

The notion of artificiality and constructedness is further strengthened through the young man's incoherent use of language. The linguistic alienation is brought forth by Stillman's frequent use of antitheses, senseless repetitions, and tautologies, i.e., statements that are redundant as they have no meaning or message-value. Remarks such as "Perhaps I am Peter Stillman and perhaps I am not" (20) or "Dark. Very dark. As dark as very dark" (16) disrupt the natural flow of communication, reminding of a synthesized model of speech that is not yet fully developed. Stillman's account of his childhood drama sounds as if constructed or controlled because he is constantly oscillating between two different narrative modes, first-person and third-person narration. The sudden switch of perspectives also indicates an outside 'other' that seems to control his account. Stillman's intuitive foregrounding privileges form over content and, again, make the familiar strange and spooky. Furthermore, and as noted earlier, Stillman's use of language is also uncanny because it signals the return of the pre-linguistic, and thus of a mythic (fictional) past.

What is far more interesting, however, is why Quinn or, respectively, the reader experiences the professor's son as uncanny. Whereas Freud disregards the possibility that Hoffmann's Olympia, the wooden doll that comes to life in "The Sandman," contributes to the uncanny effect of the story, Jentsch believes that feelings of uncanniness are invoked when we are uncertain of whether something is animate or inanimate. Jentsch, in this respect, foreshadowed what today has become one of the most existential threats of the century: artificial intelligence and robotic technology. In Japan, roboticists have started to work on humanoid robots that are supposed to take care of the elderly, in order to be prepared for a predicted shortfall in nursing staff. Nowadays, robots cannot only walk on two legs but can also recharge themselves, simulate empathy, and look uncannily like humans (Markoff, para. 1).

Approximately ten years prior to the publication of *City of Glass*, a Japanese scientist named Masahiro Mori presented a theory which concerned the question why we sometimes feel unease and discomfort when looking at objects that have human-like qualities. Mori argues that the more realistic or human-like an object (or creature) appears to us, the more positive is our emotional response towards it. However, if the lifeless object becomes almost indistinguishable from a real person, our emotional response suddenly changes and we experience a feeling of unease and eeriness. As illustrated in the following graph, Mori calls this sudden change from positive to negative familiarity 'the uncanny valley.'

The uncanny valley manifests itself because the object, at a certain point, enters into a dialogue with the real and the mechanic and thus also transgresses the boundary between the living and the dead. Also for Mori, the uncanny valley is related to our fear of death. In his paper he explains: "When we die, we fall into the trough of the uncanny valley. Our body becomes cold, our color changes, and movement ceases. [...] It may be important to our self-preservation" (Mori 35). In other words, Mori and Freud do agree on the fact that people experience doubles and lifelike dolls uncanny because they remind us of our own mortality, or using the Freudian idiom, they become "harbingers of death" (U 142).

On the very first sight of Stillman Jr., Quinn "thought of his own dead son. Then, just as suddenly as the thought had appeared, it vanished" (*COG* 14). Quinn's use of the word 'own' further indicates that he perceives Stillman from the very beginning as dead. Interestingly, it is Stillman Jr. as "a young man, dressed entirely in white, with the white-blond hair of a child" (14) that triggers in Quinn the (mirror) image of his dead son Daniel. Apart from Stillman's robot-like qualities, his appearance is almost transparent or ghost-like:

> Against the pallor of his skin, the flaxen thinness of his hair, the effect was almost transparent, as though one could see through to the blue veins behind the skin of his face. [...] Stillman had become invisible. He could see him sitting in the chair across from him, but at the same time it felt as though he was not there. (*COG* 15)

Stillman is described as both absent and present, thus he is rather an apparition, which rises also (metaphysical) questions about his status as a human being. Following Derrida, the young Stillman embodies *différence*, the simultaneous existence of absence and presence but also, linguistically speaking, of difference (spatial) and deferral (temporal). In chronotopic terms, Stillman's character performs *Stadtzeit* in that he constantly reenacts his trauma of being trapped in a windowless room. Hence, he represents the transcendental state of the in-between, which not only suggests a simultaneous presence in the past and the present but also a constant revisiting of his dark childhood prison.

QUINN'S *CAMERA OBSCURA*

Throughout *City of Glass*, the dark room (in Latin *camera obscura*) recurs as a chronotopic motif that also frames the story. Chronologically speaking, it is a dark room which initiates the crime, i.e., the imprisonment of Stillman's son in "darkness, isolated from the world" (*COG* 27), and it is a dark room from which Quinn mysteriously disappears at the very end. More specifically, Quinn's final journey ends in a "windowless cubicle" (*COG* 127) in the Stillman apartment, in which he strips himself of all his clothes, lies down on the floor and continues to take notes in his notebook until he finds no more paper to write. His naked positioning in dark space, as noted earlier, is the symbolic reenactment of the final breakdown of the search for truth and meaning, and the impossibility of reversing the Fall of Man from the state of innocence in paradise. However, for Quinn this realization is not a defeat but more like a victory as "[h]e regret[s] having wasted so many pages at the beginning of the red notebook, and in fact [feels] sorry that he [...] bothered to write about the Stillman case at all" (*COG* 131).

Quinn's new urge to write about more transcendental matters, or a more natural order, i.e., "about the stars, the earth, his hopes of mankind" (ibid.), is accompanied by a gradually growing darkness that finally wins over daylight:

Quinn observed that the periods of dark nevertheless kept gaining on the periods of light. It seemed to him that he had less and less time to eat his food and write in the red notebook. The next time there was light, he could only manage two sentences. He began to skip his meals in order to devote himself to the red notebook, eating only when he felt he could no longer hold out. But the time continued to diminish, and soon he was able to eat no more than a bite or two before the darkness came back. He did not think of turning on the electric light, for he had long ago forgotten it was there. (ibid.)

The fading of daylight signals his journey into another dimension, a dimension in which "night and day [are] no more than relative terms" (*COG* 128). By entering the dark empty room, Quinn symbolically enters his grave, buries himself alive in darkness and takes "an aporethic decision between death and slumber" (Royle 159). Already at the very beginning of the novel, the narrator describes Quinn's life as "posthumous" (*COG* 5), which also implies that he conceives of himself as dead. His symbolic act of live burial is a reference back to the funeral of his son, back to "the little coffin that held his son's body and how he had seen it [...] being lowered into the ground" (*COG* 35), that lies at the origin of Quinn's trauma.

Ever since Poe's "The Premature Burial" or "The Fall of the House of Usher," the notion of live burial has been a prevalent theme of American Gothic writing. For Freud, being buried alive is one of the most uncanny fantasies of all. It signifies the liminal state between life and death that is evoked by the most radical spatial confinement in the dark: being entrapped in a coffin that is lowered into the earth. Yet, for Freud, the act of being buried alive always entails a positive connotation, that of the return to pre-natal existence:

> Some would award the crown of the uncanny to the idea of being buried alive, only apparently dead. However, psychoanalysis has taught us this terrifying fantasy is merely a variant of another, which was originally not at all frightening, but relied on certain lasciviousness; this was the fantasy of living in the womb. (U 150)

Quinn, by stripping naked and positioning himself horizontally onto the floor in a dark room, symbolically returns to the womb and thus to an innocent state. The dark room, therefore, is not simply a grave, but rather a realm where something new can originate. Similarly, the isolated room in which Stillman locks up his son represents more than just a space of confinement. For Stillman, it is the complex sphere of all origin, an "ultra-cellar" (20), to use Gaston Bachelard's term, a multi-layered and interconnected underground world with endless steps and reduplicated cells. Quinn's act of live burial, therefore, resembles a journey into the realm of transcendental irrationality and thus into the sphere in which not only the repressed, but also dreams, fantasies, and the imagination have their origin.

When the unnamed narrator of *The Locked Room*, the third part of Auster's trilogy, discovers that the "[locked] room was located in [his] skull" (293), Auster clearly makes a reference to Locke's conception of the dark room as an architectural metaphor of the mind, as formulated in *An Essay Concerning Human Understanding* (1690):

> The understanding is not much unlike a closet wholly shut from light, with only some little opening left, to let in external visible resemblances, or ideas of things without: would the pictures coming into such a dark room but stay there, and lie so orderly as to be found upon occasion, it would very much resemble the understanding of a man, in reference to all objects of sight, and the ideas of them. (96)

What Locke wants to say here is that, apart from our senses, we are only connected to the external world through projected images that enter our mind through a tiny opening in the dark room. In other words, we see the world as projections, not much unlike the prisoners in the Platonic cave for whom the shadows on the stone wall constitute their one and only reality. What this implies is that we can only be certain of what is going on in the cave, or rather in our subjective mind. Thus, we are prisoners of our own phantom-show, never gaining access to an outside reality. Quinn's and Stillman's world is uncanny because they are authors who "se[e] the world only through words, liv[e] only through the lives of others" (Auster, *Ghosts* 171-172). More specifically, Quinn falls victim to uncanny mirrorings and the 'unhomely' because he perceives the city through the lens of trauma. Quinn's subjective gaze upon the city projects nothing but an x-ray picture of himself onto the 'wall' of his skull, an uncanny image showing a living person as if already dead.

Locke's famous conception of the dark room can be conceived of as an analogy to the architectural structure of one of the earliest photographical devices – the *camera obscura*. As the precursor of modern photography, the *camera obscura* denotes a dark chamber in which external light can pass through a tiny hole, thus, producing an upside down image of the outside world on the opposite wall. Many great thinkers (among them Euklid, Aristotle, Kepler or Leibnitz) compared this optical phenomenon to the workings of human sight and used it as a metaphor for rational observation of the outside world. The *camera obscura* provided knowledge and insights about the world that were not, as usual, the result of the natural sciences but the result of a man-made apparatus. According to Jonathan Crary, the *camera obscura* defines the observer as an autonomous, isolated, and privatized subject: "It impels a kind of *askesis*, or withdrawal from the world, in order to regulate and purify one's relation to the manifold contents of the now 'exterior' world" (39).

Quinn decides to enter the *camera obscura* of the Stillmans' apartment because he wants to strip himself of all the multiple personae and mirror images that the detective case and the chaotic urban world have generated. When Quinn disappears from the dark room and from the story, he puts himself into the role of the observing subject within the *camera obscura* and becomes "a disembodied witness to a mechanical and transcendental re-presentation of the objectivity of the world" (Crary 41). Quinn's spatial disengagement with the outer world also signals his devotion to psychological inwardness. Being reduced to the 'observing I,' Quinn, finally, succeeds in bringing forth the divorce between subject and object, or subject and image. What remains is only the inverted representation on the opposite wall. In other words, when Quinn retreats into the darkened room he retreats into the book itself, or in Lacanean terms, into the sphere of the imaginary, the sphere of representation.

As Quinn disappears at the end of the story, a first-person narrative voice takes over, claiming to be a friend of 'Auster.' We learn that it was him who had found Quinn's notebook and that he, in the process of transcription, "followed the notebook as closely as [he] could" (*COG* 133). He further informs us that "the text was difficult to decipher" (ibid.). Using the notebook only as a blueprint, we as readers realize that we have just read a copy for which there is no original account, i.e., a simulacrum. At the end, however, Auster needs to introduce the narrative entity as Quinn, having retreated into the *camera obscura*, is no longer able to represent or even see himself. However, what remains is the inverted image on the dark wall, the very ideas that enter through the pinhole. Auster deliberately depicted New York City as a space lacking depth because it is nothing but a projection of Quinn's mind.

One of the very last images of the novel is that of a city buried in snow: "The city was entirely white now, and the snow kept falling, as though it would never end" (*COG* 133). Interrelating Quinn's 'death' or his existence in darkness with the image of snow, Auster charges the ending with the color of innocence, hence, suggesting a blank page upon which a new story can be composed. Here, the white space is symbolic for the process of creative writing that has the power to bring to light one's repressed thoughts. As Auster himself has argued, the act of writing often resembles an unconscious translation of (traumatic) experiences into words:

One has many memories which are deeply entombed. It is the process of writing which brings these small bits of memory to the surface. But one isn't aware of it. One doesn't know where they come from. One cannot put them into focus. From time to time one is able to retrace the path and reach the origin he writer's works are born from these hidden springs. ("Interview with Gérard" 23)

Thus, the black (or white) space in the end does not necessarily continue the theme of nihilistic despair but rather confronts the reader with many subjective truths. Quinn's post-traumatic disorders he experienced outside the dark room was necessary for the reader to grasp the workings of the 'inside.' In this respect, *City of Glass* is a mind-text that, in fact, also comes to stand for the intellectual, mental space of reader and writer.

Auster's latest book *Man in the Dark* (2008) continues the chronotopic motif of the dark room. Suffering from insomnia, protagonist August Brill kills "another white night in the great American wilderness" (*Man in the Dark* 1) by imagining a story in which America is at war not with Iraq, but with itself. Brill lets his first story enfold with the image of a young magician called Owen Brick, who one day wakes up in a burrow wearing a uniform. However, what is more uncanny than the theme of live burial is the fact that it is former US-president Bush who again pulls the strings of this brutal war fought between republicans and democrats. For Auster, it was the 2000 US elections that transformed the nation into a twilight zone in which a civil war comes to symbolize the loss of a common discourse. Hence, it is also Auster who is the man in the dark, not being able to grasp why Americans could quietly acquiesce in Bush's politics of fear and warfare ("Interview with Dominik" A5).

Even if the *camera obscura* is frequently used as a metaphor for the workings of our mind, for the very locus of our repressed fears and wounds or for a nation's symbolic blindness, one must not forget that it has also been used as a means of popular entertainment. At a crucial point in *Ghosts*, the narrator conceives of the dark room as a funhouse: "There is something nice about being in the dark, [...] something thrilling about not knowing what is going to happen next. It keeps you alert, [...] and there's no harm in that, is there?" (154). Whereas modernists are lost in the dark room, postmodernists play hide and seek in it. As the city made of glass fools Quinn's eyes, the novel fools the reader by revealing itself as a literary *trompe-l'œil,* a representation that only simulates a three-dimensional space. The true setting of *City of Glass*, therefore, is not New York City but Quinn's dark room of the mind. Next to the flood of metareferential play, the construction of the illusionary city as a projected image is an intentional act of mimicry that is aimed at keeping the reader in the dark. Accordingly, Auster continues the tradition of early literary postmodernists who also made the familiar strange by means of an ironic and experimental rethinking of the past.

THE UNCANNY COMIC

Karasik and Mazzucchelli's graphic adaptation of Auster's novel, according to Art Spiegelman, "created a strange *Doppelgänger* of the original book" (ix). The strangeness that Spiegelman attributes to the work relies on the aspect of format. "You cannot scare people more," say Coop and Himmelblau, "than when you are going to dissolve form" (qtd. in Laurence et. al. para. 25). The founders of the Viennese Architectural Design Firm that are famous for their provocative building style articulate an aesthetic dilemma that is also true for literature. When, in the 1980s, Art Spiegelman used a medium of pop-culture to tell a personal story about the Holocaust, using mice to impersonate the Jews and cats to impersonate the Nazis, people were shocked, because the familiar has been made uncannily strange. How can an author use the 'comic form' in order to broach the issue of genocide? Especially in the US, the medium of graphic narrative has for a long time been associated with carefree children's literature, i.e., funny cartoons such as *Mickey Mouse*, which is why Spiegelman's work signaled a radical break with traditional representations of historical trauma. Similarly, *City of Glass* is not supposed to be read by children nor is it intended to be comical in tone.

The shift of popular culture into the domains of high culture was part of a democratization process of art that characterized the postmodern period (Malpas 20). This process was also fuelled by the visual turn, which likewise saw an embedding of the visual in the literary text. For example, the emergence of concrete poetry or the ekphrastic poetics of early postmodernists such as John Barth, William Gass, or Donald Barthelme, clearly signaled that the visual had found entry into the domain of the literary text. In the preface to the graphic version of Auster's novel, Spiegelman points out that "*City of Glass* is a surprisingly nonvisual work at its core" (vii), because it is first and foremost concerned with linguistic signs. Why then take the challenge of translating this book, "this complex web of words" (ibid.), into a visual narrative? Although Spiegelman rightly claims that it is a book about 'words,' *City of Glass* is as much about the more general concept of signification. Written language, as we all know, came into existence as a collection of pictorial signs (e.g., hieroglyphs) and, for example, in Japanese calligraphy, language is still treated as a system of images. Text and image, thus, are not entirely separate domains.

The visual doubling of Auster's story might be the result of the postmodern's affection with the visual. More importantly, however, the visual translation of Auster's novel not only adds another (metafictional) layer of signification but also points to the uncanniness of visual discourses as such. "When visual culture tells stories," writes Nicholas Mirzoeff, "they are ghost stories" (239). Obviously, Mirzoeff's argument is based on postmodernism's concern with visual plurality in the form of simulacra and other phantasmagoric products and events that dominate contemporary culture. For Mirzoeff, postmodern visuality is first and foremost uncanny because it is concerned with questions of ontology: "The ghost is [...] an assertion that the virtual is in some sense real, and the paranormal normal, as what was formerly invisible comes into visibility" (ibid.). Auster's novel, as we have seen, is very much concerned with visual and perceptional ambiguities that affect both characters and readers. Many story-related elements of *City of Glass* are dominantly visual: For example, Quinn's function as a private *eye* (that also comes to stand for "the physical eye of the writer, the eye of the man who looks out from himself into the world" (*COG* 9), his positioning in dark or transparent spaces, or Quinn's projection of his unconscious fears onto the city. The uncanny thus is, similar to Hoffmann's "The Sandman," also largely constructed upon tropes of visibility and the optical.[25]

Long before the visual turn was declared in the humanities also Walter Benjamin, along with other representatives of the Frankfurt School, such as Siegfried Kracauer or Ernst Bloch, recognized the uncanny link between words and (mental) images. His so-called *Denkbilder*[26] – prose miniatures in which impressions of (pre-

---

25 Freud's interpretation focuses on Nathanael's fear of blindness that Freud regards as a metaphor for castration anxiety.

26 It has often been noted that Benjamin's *Denkbilder* ('thought-images') follow the structure of the baroque emblem which also consist of a title (*inscriptio*), an image (*pictura*), and a comment in prose (*subscriptio*) and which in combination reveal a philosophical or moral truth. Also Ernst

dominantly urban) everyday life and philosophical thought were condensed into fragmentary, diary-like entries – captured visual moments of experience. For example, Benjamin's *Denkbild* entitled "One Way Street" – whose title alone evokes the visuality of a traffic sign – is, stylistically speaking, not a diegetic, but rather a mimetic representation of Berlin because it is structured not according to plot, but rather according to the city's visible architecture (Schütz 36).

In "Modernist Miniatures: Literary Snapshots of Urban Spaces," Andreas Huyssen points out that it is the visual's encounter with the verbal that enforces estrangement: "The visual dimension disturbs legibility, and the promise of linguistic transparency is denied in the complex texture of ekphrasis, metaphor and abstraction" (31). For Benjamin, however, the 'writing of images' does not so much refer to rhetorical techniques such as the use of figures of speech, but rather to a constellation of images that freeze the immediateness of certain (historical) moments. Similar to the Imagist tradition, Benjamin's goal was to intellectually capture the moment of direct perception; however, unlike the Imagists, he did not compose his *Denkbilder* according to the rules of the musical phrase. Instead, his compositions rely on the associative and dream-like character of modern city life and are therefore always chronotopically constructed. Benjamin's thought-images are, of course, based on his famous conception of the dialectical image, an ambiguous image which contains past experiences that are important in the present. In convolute N of the *Arcades Project*, Benjamin writes:

It's not that what is past casts its light on what is present, or what is present its light on what is past; rather image is that wherein what has been comes together in a flash with the now to form a constellation. In other words, image is dialectics at a standstill. For while the relation of the present to the past is a purely temporal, continuous one, the relation of what-has-been to the now is dialectical: it is not progression but image, suddenly emergent. Only dialectical images are genuine (i.e., not archaic); and the place where one encounters them is language. (462)

Bloch, Siegfried Kracauer, and Theodor Adorno made use of the genre in order to depict the discomforts of the modern experience.

Language, thus, is the space in which the dialectical image can be located. More precisely, it is the immediate act of speaking or communicating that, for Benjamin, has the power to 'awake' the bourgeois urban society from their dream, or their paralysis evoked by phantasmagoric commodity culture. The dialectical image, in Benjamin's words, "comes about through action and is action" (qtd. in Wohlfarth 263).

For Benjamin, it was the notebook that served as the most important tool for his *Aufzeichnungen*. "Let no thought pass incognito," he advises us, "and keep your notebook as strictly as the authorities keep their register of aliens" ("One Way Street" 81). The defining feature of a notebook is, as we all know, to be able to immediately sketch or write down something we perceive so that it does not escape from our memory. Anke Te Heesen rightly argues that the act of 'taking notes' is automatically accompanied by the process of direct perception:

Something is noted, generally by hand, and thus taken note of. Therefore, apart from the actual act of writing, noting also describes a particular kind of perception: *taking notice of something.* Etymologically, here writing and taking notice are contained in one procedure, which at the same time implies habitual forming of a person and results in a praxis with paper that requires certain gestures, performed acts, rituals and tools. (584)

As evidences of past moments, notebook entries resemble the direct translation of visual images into a fragmentary text. It is thus the (mental) image that serves as the transitory link between an object's materiality and its verbal description. It is the notebook that anticipates the fleetingness of an image, as it is the medium that can best capture the 'now' of recognisability.

This philosophical link that Benjamin establishes between image and language is crucial for understanding the uncanny quality of the graphic adaptation of Auster's novel. Most basically, the graphic novel visualizes the dialectical image at various points. For example, the dialectical image, evoking the sudden moment when past and present merge, manifests itself when Quinn (or the reader) is experiencing sudden moments of involuntary memory. For example, the unexpected and sudden recurrence of a panel showing a child's face screaming disrupts the narrative flow and structural logic and thus visualizes

Quinn's return of the repressed. As Shakar argues, the screaming child is

> the center of the book [...] It will appear again and again, each time in a surprising context which will add to its significance and to its visceral impact. Thus, it will come to signify [Quinn's] dead child; Peter Stillman; his anger at Stillman Sr. ... Quinn's own childhood; a generalized sense of lost innocence; and the alienation of man from his fellow man and from himself. (qtd. in Coughlan 847)

Baudellaire's quote[27] that accompanies a triad of panels in which the image of the screaming child interrupts the depiction of the homeless wanderers also follows the same logic as Benjamin's *Denkbild*. The text embeds an image (and *vice versa*) in order to concisely articulate a complex philosophical thought. Baudelaire's verbal paradox and its translation that frame and structure the three panels suggest a hidden philosophical connection between New York's fallen people and the death of Quinn's son. What connects text and images is the notion of inwardness or 'involuntary memory' that torments not only Quinn but also, on a more collective level, the homeless population of New York as such. Quinn as well as the homeless are "locked inside madness" (*COG* 110) because they try to overcome the effects of trauma. By bringing together subjective and collective traumata, the graphic novel succeeds in (re-)evoking and juxtaposing various cultural and literal narratives. The graphic novel, as a whole, is also a metafictional pun towards the dialectical image as the signifier of multiple meaning. As Iva Jevtic suggests: "The multiplicity of perspectives and insecure positions within an image points towards the relativity of discourses, a certain absence at the heart of what we expected to be full and absolute, to contain an unequivocal meaning" (6).

In graphic narratives, pictorial signs support the verbal signs in order to sensually intensify the readerly perception. This intensification is also the result of a more immediate or direct, as visual, representation of things. As all mimetic forms of narration, also comic

---

27 "Il me semble que je serais toujours bien là où je ne suis pas. In other words: It seems to me that I will always be happy in the place where I am not. Or, more bluntly: Wherever I am not is the place where I am myself" (*COG* 110-111).

books are much more concerned with spatial composition, since a page in a graphic narrative is a "multi-frame" (Atkinson 113) in the sense that it brings together and separates a multiplicity of images. In *City of Glass*, this framing through the device of the panel wonderfully serves the purpose to visualize or indirectly comment on the novel's chronotopic motives which, as shown earlier, deal with confinement, aberration (i.e., the search for and the loss of order and wholeness), or the fragmentation of the self. The visual recurrence of New York's grid, for example, in the form of prison bars, windowpanes, or the books' panel division, brings back to mind the imprisonment of Peter Stillman Jr. that initiated Quinn's case, as well as Quinn's own psychic imprisonment; but also, more broadly speaking, it reminds us that devices of structural order do not necessarily point to a common 'truth' but can result in chaos.

Also the visual translation of Auster's novel makes us aware that signification is always metaphoric. Apart from the depiction of Grand Central Station and the skyline, iconic markers of New York are absent from the graphic narrative. This indicates that the city is nothing but an empty signifier that could be filled with any subjective content. Thus, what is placed in the foreground is Quinn's psycho-space that is, in its essence, postmodern as it gives priority to "the ambivalent potentiality of the sign" (Herzogenrath 19).

This ambivalence of the sign is also expressed in relation to authorship and narrative authority. The fact that the empirical author (Paul Auster) is visually present as his fictional double conjures up intellectual uncertainty about who functions as the guiding or 'implied' voice of the text. According to Paul Atkinson, Auster's strategy to bring to the surface his own empirical persona is related to the postmodern notion, as famously articulated by Roland Barthes, that 'the author is dead': "The only way to kill the author is to create a fictional double in the text, which undermines the author's position as an invisible, guiding principle for the text as a whole" (Atkinson 116). Accordingly, in the graphic novel, the reader, when looking at Auster's drawn alter-ego, is trapped in the complex web of unnamed narrators and multiple and multiplied authors who all seem to be on the same level. Although Paul Auster's comic alter-ego (resembling the 'real' Paul Auster in terms of physiognomic features) is drawn with much more care and detail than Quinn, this does not tell us anything about authorial hierarchies or degrees of reality. As Quinn's identity constantly changes, also the drawing style in which he is depicted does. As soon as Quinn has turned into a homeless, his facial features do no longer consist of simple dots and lines. What disturbs us intellectually is that we cannot rely on a clear distinction of fact and fiction, nor can we rely on the medium of visibility. As Foucault has pointed out, "[v]isibility is a trap" (qtd. in Mirzoeff 240). For Foucault, architectures like the panopticon expose the (imprisoned) subject to a public gaze while inflicting the supervising subject with the privilege to hide. Similarly, Auster, by employing metafictional elements, also plays with the crucial interrelationship of visibility and power.

At the story's end, when Quinn runs out of pages of his red notebook, also the graphic novel's grid division disintegrates and page numbers disappear into black nothingness. In fact, stable panels dissolve into flexible pages, fluttering down a dark abyss. At the abyss' brink, we see the shadowy silhouette of a witness of the scene, whose identity, of course, is unknown. What we experience is a chronotopic collapse that manifests itself in the inversion of inside and outside. Whereas earlier in the graphic novel the panels served as the major framing device of content, it is now the black hole that accommodates the panels. Uncannily, the gutter – the empty space separating one panel from another – now fills the page. The loss of page-numbering, visually echoing Quinn's dilemma that "there are no more pages in the notebook" (*COG* 132), leads the reader to suspect that what s/he is or has been reading, is nothing but (a copy of) Quinn's red notebook. This assumption is finally confirmed when the reader arrives at the books inside cover page which exhibits the same rhizomatic print as Quinn's notebook in the story.

This ending, again, rearticulates Benjamin's goal to establish via the image a connection between words and the material object. The notebook that uncannily materializes in our hands serves as the medium of the dialectical image that always captures experience *per se*. Quinn's moment of intense insight also triggers in us a "profane illumination," as Benjamin has it, in which we realize that truth, meaning, and representation can never be conceived of as singular or unified concepts. According to Paul Stephens and Robert Hardwick Weston, Benjamin's *Denkbilder* also entail a didactical purpose: "To *denkbild* is […] to build upon oneself, to educate oneself in the sense of *Bildung;* here the notebook serves, like the ancient *hupomnemata*, not merely as a spur to memory, but as the autodidact's writing of the self, as the chronicle of his intellectual life" (138). What is true for Benjamin's use of the notebook is also true for Quinn's. It is the act of (free) writing that brings Quinn closer to his true self that slumbers in the dark realm of the unconscious, and thus closer to the reprocessing of trauma. "For it is only in the darkness of solitude," as Paul Auster writes, "that the work of memory begins" (*The Invention of Solitude* 164).

However, it is a less metaphysical image that constitutes the very last page of Karasik and Mazzuchelli's adaptation. Instead of leaving the readers with questions of ontology, they are, once again, confronted with a metafictional device. The radical narratological shift that is marked by Quinn's disappearance and the emergence of an outside narrator is visualized with the image of a manual typewriter and a page covered with lines in Courier font. Typewriter fonts are, according to Marion, often a sign of authorial "*objectivité* that is often associated with the instrument" (qtd. in Atkinson 224). This change in font and format is a visual signal that denotes a transition to another (maybe more reliable) world.

When we learn that *City of Glass* is, in fact, the narrator's reprint of Quinn's notebook, a text that for him "was difficult to decipher" (133), the boundaries between fact and fiction completely blur. We, as readers, are unable to decide whose story is the more reliable, because the text fundamentally lacks authorial control. Signs, we have to conclude, whether they are textual or visual, do not point to a common outside reality. What is visually placed in the center of the last page is Auster's instrument, i.e., language, with which he is able to evoke different worlds. Thus the graphic novel rephrases Benjamin's aphorism that it is the image constructed through language that comes closest to 'reality.'

All in all, the graphic adaptation of *City of Glass* represents both a technique and effect of the uncanny that, through the intersection of medial forms of representation, generate an eclecticism that is analogous with a spatiality of the mind in which the past, or respectively, the 'primordial story,' is constantly revisited. The heap of trash beneath the typewriter points to the remnants of the past that burst into flames as the story comes to an end. The broken and useless objects evoke decay and chaos and also the disintegration of epistemic coherence. Yet, we must not lament this loss of coherence, but rather celebrate the newly gained freedoms and joys that speculative games entail. Auster leaves us with a short scribbled note placed at the very right corner of his last page, telling us that Quinn's story, which we can no longer witness, might continue elsewhere.

Haunted Harlem:
Toni Morrison's *Jazz*

> They lean over me and say:
> "Who deathed you who,
> who, who, who, who ...
> I whisper: "Tell you presently...
> Shortly...this evening...
> Tomorrow..."
> Tomorrow is here
> And you out there safe.
> I'm safe in here, Tootsie.
> OWEN DODSON

As part of James Van der Zee's photo-collection *The Harlem Book of the Dead*, Owen Dodson's verse accompanies a photograph of a dead black girl lying in a coffin, her chest covered with a bouquet of white flowers. According to Van der Zee, "the girl was shot by her sweetheart at a party with a noiseless gun" (84) and in an act of altruism shortly before her death refused to give the name of her murderer. It was the girl's portrait infused with this tragic story that served as the main inspiration for Toni Morrison to write *Jazz* (1992), the second novel of her trilogy that starts with *Beloved* (1987) and ends with *Paradise* (1998).

As with *Beloved*, her Pulitzer Prize winning masterpiece, Morrison uses an actual incident of homicide to initiate *Beloved*'s sequel *Jazz*, a story that continues the theme of 'rememory'[1] of African American

---

1   Morrison coined the term 'rememory' to denote the process of actively reliving or re-picturing experiences of the past. In *Beloved*, Sethe explains

history. In the foreword to Van der Zee's photograph collection, Morrison describes the funeral portrait as "so living, so 'undead'" (x), thus alluding to the work's uncanny aura. Owen Dodson's verse provides the dead girl with a voice and thus further intensifies the eerie liminality between life and death that the photograph radiates. Van der Zee's illustrated book follows the same artistic aim as much of Morrison's *oeuvre*: to revive the stories of a past that (deliberately) has been forgotten in traditional accounts of American historiography.

Often labeled "historiographic metafiction" (Hutcheon 122), the novels of Morrison's trilogy fuse historical fact with folklore myths and supernatural elements, thus questioning the idea of an objective truth as such. Margret Garner's case of infanticide upon which Morrison modeled the story of *Beloved*, for example, is remembered through the fictional construction of a *Poltergeist* that first haunts the house of the ex-slave Sethe and later manifests itself in the form of a mysterious young woman. In a conversation with Mel Watkins, Morrison was asked whether she believed in ghosts, and she answered: "Yes, it is part of our heritage" ("Talk with Toni Morrison" 46). Accordingly, Morrison's interest in the supernatural can largely be attributed to the African American genealogical belief system, in which the living and the dead do not necessarily form separate entities. In African and African American cultures there is a rich mystical tradition that includes Hoodoo practices and contact with ancestor spirits. In "Toni Morrison's Folk Roots," Barbara J. Wilcots asserts: "*Beloved* is firmly rooted in the African world view that death is the threshold to a parallel existence and that spirits continue to exist and interact with living loved ones" (694). Therefore, for Africans and African Americans, as Smith-Wright argues, "[g]hosts are not strange beings from the netherworld [...] They hover just outside of documentable experience" (155).

In "The Ghosts of Place," Michael Mayerfeld Bell defines ghosts as "the scary spirits of the unsettled dead – [...] disturbed souls who came to a bad and frequently unjust end, and who haunt our anxious

---

the concept to Denver as follows: "Some things just stay. I used to think it was my rememory. Some things you forget. Other things you never do. But it's not. Places, places are still there. If a house burns down, it's gone, but the place-the picture of it-stays, and not just in my rememory, but out there, in the world" (43).

memories [...] a felt presence – an anima, *geist*, or genius – that possesses and gives a sense of social aliveness to a place" (815). Hence, it is the phenomenological presence of Garner's child and the nameless dead black girl on Van der Zee's photograph that hovers over the first two stories of Morrison's trilogy. What is more, by giving life to these dead girls, Morrison provides them with a voice that enables them to articulate their personal 'truths.' At the same time, however, they simultaneously lend their voices to all those African Americans who, in the course of the Middle Passage, the pre-Civil-War period, Reconstruction and post-Reconstruction, have been silenced and 'forgotten' by a white supremacist 'master' discourse. For example, in 1856 Margret Garner's prosecutors refused to acknowledge the necessary background of the case and wanted to jail and hang Garner not only for the act of murder she committed but primarily for the destruction of private property, as the baby-girl was also meant to be returned to a Kentucky plantation (Tally, *Toni Morrison's Beloved* 6). The process of silencing or editing the 'true' stories of (ex-)slaves also forms a crucial theme in *Beloved* and is symbolically alluded to when Morrison, for example, describes Paul D's literal silencing through the iron-bit, a piece of metal that kept the tongue of slaves pressed down and that masters forced slaves to wear as a means of punishment.

In depicting 'the unspeakable,' Morrison's fiction powerfully captures personal memories or, rather, traumata, thus radically challenging traditional slave narratives, accounts that largely repressed the 'truth' as they had to be adapted according to the authentication politics exercised by white sponsors. Accordingly, one can conceive of Morrison's fiction as vivid examples of the phantom text[2], i.e., a text which, according to Nicholas Royle, lays emphasis on "what it does *not* say, or says (perhaps) without saying" (278). It is through the insertion of blank pages or visual gaps in the typography that Morrison visualizes these "areas of silence" (Royle 279) which in an African American context are related to the process of (cultural) mourning. In

---

2   In *The Uncanny*, Nicholas Royle defines the phantom text as follows: "Phantom texts are fleeting, continually moving on, leading us away, like Hamlet's ghost, to some other scene or scenes which we, as readers, cannot anticipate" (280).

his essay "Notes on the Phantom: A Complement to Freud's Metapsychology," Nicholas Abraham notes that the phantom

> [i]s nothing but an invention of the living. Yes, an invention in the sense that the phantom is meant to objectify, even if under the guise of individual or collective hallucinations, the gap that the concealment of some part of a loved one's life produced in us. The phantom is, therefore, also a metapsychological fact. Consequently what haunts us are not the dead, but the gaps left within us by the secrets of others. (287)

In the epigraph to *Beloved*, Morrison devotes her ghost story to the "[s]ixty [m]illion and more" African slaves who lost their lives during the Middle Passage, a historical event largely ignored by a hegemonic national historiography. As a consequence, Morrison introduces the ghost-character of Beloved who, being able to travel back and forth in time, verbalizes the horrors experienced on the slave ships:

> I am always crouching   the man on my face is dead   his face is not mine   his mouth smells sweet but his eyes are locked
>
>   some who eat nasty themselves   I do not eat   the men without skin bring us their morning water to drink   we have none   at night I cannot see the dead man on my face   daylight come through the cracks and I can see his locked eyes I am not big   small rats do not wait for us to sleep   someone is thrashing but there is no room to do it in   if we had more to drink we could make tears (*Beloved* 248)

The gaps in the typeface that mark her stream-of-consciousness narration are also a visual allegory of what Morrison calls "national amnesia," i.e., the intentional forgetting or erasure of a past that not only represented the incompleteness of recorded history but also and, more importantly, fragments of a past that for most African Americans were too cruel to remember. By creating her female protagonist as a ghost, Morrison wants to remind us that the remembering of an enslaved past is, as Avery F. Gordon puts it, "not history, but haunting" (165).

This haunting, most obviously, is analogous to the Freudian notion of the return of the repressed, the manifestation of the uncanny, in which the past actively determines one's present state of mind. More specifically, however, the uncanny, when discussed in an African

American or Morrisonean context should, in a further step, be conceived of in its German literal sense of *unheimlich*, translating into the English 'unhomely.' Freud's extensive etymological study of the term also revealed the *unheimlich* – as the negation of everything that "belongs to the house, not strange, familiar, tame, dear and intimate, homely" (U 126) – as fundamentally related to the domestic, or rather *un*domestic sphere.

In *The Location of Culture*, Homi Bhabha applies Freud's theoretical foundations to his field of postcolonial studies and defines the 'unhomely' as "a paradigmatic colonial and post-colonial condition" (9). Enforced deterritorialization and hegemonic power relationships that characterize colonial rule have brought forth a history of displacement in which, according to Bhabha, "the borders between home and world become confused; and, uncannily, the private and the public become part of each other, forcing upon us a vision that is as divided as it is disorienting" (ibid.). Ghosts, for Morrison, are most apt to provide this phenomenological transition between the external and the internal spaces that characterize the African American experience. This external/internal dichotomy, as we will see in the following chapters, comprises manifold sub-binaries such as the official and the personal, the conscious and the unconscious, the South and the North, the private and the public, the real and the unreal or, maybe most importantly, the self and the other.

RURAL PASTS, URBAN PRESENTS

What makes *Beloved* radically distinct from *Jazz* is, first and foremost, its temporal and spatial setting. Whereas in *Beloved* the haunting occurs in a humble house located in the rural South during the Reconstruction era, in *Jazz* ghosts signal their presence in 'the City' which, even though unnamed, clearly refers to Harlem during the 1920s. Initiated by the Great Migration, an event starting in the late nineteenth century during which roughly 1.5 million Southern blacks fled to Northern cities in order to escape Jim Crowism and poor working conditions, African Americans experienced a significant reconfiguring of space from the rural to the urban. Charles Scruggs gives particular attention to the fact that the Great Migration "was a phenomenon unlike any other migratory movement in American history. It was a displacement of a people on so vast a scale and in so short a time that the mythical westward movement in the nineteenth century seems small by comparison" (14). According to Gilbert Osofsky, the demographic shifts were most prominent in Harlem, where between 1910 and 1920 the population of African Americans rose to 66 percent, further increasing in the years from 1920 to 1930 (310).

At the beginning of the century, Harlem's white population – primarily Jews and Italians – started to move to more wealthy boroughs, leaving behind a great number of empty apartments, which consequently forced the real estate industry to open the Harlem market for black tenants. The vast number of available housing was also caused by a miscalculation of urban planners who expected a flood of (white) residents triggered by the opening of the Lenox subway line in 1904. However, the hoped-for boom failed to materialize, so that the large number of available brownstone real-estate was made available for blacks. However, as more and more African Americans followed the 'Opened for Colored' signs attached to apartments for rent, the remaining white population of Harlem gradually decreased. Similar migratory movements could be observed in other American cities in the North, such as Chicago or Philadelphia. In "Connecting Memory, Self, and the Power of Place in African American Urban History," Earl Lewis remarks that the Great Migration primarily denoted the transition from pre-modern rurality to modern urbanity, as "[i]n 1900, the least urbanized segment of the population, African Americans, by 1960 were the most urbanized" (118).

With the economic shift from agriculture to industry at the turn of the century, the city promised to be a safe haven, offering better working conditions and also, what was maybe more important, a cultural and political voice. Again, it was Harlem that emerged as what Alain Locke termed the "race capital" (72) of the nation, in which a new black self could be born. In his famous anthology *The New Negro*, often regarded as the manifesto of the Harlem Renaissance, he comments on the great potentialities of Harlem's heterogeneous black community to renew black self-esteem and self-expression:

Here in Manhattan is not merely the largest Negro community in the world, but the first concentration in history of so many diverse elements of Negro life. It has attracted the African, the West Indian, the Negro American; it has brought together the Negro of the city and the man from the town and village; the peasant, the student, the business man, the professional man, artist, poet, musician, adventurer and worker, preacher and criminal, exploiter and social outcast. Each group has come with its own separate motives and for its own special ends, but their greatest experience has been the finding of one another. Proscription and prejudice have thrown these dissimilar elements into a common area of contact and interaction. Within this area, race sympathy and unity have determined a further fusing of sentiment and experience. [...] In Harlem, Negro life is seizing upon its first chances for group expression and self-determination. (5)

Indeed, in the 1920s, life in Harlem was characterized by the flourishing of black arts and entertainment, e.g., the cabaret, poetry, and the rhythms of blues and jazz, which made the urban scene a "spectacular urban playground" (Balshaw, "Black Was White" 313). As a result, many musicians, actors, writers, as well as colourful eccentrics gathered in Harlem not only to celebrate African American folklore but to "reformulat[e]" (ibid.) their cultural production. In many of the literary accounts that sprung from the Jazz Age years, Harlem was largely imagined as a heavenly city, a place resembling "a miracle straight out of the skies" (Johnson 3-4). This imagery of rebirth and renewal also manifested itself in the cultural movement's name, 'The Harlem Renaissance,' celebrating Harlem as "the privileged site of a positive construction of blackness countering the white construction of blackness and enslavement" (Paquet-Derris 223). In *Jazz*, Morrison makes her main characters, Joe and Violet, "traindance" (*JZ* 36) on their way North:

They weren't even there yet and already the City was speaking to them. They were dancing. Like a million others, chest pounding, tracks controlling their feet, they stared out of the window for first sight of the City that danced with them, proving already how much it loved them. Like a million more they could hardly wait to get there and love it back. (*Jazz* 32)[3]

By the 1930s, however, the idealized account of Locke had already given way to more sober and darker representations of the city.

---

3   Throughout this paper the reference entry for *Jazz* will be abbreviated with JZ.

Already in the late 1920s, Claude McKay's *Home to Harlem* (1928) or Carl Van Vechten's *Nigger Heaven* (1926) introduced Harlem's underworld as an allegoric vision of a dark and primitive jungle and foreshadowed that Harlem's heyday was soon to come to an end. Although many whites participated in the colorful spectacle of Harlem, the majority never stopped viewing African Americans as the exotic, primitive other.

The Great Depression of the 1930s caused rapid declines in production and sales, which led to unemployment on both sides, black and white. The fierce competition for jobs enforced racism even more, as many whites believed that black people were stealing their jobs. In addition, the crisis of the 1930s involved the decline of the cityscape itself, as the authorities ceased to take care of real estate. As employment and living conditions became more and more miserable, a great number of black artists and intellectuals left Harlem. By the 1940s, Harlem had become the exemplary postwar ghetto. Featuring social "pathologies" (Rotella 221) such as poverty, unemployment, poor living conditions, drug addiction, homicide, and unstable family units, the black Metropolis became the epitome of urban crisis.

The sudden transformation from a city of heaven to a city of hell is also illustrated in the writings of Rudolph Fisher. As already described in his 1925 short-story "The City of Refuge," Gillis perceives Harlem as "the land of plenty" (36) where "black was white" (ibid.) and where "cullud policemans [*sic*]" (ibid.) passed his way. However, in his short story "Vestiges: Harlem Sketches," Fisher's Harlem is depicted as the "city of the devil – outpost of hell" (75), depriving its inhabitants of their souls. Understandably, the nightmarish reality of the big city left its traces in the psyches of many African Americans. In his essay "Harlem is Nowhere," Ralph Ellison writes:

> [T]he most surreal fantasies are acted out upon the streets of Harlem; a man ducks in and out of traffic shouting and throwing imaginary grenades that actually exploded during World War I; a boy participates in the rape robbery of his mother; [...] two men hold a third while a lesbian slashes him to death with a razor blade; boy gangsters wielding homemade pistols [...] shoot down their young rivals. Life becomes a masquerade, exotic costumes are worn every day. (295-296)

Describing Harlem as a place of terror and confusion, Ellison captures a surreal city experience where it is impossible to distinguish between the real and the unreal. Especially in the 1940s and 1950s, most African Americans were caught in a world of social injustice and were desperately longing for a reality they could make sense of. Finally, the social and economic illnesses of the black folk developed into a collective psychological disease, leaving the black urbanite in a state of mental confusion. In 1946, the Lafargue Psychiatric Clinic in Harlem began to offer psychiatric care for everyone, regardless of race or ability to pay. Ellison points out that the clinic became the refuge for many black city dwellers "who in responding to the complex forces of America ha[ve] become confused" ("Harlem is Nowhere" 295). This confusion, depicted by Ellison, mainly relies on the fact that Harlem was conceived as heaven but lived as hell. In her book *Looking for Harlem* (2000), Maria Balshaw writes about this dialectic notion of Harlem:

On the one hand we find a passionate urbanism, where the city stands for the future and more particularly the future of the race. On the other hand we see the city painted as the site of deprivation, squalor and discontent, a version of racial urbanism we are perhaps more familiar with in our contemporary era. (1)

Whereas in reality the colourful period of the Harlem Renaissance ended with the Great Depression, it lived on as a fictional construct in the minds of many black Southerners for much longer. Morrison's *Jazz* captures this paradox of Harlem, "the tension between this projection of dream and its failure" (ibid. 2), in that she makes her characters involuntarily relive their traumatic experiences from the past. As Ryan and Májoza eloquently put it: "In *Jazz*, the American South is the *milieu de mémoire* newly jeopardized by the racist backlash of the post-Reconstruction era, and whose 'remains' survivors in the North must access through memory in order to re-create themselves in the city" (133). It is 'the City' that presents itself strangely in disguise, being illusive, seductive, beautiful, and frightening at the same time. It thus alludes to both the city of the mind, that for many African Americans translated into the Promised Land, but also to the material urban reality of poverty, oppression, and limited opportunities – a socio-economic condition which Langston Hughes powerfully translated into his poem "Harlem: A Dream Deferred"

(1951) and which Lorraine Hansberry, inspired by Hughes figurative language, converted into her 1959 play *A Raisin in the Sun*.

Many African American writers expressed this paradoxical quality of Harlem representing both dream and nightmare. In the first lines of his poem "Return of the Native," Amiri Baraka powerfully evokes the dialectic of beauty and viciousness: "Harlem is vicious/modernism. BangClash/ Vicious the way it's made. / Can you stand such beauty. / So violent and transforming" (217). Similarly, James Baldwin's protagonist of *Go Tell It On the Mountain* (1953) is torn between the two archetypal notions of heaven and hell when he looks at Manhattan's skyline, standing on a hill in Central Park:

There arose in him an exultation and a sense of power [...] he would live in this shining city which his ancestors had seen with longing from far away [...] And still, on the summit of that hill he paused. He remembered the people he had seen in the city, whose eyes held no love for him [...] Then he remembered his father and his mother, and all the arms stretched out to hold him back, to save him from this city where, they said, his soul would find perdition [...] It was the roar of the damned that filled Broadway. (33-34)

Also, Claude McKay, a forerunner of Hughes and Ellison, highlighted the black emotional dilemma of loving and hating the city. In his poem "The White City," he describes the city as "white world's hell" (ibid.) and uses vampire imagery in order to illustrate his social entrapment in the American metropolis. The city makes him a victim that has to be "f[ed] with vital blood" (ibid.). At the same time, however, it is his hate for the city that keeps him alive. In the one but last couplet, he visually experiences the beauty of the physical cityscape, admiring its "vapor-kissed" (ibid.) towers (Maxwell, Section 2, para. 1). Since the lyrical I is entrapped in 'Zoo York,' he can only experience the city's beauty by hating it.

Also at the beginning of *Jazz*, the nameless narrator figure depicts Harlem in highly ambivalent terms. Although the narrating I explicitly describes the city as a place which makes one "dream tall and feel in on things" (*JZ* 7), the morbid and violent imagery used in the depiction of New York's architecture subliminally alludes to a harsh social reality characterized by racial segregation:

Daylight slants like a razor cutting the buildings in half. In the top half I see looking faces and it's not easy to tell which are people, which the work of stonemasons. Below is shadow where any blasé thing takes place: clarinets and lovemaking, fists and the voices of sorrowful women. When I look over strips of green grass lining the river, at church steeples and into the cream-and-copper halls of apartment buildings, I'm strong. Alone, yes, but top-notch and indestructible-like the City in 1926 when all the wars are over and there will never be another one. The people down there in the shadow are happy about that. At last, at last, everything's ahead. The smart ones say so and people listening to them and reading what they write down agree: Here comes the new. Look out. There goes the sad stuff. The bad stuff. [...] History is over, you all, and everything ahead at last. (ibid.)

The social hierarchies manifest themselves in built form, in particular, in skyscrapers being the most visible symbols of white hegemonic control. From a god-like perspective, it is the African American city dwellers that inhabit a dark space of shadows 'down below,' a spatial metaphor designating both the African American dream of equality that is overshadowed by racist power structures and the undying hope for a future of racial uplift that Alain Locke had once proclaimed in *The New Negro* (Kennedy 74). Here, the uncanny does not yet reveal itself as the return of the repressed, but rather as the sublime, a quality of greatness that presents the city as both empowering and daunting or, in Chadwick-Joshua's words, as both "nurturer and agitator" (169).

The chronotopic motives of Morrison's Harlem are, as mentioned earlier, concerned with the dissolving of boundaries. Especially the (construction of a) notion of home in the city is constantly contested in Morrison's fiction, as all the characters are psychologically unable to leave behind a communal Southern (and also African) past. Through unconscious acts of 'rememory,' Morrison's characters constantly travel back to their ancestral homeland so that the city, in fact, as Richard Wright writes in *Black Boy*, becomes an alien place into which a part of the South was "transplanted" (284). This transplantation of a painful past also manifests itself in Morrison's depiction of a spatial setting that takes us to dark, private spaces of confinement as well as to the surreal sidewalks of Jazz Age Harlem.

In Morrison's *Jazz*, the chapters are unnumbered, i.e., they do not underlie a structural chronology that helps to formulate a coherent story. Most critics have read this formality as analogous to the composition of a jazz piece or a jazz session in which transitions are loose, fluid, and often improvisational. However, when applying a chronotopic reading to Morrison's text, the non-hierarchal structuring and fluid overlap of chapters also suggest a democratization of narrated space in which the stories about the remembered South are as important as the stories about the experienced North. This structural device also pays tribute to the conception of postmodern landscapes as such, which are, according to Mike Crang and Penny Travlou, "a juxtaposition of asynchronous moments where space forms a container for different areas producing a depthless world where time as process is erased [...] and which demands cognitive mapping" (161). Indeed, Morrison's *Jazz* presents cognitive representations of Harlem, maps drawn by characters who have difficulties making the city their home because dislocation, for them, is not only a geographical but mainly a psychological phenomenon. Similarly to the exile who, according to Said, "is always out of place" (180), the African American migrant struggles in order to develop a sense of belonging. In Harlem, writes Ralph Ellison, "[o]ne's identity drifts in a capricious reality in which even the most commonly held assumptions are questionable. One 'is' literally, but one is nowhere; one wanders dazed in a ghetto maze, a 'displaced person' of American democracy" ("Harlem is Nowhere" 298).

JAZZ SPACE

"There is no question," writes Justine Tally, "but that in *Jazz* the City is so vividly alive that it takes on the status of character" (*The Story* 34). Always spelled with a capital 'C,' the City is clearly anthropomorphized[4] – also in the sense that it operates analogously to the human heart which, by its rhythmic contractions, maintains the life force in human beings. By rhetorically comparing Harlem to the pulsating center of the human body, Morrison conceives of the City not only as the nation's symbolic 'heart of darkness' but also as a spatial translation of an essentialism that saw blues and jazz music as the driving cultural force (or voice) of authentic blackness. When

---

4   When Joe and Violet migrate to New York City, the City "speak[s] to them [...] dance[s] with them [and] love[s] them" (*JZ* 32).

Morrison uses the city as "an instrumental space" (Paquet-Deyris 2) she is clearly aware of the spirit of the Black Arts Movement of the 1960s, which advocated the notion, as articulated by Amiri Baraka in "The Myth of a Negro Literature," that "[t]he development of the Negro's music was [...] direct and instinctive" (168) because it grew out of "the depths of the black man's soul" (165) tormented by the experience of captivity and bondage.

Early on in the Harlem Renaissance, black music signified not only the folk aesthetic of black Southerners but an art form of artistic resistance against white hegemonic control. For example, in *Jazz*, the streets and sidewalks of Harlem form a system of intersections whose lively dynamism is expressed by Morrison's narrative voice through the use of staccato speech:

[T]he sidewalks, snowcovered or not, are wider than the main roads of the towns where they were born and perfectly ordinary people can stand at the stop, get on the streetcar, give the man the nickel, and ride anywhere you please, although you don't please to go many places because everything you want is right where you are: the church, the store, the party, the women, the men, the postbox (but no high schools), the furniture store, street newspaper vendors, the bootleg houses (but no banks), the beauty parlors, the barbershops, the juke joints, the ice wagons, the rag collectors, the pool halls, the open food markets, the number runner, and every club, organization, group, order, union, society, brotherhood, sisterhood or association imaginable. (*JZ* 10)

The narrator of *Jazz* depicts Harlem's built environment as a place that "pumps desire" (*JZ* 34). However, the steady pumping rhythm that is evoked by the enumeration enforces not only the musicality of improvised jazz style apparent throughout Morrison's text but also the social inscriptions of the Harlem Renaissance cityscape, i.e., the dominating infrastructure of spectacle and political activism. Yet, Harlem lacks banks and high schools, institutions upon which white hegemonic control is built upon. In this way, Harlem is both liberating and restrictive, hence forming a space of contradiction that estranges the characters and allows for the uncanny to surface. More specifically, jazz music becomes the major chronotopic tool for Morrison to evoke the uncanny moments in the story. More broadly speaking, it is the musicality of jazz (with its improvisational style and its unexpected repetitions) which haunts the literary text and thus makes the familiar strange. Furthermore, jazz music serves as an apt stylistic element to depict uncanny forces because it has always been associated with 'repressed' or 'forbidden' desires that were considered amoral in the white man's imagination.

The critic's opinions over whether jazz emerged as a rural or urban phenomenon differ extremely. Many people claim that jazz as an art form developed out of the blues, a genre that emerged in the American South, and more specifically in the Mississippi Delta, at the turn of the nineteenth century. Often defined along the lines of individual experiences of grief or hardship, the blues, by assimilating field hollers, call and response patterns and Negro spirituals, clearly pays testimony to the history of slavery in the Deep South. "It is only in his music," writes James Baldwin, "that the Negro of America has been able to tell his story" ("Many Thousands Gone" 24). Whereas the blues is associated with the rural South, now jazz is rather connected to the urban North, mainly because it was in cities such as New York or Chicago where an infrastructure and audience for musical entertainment made possible a further cultivation of jazz as an art form. Especially the Harlem of the 1920s was regarded as "the commercial hub of jazz activity" (Ramsey 113), producing legends such as Edward Kennedy Ellington or Billie Holliday. However, even during the 1920s, the cultural elite looked askance at an art form that sprung from the black urban proletariat[5]. Justine Tally notes that "jazz was associated with moral anarchy, cultural backwardness and illicit sexuality, particularly black female sexuality" (*The Story* 65). Jazz was often performed in secret spaces and for many denoted nothing but forbidden underground entertainment. During the prohibition era, jazz was the dominant musical genre played in speakeasies,[6] i.e., illegal nightclubs in which alcohol was sold and consumed, which enforced

---

5 Questioning the aesthetic value of jazz, also black intellectuals and literati such as Countee Cullen, who strongly advocated a post-racial attitude, believed that the music's association with the lower social stratum as well as with a tragic past would counteract the advancement towards a color-blind nation.

6 The name "speakeasies" derives from the phrase "to speak easy" (to whisper) – a necessity during the prohibition era in order to keep the illegal drinking joints secret.

associations of the black subject with amorality, primitivism, and exotic spectacle. Although for many urban blacks this (underground) popularization and celebration of jazz went in accordance with the expression of a new freedom, jazz always subliminally conjured up, as Ralph Ellison formulates it, "the painful details and episodes of a brutal experience alive in one's consciousness" (*Shadow* 78).

In *Jazz*, Morrison's narrator articulates this presence of the past that is inscribed in African American music by using an architectural imagery of fear right at the beginning of the novel: "Word was that underneath the good times and the easy money something evil ran the streets and nothing was safe--not even the dead" (*JZ* 9). Alluding to the very beginning of *Jazz*, in which Violet's attack on Dorcas, her husband's young dead mistress, is described, the narrator juxtaposes the creative atmosphere of Jazz Age Harlem with the present psychological pathologies the history of bondage has left behind. At the same time, the phrase foreshadows encounters with the uncanny, suggesting that all that which should remain secret, hidden, or suppressed in the glittering world of jazz is about to resurface. It is the music that paradoxically does both, makes the characters forget and remember the past at the same time. Alice Manfred, Dorcas' aunt and guardian, conceives of the blues as an illusionary tool, fooling too many African Americans to believe that the time of racial intolerance is over:

[Alice] heard a complicated anger in it; something hostile that disguised itself as flourish and roaring seduction. [...] It faked happiness, faked welcome, but it did not make her feel generous, this juke joint, barrel hooch, tonk house music. It made her hold her hand in the pocket of her apron to keep from smashing it through the glass pane to snatch the world in her fist and squeeze the life out of it for doing what it did and did and did to her and everybody else she knew or knew about. (*JZ* 59)

In contrast, Joe and Violet fall victim to the lure of Jazz Age Harlem and deliberately exchange their rural past for an urban future. Joe's desperate need for 'young loving' is temporarily satisfied by his sexual relationship with the teenage girl Dorcas, who has "all the ingredients of pretty" (*JZ* 201) and wears "vampy underwear" (ibid.), and Violet at first admits that city life is so much better without children. Still, it is through unconscious acts of 'rememory' that Morrison's characters gradually learn that 'something evil' is at work in the city, driving them to commit illogical acts of violence: Joe's murder of his beloved Dorcas and Violet's attack on the dead girl's body.

The music of jazz, in articulating personal stories of unbearable loss and displacement, provides, as Ann-Marie Paquet Derris points out, "the historical background the narrative voice incompletely supplies" (221). The unreliable narrator refers to the city as a place where "history is over [...] and everything's ahead" (*JZ* 7), thus repressing the major subtext of cultural mourning. The fear of remembering a cruel past results in what Morrison calls 'national amnesia,' a self-induced forgetfulness which defers a confrontation with the past and also the process of healing. Hence, Morrison makes jazz function as an *ars memoriae*, i.e., the art to 'properly' memorize a certain discourse of the past. To remember African American history 'properly,' Morrison once claimed in "Rootedness: The Ancestor as Foundation," means not only to recall how it was like but how it felt. Oral art forms such as the blues or folk tales, thus, become the tools to authentically 'relive' the African American experience:

> There are things that I try to incorporate into my fiction that are directly and deliberately related to what I regard as the major characteristics of Black art, wherever it is. One of which is the ability to be both print and oral literature: to combine those two aspects so that the stories can be read in silence, of course, but one should be able to hear them as well. [...] To make the story appear oral, meandering, effortless, spoken – to have the reader feel the narrator without identifying that narrator, or hearing him or her knock about, and to have the reader work with the author in the construction of the book – is what's important. ("Rootedness" 59)

Morrison uses jazz as both a discursive technique and a narratological theme also because it is said to be able to capture the emotional truth of individual pasts. The fact that jazz operates similarly to the uncanny can be seen in the very first word that opens the story. In "Sth, I know that woman," (*JZ* 1) the narrator records the sound *sth*, suggesting a certain silence or secrecy which implies that the story which is about to follow (or resurface) is one that should rather remain secret.[7] At the

---

[7] There is also the phonetic similarity of "Sth" to "Shhh", "Shhh" being also the title of a jazz composition by Patrice Rushen, female R&B singer and

same time, the sound evokes an orality that, as Mariangela Palladino notes, "throws the reader into a world of gossips, rumours, and stories" (6). Many critics have noted that Morrison applies *skaz* – a Russian Formalist literary device denoting oral narration – into her writing. Accordingly, she makes orality strangely appear in the text. Palladino further states that Morrison's novel "'sounds' like a chant and its flat printed words seem to have an inner rhythm crying out to be sung" (3).

The epigraph of *Jazz*, which Morrison takes from "Thunder, Perfect Mind," deriving from a corpus of texts referred to as The Nag Hammadi, upon first examination, seems to foreshadow Morrison's attempt to fuse the oral with the written. In the epigraph, it says: "I am the name of the sound/ and the sound of the name./ I am the sign of the letter/ And the designation of the division" (*JZ* xi). Whereas the first two lines clearly invite a phonocentric reading, the last two lines, however, suggest a disconnection between the sound and the letter and thus also the impossibility of what Henry Louis Gates Jr. has called "the speakerly text" (xxv). The intellectual ambiguity the epigraph evokes, however, is rather a paradoxon which upon closer examination holds some truth. If we conceive of *Jazz* as "a story about the ways and means of storytelling itself and the language of the narrative process" (*The Story* 29), as Justine Tally suggests, and if we accept that "the voice [of the epigraph] is language/logos itself" (ibid. 26), the division between the sign and the letter is not something limiting or restrictive, but rather something liberating that points to the endless possibilities of storytelling (ibid.). How a story is told is always determined by the relationships of speaker and listener in a certain society, just as much as the (truth) value of a sign is determined by its relationship to other signs in a certain system.[8] Language, hence, does

---

pianist, who performed the piece together with Wayne Shorter at the Montreux Jazz Festival in 1988.

8   In *Course in General Linguistics*, Saussure writes: "The notion of value [...] shows us that it is a great mistake to consider a sign as nothing more than the combination of a certain sound and a certain concept. To think of a sign as nothing more would be to isolate it from the system to which it belongs. It would be to suppose that a start could be made with individual signs, and a system constructed by putting them together. On the contrary, the system as a united whole is the starting point, from which it becomes

not correspond to reality as such, and the stable bond between a signifier and a signified, as suggested *avant* Saussure, is nothing but phantasmal.

In similar terms, as Ann Banfield in her definition of *skaz* reveals, 'true' orality in a text is a simulacrum:

> The skaz narrative is not orally composed; it is a written imitation of an oral narrative, and it is only conceivable if it is written. In a real act of oral composition, the voice and accent of the storyteller is perhaps as equally transparent as the narration of a written text; nevertheless, it is produced concurrently with the story and can be heard as well. (253)

Rather, what Morrison wants to say with her epigraph is that we have to conceive of this textual orality as a haunting, an absent presence or present absence that makes itself strangely felt in the written text. Conceiving of the notion of *skaz* as haunting also makes possible for Morrison to let phantom-stories, i.e., all the stories untold resurface in unexpected and mysterious ways. *Skaz*, thus, is the repressed voice of the unconscious mind that makes us aware of the importance of oral storytelling in African and African American folk cultures.

Skaz and jazz, both contribute to a novelistic chronotope that is defined through repetition and simultaneity. Jazz is characterized by the stylistic principle of repetition, repeating "a stanza of twelve bars with a variation of three chords" (Palladino 2). Similarly, with *skaz* or oral storytelling, the repetition of verbal elements enables memorization, and thus their preservation in the human mind. In *Jazz*, plot lines and stories repeat themselves, such as the episode about Golden Gray's arrival at his father's house:

> When he gets to the house, he pulls into the yard and finds a shed with two stalls in back. He takes his horse into one and wipes her down carefully. Then he throws a blanket over her and looks out for water and feed. He takes a long time over this. (*JZ* 146)
> [...] Certainly the owner never expected a horse and a carriage to arrive – the fence gate is wide enough for a stout woman but no more. He unharnesses the horse and walks it a way to the right and discovers, behind the cabin and under

---

> possible, by a process of analysis, to identify its constituent elements" (112-113).

a tree he does not know the name of, two open stalls, one of which is full of shapes. Leading the horse he hears behind him a groan from the woman, but doesn't stop to see whether she is waking or dying or falling off the seat. Close up on the stalls he sees that the shapes are tubs, sacks, lumber wheels, a broken plow, a butter press and a metal trunk. There is a stake too, and he ties the horse to it. Water, he thinks. Water for the horse. (*JZ* 151)

Although the same story is repeated, the two versions are not the same, as told from two different perspectives and in different narrative modes. While the first version features a diegetic narrative mode, summarizing the most essential events in a thematically focused and orderly account, the second version is told in a mimetic narrative mode (or scenic presentation) in which events are presented as reflected in a character's consciousness. Whereas the first account clearly suggests a camera-eye narration, the second allows us a deeper insight into Golden Gray's perceptions and the workings of his mind. What is doubled is only the story's *histoire*, but not its *discours*. In *Jazz*, the repetition of Golden Gray's arrival at Henry LesTroy's cabin is crucial because it signifies his split racial identity, i.e., the fact that he is neither black nor white. Yet, the doubling of the story also fulfills a metafictional function.

Justine Tally contends that "the outstanding concern of the novel is not the stories that are told but the examination of how these (in fact, all) stories are told" (12), and that in the novel "[t]he process of storytelling is foregrounded conscientiously" (10). As already noted in the previous chapter of this study, repetition always occurs, as Deleuze says, "in relation to something unique or singular which has no equal or equivalent" (1). In *skaz*, unlike in written narration, there can never be an exact reduplication of a story, as stories can be interrupted or changed unexpectedly. The same, of course, applies to the 'cut' and improvisation techniques in jazz music. Morrison, at various instances in the novel, captures this repetitive improvisational style and polyrhythmic tone in her diction, as indicated in the following passage: "Blues man. Black and bluesman. Black therefore blue man. Everybody knows your name. Where-did-she-go-and-why-man. So-lonesome-I-could die man. Everybody knows your name" (*JZ* 119).

If there is a character in *Jazz* that anthropomorphizes the flexible and open mechanics of *skaz* (and jazz), it is certainly the character of Henry LesTroy, the skilled huntsman, who is the substitute father for

Joe in his childhood years and whose identity is as fluid and fragmented as the novel's overall structure. Although he might, at first sight, not stand in direct relation to the urban uncanny, he is an intrinsic part of Morrison's rhizomatic memory discourse that shapes the novel as a whole. Referred to as Henry LesTroy, but at times also as Henry Lestory, he comes to personify the inextricable triad of history, destruction (as symbolized in Troy), and storytelling that shapes and defines all of the character's actions. Moreover, Henry LesTroy/Lestory is known among his community as Hunter's Hunter, a name suggesting a *Doppelgänger* identity or split consciousness. According to Philip Page, his name explicitly reveals the complexity of his character:

> Henry is the archetypal father figure, the 'father' of the novel. He is 'Hunter's Hunter', who enjoys perfect knowledge of and union with nature. [...] He is a griot, a spiritual guide, like Pilate in Song of Solomon and Therese in Tar Baby, and like them his harmony with nature corresponds with his inner harmony and fulfilled self-knowledge. (58)

As a woodsman and hunter, LesTroy represents the rural Southern home and thus also Joe and Violet's roots that have become even more severed in the city. LesTroy/Lestory possesses the skills that all of the characters desperately long for. His ability to understand and feel in on the animal's codes and their natural habitat makes it easy for him to trace and catch the precious prey. In Morrison's words: "He was so good they say he just carried the rifle for the hell of it because he knew way before what the prey would do, how to fool snakes, bend twigs and string to catch rabbits, groundhog [*sic*]; make a sound waterfowl couldn't resist" (*JZ* 125). LesTroy/Lestory's hunt for wild animals becomes an allegory for Joe and Violet's hunt for family ties that, in the course of history, have become lost or too loose.

At the same time, however, LesTroy/Lestory's *raison d'être* makes him a constant transient so that his home, the empty cabin Golden Gray arrives at, becomes the chronotopic metaphor for absence itself, in other words, "the place where he [i.e., LesTroy/Lestory] should have been and was not" (*JZ* 158). It is Golden Gray's awareness to have come to the spatial evidence of his father's existence that conjures up the pain of loss he had repressed until this point. Morrison illustrates this return of the repressed by using the powerful imagery of amputation:

Before, I thought everybody was one-armed, like me. Now I feel the surgery. The crunch of bone when it is sundered, the sliced flesh and tubes of blood cut through, shocking the bloodrun and disturbing the nerves. They *dangle and writhe*. Singing pain. Waking me with the sound of itself, thrumming when I sleep so deeply it strangles my dreams away. There is nothing for it but to go away from where he is not to *where he used to be and might be still*. Let *the dangle and the writhe* see what it is missing; let the pain sing to the dirt where he stepped in the place *where he used to be and might be still*. (ibid., my emphasis)

Morrison's stylistic 'repulsion to repeat' enforces the mental processing of Golden Gray's feelings of parental loss; a loss so painful that he imagines it as losing a body part. What he comes to realize in this uncanny moment is the fact that he never had a father – an epiphany that, triggered by the sight of the empty cabin, hurts him like a blade cutting his flesh. The uncanny moment is also evoked because something unreal or illusionary (i.e., the father figure) suddenly takes on materiality (i.e., his domestic space). Or in Freud's terms: "[The] uncanny effect often arises when the boundary between fantasy and reality is blurred, when we are faced with the reality of something that we have until now considered imaginary" (U 150). Interestingly, Freud also considers "[s]evered limbs, a severed head, a hand detached from the arm [...], feet that dance by themselves" (ibid.) as particularly uncanny, "especially when they are credited [...] with independent activity" (ibid.). Golden Gray also imagines the detached arm to come to life: "Perhaps the arm will no longer be a phantom, but will take its own shape, grow its own muscle and bone, and its blood will pump from the loud singing that has found the purpose of its serenade. Amen" (*JZ* 159). Just like Harlem, the arm gains its life force from music, the cultural tool and expression of identity (re-)formation. As Michael Nowlin makes clear: "Golden Gray doesn't just affirm his own castration here; he discovers the meaning of the blues and the tragic mode of reconnection they afford" (63). Golden Gray's "gone-away hand" (*JZ* 158) is used by Morrison as a *pars pro toto*,[9] coming to stand for all the painful parental losses that connect the family histories of Joe, Violet, Alice, Dorcas, Felice, and Wild. Consequently, the question posed by the black boy who Golden Gray encounters at his father's house – ""Might you be related to Lestory?" (*JZ* 149) – is, in fact, a rhetorical question not only directed to the hunter but to all of the characters in the novel. It is through the rhythms of black music that the rural South, as personified through LesTroy/Lestory (and Wild), and the urban North, as personified through Dorcas, are chronotopically related.

As illustrated in the following chapters, the jazz space the reader enters in the novel is not exclusively urban. Rather, Morrison constructs a "phantomistic topography" (Royle 279) of New York City that makes the black, sorrowful voices of the rural South (and its history) uncannily resound. It is a text that, as the narrator of *Jazz* suggests, imagines the past as "an abused record with no choice but to repeat itself at the crack" (*JZ* 220).

MEMORY TRACKS AND SIDEWALK CRACKS

"One thing for sure," the narrative voice claims, "the streets will confuse you, teach you or break your neck" (*JZ* 72). In *Jazz*, Morrison frequently alludes to the fact that the city is an ambiguous, incomprehensible and therefore dangerous landscape in which dwelling in the traditional sense has become impossible. However, whereas Western scholars such as Heidegger or Adorno attribute the loss of 'home' to the condition of modernity as such,[10] for Morrison, home-

---

9   Throughout the novel, also other images of fragmented black bodies recur, for example, Neola's paralyzed "frozen arm" (*JZ* 62).

10 In *Minima Moralia: Reflections on a Damaged Life*, Adorno compares the modern condition as such to a state of collective homelessness: "Dwelling, in the proper sense, is now impossible. The traditional residences we grew up in have grown intolerable: each trait of comfort in them is paid for with a betrayal of knowledge, each vestige of shelter with the musty pact of family interests. The functional modern habitations designed from a tabula rasa, are living-cases manufactured by experts for philistines, or factory sites that have strayed into the consumption sphere, devoid of all relation

lessness is clearly tied to the issue of race. In many of her works, lacking a home, temporally or permanently, correlates with the loss or fragmentation of black subjectivity (and sometimes even with the loss or fragmentation of a unified body). The confusion radiating from the streets, therefore, symbolizes the confusion of the self that was enforced by the expectation that, in Harlem, a 'new', more positive and stable black self can be developed. According Donald B. Gibson, "the New Negroes were not only 'new' to the world; they were new to themselves" (46). However, the act of self-definition and renewal represented a difficult endeavor because most African Americans had radically been disconnected from their roots and family ties, or chronotopically speaking, from a Southern past. Throughout the novel, Morrison clearly associates this rural past with the notion of wholeness and, in particular, psychological stability. For example, Violet observes at one point: "Before I came North I made sense and so did the world" (*JZ* 207).

In *Jazz*, Morrison presents cognitive maps of Harlem. Hence, in the City, spatial practices are acted out as a translation of subjective obsessions. For example, Joe conceives of New York as an urban jungle through which he desperately "hunt[s]" (28) for Dorcas because he unconsciously repeats the search for his lost mother Wild. Violet's urge for mothering manifests itself in a dark, cold, and empty city, a space where she is unable to find rest. What lies at the very heart of the characters' obsessions repeats itself in the actual construction of New York City which, according to Gaston Bachelard, architecturally lacks a solid foundation: "[Sky-scrapers] have no roots and, what is quite unthinkable for a dreamer of houses, sky-scrapers have no cellars. From the street to the roof, the rooms pile up one on top of the other, while the tent of a horizonless sky encloses the entire city" (27).

In similar terms, Morrison draws New York City as a place with "no foundation at all" (*JZ* 23) and also makes her narrative voice use nature imagery in order to subliminally criticize the artificiality and depthlessness of the urban landscape:

> to the occupant: in them the nostalgia for independent existence, defunct in any case, is sent packing. Modern man wishes to sleep close to the ground like an animal, a German magazine decreed with prophetic masochism before Hitler, abolishing with the bed the threshold between waking and dreaming" (38).

[T]here is nothing to beat what the City can make of a nightsky. It can empty itself of surface, and more like the ocean itself, go deep, starless. Close up on the top of buildings, near, nearer than the cap you are wearing, such a citysky presses and retreats, presses and retreats, making me think of the free but illegal love of sweethearts before they are discovered [...]. Otherwise, if it wanted to, it could show me stars cut from the lame gowns of chorus girls, or mirrored in the eyes of sweethearts furtive and happy under the pressure of a deep touchable sky. But that's not all a citysky can do. It can go purple and keep an orange heart so the clothes of the people on the streets glow like dance-hall costumes. (35-36)

Here, the city is portrayed as if inflicted with a transcendental power that can transform the nightly sky into a vast and mysterious void or a colorful spectacle of shades. As the modern city replaces awe-inspiring images of nature, Morrison subverts traditional Romantic notions of sublimity. The city, upon first glance, seems to be great and irresistible; however, at the same time it also represents an uncontrollable, incomprehensible, and most likely dangerous force. The "booming nightsky" (ibid.), for example, produces a confining and oppressive atmosphere that is clearly frightening. Morrison's vivid color imagery, which counteracts the image of dark confinement, alludes to the unreality of the African American urban experience, an experience characterized by a spectacle in which people participate like actors on a stage. Depicting the urban (black) crowd as people wearing glittering costumes, Morrison indicates that, in the City, colored people are still manipulated by the dominant culture of imperialism that is operating behind the scenes (Scruggs 73).

Even though the characters of Morrison's novel initially display their "stronger, riskier selves" (*JZ* 33) in the city, they are trapped in an environment of displacement – an asphalt jungle in which black migrants can neither detect nor leave foot prints. As Shirley Ann Stave remarks: "The City lives in the moment, with [...] no contingency plan that indicates an understanding of the ongoing cycle of existence, in which people give birth, grow old, and die. Hence, it is rough terrain on which to battle those ghosts who refuse to remain buried in the past." (61) Accordingly, the city is, first and foremost, depicted and perceived as a "non-place," (Augé 78) a space of ongoing transit and/or transition, lacking myth, history, or identity, and which perfectly underlines the difficulties of identity (re-)formation which the characters undergo in the novel. Joe and Violet's local reality in Harlem is distorted because both were uprooted from their rural villages in the South, a process that both characters directly connect with the loss of their mothers. Both, Joe and Violet, remain haunted by their absent mother-figures and images of their former rural homes.

Joe Trace

Joe Trace is the prototypical transient, i.e., a character whose identity is built upon the notions of restlessness and displacement. Already before he moves to the city, he is constantly denied a stable home or place to dwell: After his hometown had been burned, he "went running from one part of the country to another – or nowhere" (*JZ* 126) only to become a victim of the debt environment of sharecropping in Palestine. Moving from Palestine to Rome, further up to Tenderloin and arriving in New York, Joe "thought [he] had settled into [his] permanent self, the fifth one" (*JZ* 127) but yet, moved another time uptown, "leaving the flesh-eating rats on West Fifty-third" (ibid.). With his wife Violet, he finally settles in Harlem but again in 1919 finds himself unable to rest, "walk[ing] all the way, every goddamn step of the way, with the three six nine [infantry]" (*JZ* 129). In depicting Joe's history of fleeting homes, Morrison again alludes to the fact that the loss of 'home' is closely related to the loss of (a stable) self.

Needless to say, Joe's constant search for a new home is fuelled by the acts of racism he encounters during and after the reconstruction era. For example, the arson attacks on his hometown, his eviction from his own parcel of land, the Harlem race riots, and the unbearable working conditions in the city, are testimonies and cruel reminders of his alleged black inferiority and white power. Even though, in 1925, he and Violet have eventually found a comfortable place to stay and better jobs, it is in the city where Joe, in his fatal hunt for his teenage-lover Dorcas, develops an inner compulsion to wander the streets. According to the narrator, his compulsion to move through the city seems to be beyond his control:

Take my word for it, he [Joe] is bound to the track. It pulls him like a needle through the groove of a Bluebird record. Round and round about the town. That's the way the City spins you. Makes you do what it wants, go where the laid-out roads say to. All the while letting you think you're free; […] You can't get off the track a City lays for you. (*JZ* 120)

Joe is hypnotized by the city's jazz impulse, suggesting the realization of a long-awaited freedom and new beginning. However, Morrison's rhetorical image that compares the city's grid to the groove of a record also evokes the notion of forceful confinement. Although Joe's route seems to be mostly dictated by Dorcas, who for Joe is irresistible "like candy" (*JZ* 120) to a kid, it is a more intricate source that keeps Joe on track. In fact, Joe's restlessness in the city, or more specifically, his hunt for Dorcas, is nothing but the reenactment of his search for his lost mother Wild. As Denise Heinze explains: "When Joe takes after Dorcas, who has left him for a younger man, he is simply reliving his earlier failed attempts to hunt down and find his mother and the rejection that her self-imposed exile symbolized" (35).

What Joe unconsciously repeats in the City has already been carried out in his Southern past. After learning from Henry LesTroy/Lestory that the mysterious woman hiding in the woods might be his mother, Joe "made three solitary journeys to find her" (*JZ* 177). In his essay "Traces of Derrida in Morrison's *Jazz*," Philip Page argues that "Joe's displacement originates with the even more radical displacement of his mother, Wild," and that "his conscious presence in the City only exists in terms of its play with, or memory, of his absent past in Vesper County" (57). As Joe's last name suggests, it is the notion of the trace that operates as the crucial chronotopic motif connecting the triad Joe, Dorcas, Wild. Thinking that he was the trace his parents "went off without" (*JZ* 124), Joe gives himself the last name Trace and thus comes to embody this seemingly endless search for his roots and, more specifically, for his lost mother.

In *Heterologies*, Michel de Certeau introduces the concept of the mnemic trace as "the return of what was forgotten, in other words, an action by a past that is now forced to disguise itself" (3-4). De Certeau, echoing the Freudian notion of the memory trace (*Erinnerungsspur*),[11] and, more specifically, the return of the repressed, discusses the trace as the result of two different temporal strategies: forgetting a past

---

11 In *The Interpretation of Dreams*, Freud writes: "The percepts that come to us leave in our psychic apparatus a trace which we may call a memory-trace. The function related to this memory trace we call memory" (403).

event and performing its return in the present. In Morrison's *Jazz*, these two operations are not only temporal but also spatial since Joe's deliberate forgetting of the past is inextricably tied to the city. It is the spectacular urban space of Harlem which seemingly intoxicates Joe, thus making it easy for him to leave his traumatic past of family loss behind:

> There is no air in the City but there is breath, and every morning it races through him like laughing gas brightening his eyes, his talk, and his expectations. In no time at all he forgets little pebbly creeks and apple trees so old they lay their branches along the ground and you have to reach down or stoop to pick the fruit. He forgets a sun that used to slide up like the yolk of a good country egg, thick and red-orange at the bottom of the sky, and he doesn't miss it, doesn't look up to see what happened to it or to stars made irrelevant by the light of thrilling, wasteful street lamps. (*JZ* 34)

By depicting the rural South of Joe's childhood almost as an Edenic home, the narrative voice reveals that Joe's rural past, however traumatic it might have been, also includes something that is too precious to forget. Morrison's use of nature imagery (i.e., the tree and the egg as symbols of nourishing) also underlines that it is the longing for his family roots in the South that lies buried in the depths of his unconscious.

Michel de Certeau regards forgetting as a temporal strategy that is not passive, or sheer coincidence, but rather as a voluntary act that is directed against the past. In the context of African American history, the forgetting of a slave past plays a crucial role, and for Joe and Violet the migration to New York is clearly connected with the desire to leave their own traumas of family loss behind. Following Freud and de Certeau, we know that we can only be haunted by something we have been involved in in the past and by something that was suppressed through the process of forgetting. When Joe 'hunts' Dorcas, he is driven by his "compulsion to repeat" (Freud), unconsciously re-enacting the fourth search for his mother. In his essay "Remembering, Repeating and Working-Through"[12] (1914), Freud explains that a traumatic patient "does not remember anything of what he has forgotten and repressed, but acts it out. He reproduces it not as a

---

12 It was in this paper that Freud first mentioned the "compulsion to repeat."

memory but as an action; he repeats it, without, of course, knowing that he is repeating it" (150).

Morrison reveals at various instances and on various stylistic levels that Joe's following of Dorcas' trail in the city is a repetition of the search for his mother in Virginia, or to put it more bluntly, that Dorcas is a reenactment of the rejection by Wild. For example, much of the descriptive vocabulary used for Wild and Dorcas is isotopically related through the semantic field of the hunt: The name Dorcas derives from Greek *dorkas* meaning gazelle; Joe does not search but 'hunts' for Dorcas; Wild lives an animal like existence in the woods, is "covered with mud and leaves" (*JZ* 144), has "deer eyes" (*JZ* 162), and a voice that "belong[s] to something wearing a pelt instead of a coat" (*JZ* 92). Furthermore, syntactic parallelism strengthens the connection between Dorcas and Wild, as the following remark by Joe indicates: "*I tracked* my mother in Virginia and it led me right to her, and *I tracked* Dorcas from borough to borough" (*JZ* 130, my emphasis). When at the end of section seven the narrator asks "But where is *she*?" (*JZ* 188), the personal pronoun printed in italics designates both women, Wild and Dorcas. When Joe shoots and kills Dorcas at the party, the narrator observes that the crowd looked like "the flock of redwings" (*JZ* 130), a certain species of birds that mark Wild's presence. Most obviously, Morrison parallels the two 'hunts' in the following section, in which Joe recounts the two events as one and the same: "I wasn't looking for the trail. It was looking for me and when it started talking at first I couldn't hear it. I was rambling, just rambling all through the City. I had the gun but it was not the gun – it was my hand I wanted to touch you with. Five days rambling" (*JZ* 130-131). Although Joe makes clear that his spatial setting is 'the City,' the reference to the hand evokes his first confrontation with his wild mother in the thickets of the woods, in which he begs her to show him her hand: "Let me see your hand. Just stick it out someplace and I'll go; I promise. A sign" (*JZ* 178).

In relating the trace to "a sign" (ibid.), Morrison alludes to the Derridean conception of the trace which signifies *différance*[13], i.e., the notion that meaning or truth is not attached to the sign but rather to the interplay of dualisms (or ambiguities), most importantly that of

---

13 Derrida's neologism is often said to fuse the sense of spatiality inherent in the word 'differ' with the sense of temporality inherent in the word 'defer.'

presence and absence (*Of Grammatology* 71).[14] In *Of Grammatology*, Derrida further points out that the trace is the "arche-phenomenon of 'memory', which must be thought before the opposition of nature and culture, animality and humanity [and which] belongs to the very movement of signification" (70). Nicholas Royle, in his book-length study of the uncanny, has noted that deconstruction, and in particular Derrida's key concept of *différance*, shares with the uncanny an attention to intellectual ambiguity. "This position of dual allegiance," Derrida claims in an interview, "is one of perpetual uneasiness" (qtd. in Royle 129).

This uneasiness or, rather, uncanniness is most effectively embodied in Wild, whose identity is not only built upon pillars of intellectual ambiguity but is defined along the lines of the primordial mother figure and thus of the origin, or meaning as such. Similar to LesTroy, Wild is a transition figure and signifies movement or displacement. Neither ghost nor part of society, she can be seen as a fundamentally liminal character who hovers between the spheres of life and death or, in Derrida's terms, absence and presence. Sharon Patricia Holland remarks about Wild that "[s]he is, unlike mortals, invulnerable to barriers of time, space and place" (52). Although she lives in a cave in the woods, the narrator claims at various instances that she has the ability of being "everywhere and nowhere" (*JZ* 178) at the same time. Furthermore, she is described at one point not as "a real women but a 'vision'" (*JZ* 144).

In fact, one can read Wild's transcendental presence in *Jazz* as the return of the repressed that even transgresses the boundaries of the trilogy in the sense that, as many critics claim, Beloved and Wild are one and the same character. Martha J. Cutter has alleged that, at the end of *Beloved*, the now grown-up and pregnant embodiment of the dead girl disappears into the woods around the year 1873 (66). In *Jazz*, the reader is introduced to the wild woman living in the woods who, in the same year, gives birth to a child – presumably Joe. However, many

---

14 In *Dissemination*, Derrida writes: "The trace is the difference [*différance*] which opens appearance [*l'apparaître*] and signification. Articulating the living upon the nonliving in general, origin of all repetition, origin of ideality, the trace is not more ideal than real, not more intelligible than sensible, not more a transparent signification than an opaque energy and *no concept of metaphysics can describe it*" (65).

other intertextual references reaffirm the assumption that Beloved and Wild are one and the same ghostly character. In the novel, it says that the mysterious woman "was close enough to scare everybody because she creeps about and hides and touches and laughs a low sweet babygirl laugh in the cane" (*JZ* 37). The crawling and the babygirl laugh are clear references to Beloved. As Martha J. Cutter notes, both women "appear to love sweet things" (68) to satisfy their hunger: Beloved's hunger is stilled with honey and Wild's paths are marked by the trace of "ruined honeycombs" (*JZ* 176).[15]

As Philip Page remarks, Wild's existence is solely defined through signs of her presence that are related to other signs:

> Wild's presence/absence lies somewhere in the play between the signifiers (the redwinged blackbirds, her song, her human utensils and clothes) and the human being those signifiers point to. Thus, her presence/absence calls attention to and calls into question the usual assumptions about the privilege of presence, self, and signified. (57)

Although Wild is not described as a supernatural being but as a physically present woman, there is something mysterious and animalistic about her. It says in the book that "her eyes are large and terrible" (*JZ* 144) and that there are always black birds that announce her presence: "Redwings, those blue-black birds with the bolt of red on their wings. Something about her they liked and seeing four or more of them always meant she was close" (*JZ* 176). The red on the bird's wings could be a reference to Sethe's cruel and bloody act of cutting through the throat of her little daughter. When Golden Gray finds her, he notices "a trickle of blood down her jaw onto her neck" (*JZ* 146), which is another trace leading back to Sethe's infanticide.

Wild is spatially assigned to the woods and to the cave which she domesticates, which is also an allusion to the role of the black woman

---

15 It has to be noted that some critics, most notably Elizabeth House, do not read Beloved as a ghost but as a flesh-and-blood person. For House, for example, *Beloved* is not a ghost story but "a story of two probable instances of mistaken identity. Beloved is haunted by the loss of her African parents and thus comes to believe that Sethe is her mother. Sethe longs for her dead daughter and is rather easily convinced that Beloved is the child she has lost" (House 19).

as the savage 'other' or beast; a role that has persisted in the minds of many whites since the days of slavery (Jones 486). The cave tunnel and the forest are usually seen as archetypal images suggesting the womb and female sexuality. At the same time, a cave is also a transitory space in the sense that it connects the external world with a mythological underworld which, in the novel, functions as the pathway to repressed experiences, to the unconscious mind.

If Beloved and Wild are the same character, Beloved continues her presence as the symbolic ancestor figure in *Jazz*, as "the haunting symbol of the many Beloved – generations of mothers and daughters – hunted down and stolen from Africa" (Holland 51-52). Wild's cave, thus, is the spatial translation of the trace that leads back to all origin and which connects the external with the internal sphere. Her spatial environment marks a sphere that is "outside of and beyond history" (Rigney 67). The cave is symbolic for the original story which, in the Platonic sense, is independent of any outside reality or authoritative perspective. At the same time, however, Plato's allegory of the cave repeats itself in the history of the Great Migration, where slaves freed from bondage arrive in the big cities of the North and are blinded by "the light of thrilling, wasteful street lamps" (*JZ* 34), not by the outer reality the lights illuminate.

Joe's mnemic trace, however, expands into a rhizomatic structure connecting his own with other traces of trauma. Through following Joe Trace, also the reader picks up and ties together the trails left behind by Dorcas (i.e., the burned dolls) and Violet (i.e., the dark well), arrives at Wild's cave in the woods and, finally, through association, returns to *Beloved*, Morrison's 'original' story about the painful loss and destruction of family ties. Freud has also noted that it is through verbal or written language (or rather the sensory perception of it) that other memory traces can be triggered in our consciousness.

Accordingly, memory traces can manifest themselves as verbal flows of thought. Morrison's overall design of the book, characterized by unnumbered chapters, the insertion of blank pages, fluid associative transitions, repetitions, a juxtaposition of incomplete individual stories and, at times, the lack of punctuation, is a materialization of the mnemic trace verbalized. As such, the book itself is an infinite, non-restrictive space that contains permanent traces and, at the same time, provides the necessary empty space for all the other memory traces that have not yet surfaced. Reading and writing, thus, become spatial practices in which, as J. Hillis Miller points out, meaning is not created by the dismantling of intricate or irrational narrative threads but by following the (non-linear) trace, which involves taking hermeneutic turns, going back and forth, or even losing one's way:

> To trace is to copy, to double, and thus to avoid the death-like closure of completion, thereby allowing for endless readings, endless reader participation, endless reversions of the text. To trace is also to write, to make physical marks on a blank surface, to set in motion the continuing flux of meaning. (6-8)

Violet Trace

While Joe is characterized through the chronotopic metaphor of the memory trace, Violet's fundamental restlessness is rather the result of "dark fissures" (*JZ* 22) and "private cracks" (ibid.) – chronotopic metaphors suggesting a break or divide that results from acts of tearing apart or processes of aging. For Violet, the city streets are marked by sidewalk cracks upon which she stumbles. As an architectural translation of her psychic wounds, the cracks in the urban landscape suggest dangerous chasms leading to "places dark as the bottom of a well" (ibid.) and thus to the location of her mother's suicide. At night, Violet is haunted and scared by the image of the well into which her mother Rose Dear threw herself. Furthermore, Violet secretly suffers from the traumatic experience of pregnancy loss but represses it. The narrator claims that, for Joe and Violet, the miscarriages were rather "inconvenience than loss [as] citylife was so much better without [children]" (*JZ* 107). Still, Violet reenacts her trauma of loss several times in the novel, for example, when she impulsively attempts to steal a baby or when she satisfies her "mother-hunger" (*JZ* 108) by sleeping with a doll in her arms. Violet also projects her desperate longing for a child onto her environment, in which "she he was already staring at infants, hesitating in front of toys displayed at Christmas. Quick to anger when a sharp word was flung at a child, or a woman's hold of a baby seemed awkward or careless" (*JZ* 107). For Violet, the New York cityscape turns into a place of memory whose semiotics conjure up the tragic loss of family, motherly love, and fertility.

Unlike her husband, Violet does not feel the urge to ecstatically follow the/a trace once lost, since she would be looking for a trace already and forever lost. As her family ties can never be reestablished, Violet's spatial practices are rather defined through her need for stasis and rest. At the beginning of the novel, the narrator recounts that one afternoon Violet suddenly decided to sit down in the middle of the street:

> She didn't stumble nor was she pushed: she just sat down. After a few minutes two men and a woman came to her, but she couldn't make out why or what they said. Someone tried to give her water to drink, but she knocked it away. A policeman knelt in front of her and she rolled over on her side, covering her eyes. (*JZ* 17)

By making the street her place to rest, Violet signals that she is literally without family ties that could mend her broken self. At the same time, Violet is unconsciously repeating the eviction of her mother Rose Dear, who was deprived of her belongings and forcefully tipped out of her chair while holding an empty cup of tea. When Violet later visits Alice in her home, she confesses over a cup of tea that she "can't find a place [to] sit down" (*JZ* 81), thus indirectly repeating the scene of eviction and articulating the wish for a stable home. Violet's compulsion to repeat, therefore, serves as the mechanism that provides the transition between the different histories of dispossession and homelessness the reader witnesses in the novel.

Violet's distorted reality puts her into the position of an outside observer who perceives her life in the city as an artificial and almost mechanical sequence of events:

> I call them cracks because that is what they were. Not openings or breaks, but dark fissures in the globe light of the day. She wakes up in the morning and sees with perfect clarity a string of small, well-lit scenes. In each one something specific is being done: feed things, work things; customers and acquaintances are encountered, places entered. But she does not see herself doing these things. She sees them being done. (*JZ* 22)

Symbolizing the deep emotional gashes that the lack of both receiving and providing motherly love has left behind, the dark fissures in Violet's mind gradually expand until they finally split her consciousness into two. As the repressed memories of the past emerge, Violet is confronted with a second self that she sees walking through the city in her skin and looking through her eyes. The narrator figure points out that it was "*that other* Violet" that pushed her to commit acts of insanity such as the knife-attack on Dorcas' dead body during the funeral service:

> *that* Violet not only knew the knife was in the parrot's cage and not in the kitchen drawer; [...] She had been looking for that knife for a month. Couldn't for the life of her think what she'd done with it. But *that* Violet knew and went right to it. Knew too where the funeral was going on, although it could not have been but one of two places, come to think of it. Still, *that* Violet knew which of the two, and the right time to get there. (*JZ* 90)

Drawing on Ernst Jentsch's study on the uncanny, Freud also mentions acts of insanity as manifestations of the uncanny because they "arouse in the onlooker vague notions of automatic – mechanical – processes that may lie hidden behind the familiar image of a living person" (U 135). Beyond doubt, *that other* Violet's actions are performed automatically, as if in a state of trance. In this context, Nicolas Royle points out that the uncanny also manifests itself within one's own body: "It [the uncanny] may thus be construed as a foreign body within oneself, even the experience of oneself as a foreign body, the very estrangement of inner silence and solitude" (2). This episode is perceived as uncanny, not only because Violet crosses the border between the self and the other, but also because she is unconsciously "carrying out the repressed desires springing from the Id" (Dolar 69).

Violet's seemingly paradoxical act to violate the dead girl's face, however, is not only driven by jealousy alone but is rather born out of the social hierarchies that privilege lighter skin as a beauty ideal. While Violet is dark-skinned, Dorcas is "[l]ight skinned [and] never used skin bleach" (*JZ* 201). With Violet's attack on Dorcas' light skin and her apotheosis of Golden Gray, a mulatto who passes as white, Morrison indirectly addresses the racial hierarchies that have also found entry into the black community. According to Denise Heinze,

> Morrison spares no feelings; she feels no compunction, to mitigate her belief that the valorization of light-skinned beauty is the most disturbing and prevalent form of colorism and thus functions as one of the greatest barriers to the spiritual and psychic health of the black community. (21)

Violet's severe fragmentation of identity that results in the manifestation of 'Violent' is also advanced because she connects her husband's unfaithfulness to the attraction of Dorcas' light skin. Violet, by (maybe unconsciously) idealizing whiteness, thus more and more distances herself from her female black body up to the point it becomes both 'self' and 'other.' From DuBois we know that African Americanness, as such, is *a priori* associated with a double-self, a dichotomy that fuses (American) self and (Black) other, "two warring ideals in one dark body" (947). While Golden Gray, as a white-looking mulatto boy, is a physical translation of DuBois' concept of double-consciousness, Violet performs this duality only psychologically. Both, however, embody what Patricia Hill Collins refers to as the social "outsider within" (526) – a status that relates to the uncanny in the sense that a person "substitutes the other's self for his [or her] own" (U 142).

While Violet silently adapts a racial attitude that assumes lighter skin to be superior, Violet's second self violently acts out Violet's repressed revenge fantasies – fantasies that are not exclusively directed toward Dorcas:

Where she saw a lonesome chair left like an orphan in a park strip facing the river that other Violet saw how the ice skim gave the railing's black poles a weapony glint. Where she, last in line at the car stop, noticed a child's cold wrist jutting out of a too-short, hand-me-down coat, that Violet slammed past a whitewoman into the seat of a trolley four minutes late. And if she turned away from faces looking past her through restaurant windows, *that* Violet heard the clack of the plate glass in mean March wind. (*JZ* 89-90)

Similar to Pecola's insanity in *The Bluest Eye* (that is also driven by an obsession with white standards of beauty), Violet's encounter with her violent double (which represents nothing but the unconscious reenactment of her repressed desires) can also be considered as the first decisive step towards a sense of wholeness. In fact, and as Justine Tally rightly argues, it is Violet's double that enforces a necessary confrontation with her unarticulated fears:

Violet must envision her other 'self' in order to establish a dialogue and strive for understanding. In doing so, she comes to recognize (through her memories of her mother's suicide and True Belle's stories of Baltimore, which become 'memories she never had') the reasons for her 'erratic' behavior and her own previous incapacity for verbalizing them. (*The Story* 114)

Even though it is this dialogic relationship between Violet and her double that encourages her to pay Alice Manfred regular visits, it is not until the healing conversations with Dorcas' aunt that Violet can get rid of her obsession with Golden Gray, who "lived inside [her] mind. Quiet as a mole" (*JZ* 208) and thus also with her silent obsession to exchange her black self for one that is "[w]hite [and] [y]oung again" (ibid.).

BLACK INTERIORS

"Situated in the middle of the building so that the apartment's windows have no access to the moon or the light of a street lamp" (*JZ* 12), the domestic space that Violet and Joe inhabit resembles a dark cell sealed off from the outside world. Morrison's depiction of the home as a sphere of darkness spatially repeats the couple's paralyzed and paralyzing relationship. The rooms, for example, are furnished with a "poisoned silence" (*JZ* 5), indicating a lifeless, solitary, and fearful atmosphere. According to Freud, it is the triad of "silence, darkness and solitude" (*U* 153) that not only evokes the state of death but also activates a sensation of fear among most children. Freud further explains that the fear of darkness goes back to the infantile anxiety of loss: "Children are afraid of the dark because in the dark they cannot see the person they love; and their fear is soothed if they can take hold of that person's hand" (Freud qtd. in Royle 110).

Morrison establishes the connection between darkness and loss through the chronotopic motif of Dorcas' photograph which Violet puts onto the (empty) family mantelpiece and which soon becomes the emotional center of the household. First, Violet perceives the unsmiling face on the picture as "greedy, haughty and very lazy" (*JZ* 12); however, for Violet, Dorcas' role as the destructive other – "the little twat [that] jumped on his back and dragged him off to her bed" (*JZ* 14) – strangely gives way to a much more positive, affectionate conception of her husband's dead mistress:

Violet agrees that it must be so; not only is she losing Joe to a dead girl, but she wonders if she isn't falling in love with her too. When she isn't trying to humiliate Joe, she is admiring the dead girl's hair; when she isn't cursing Joe with brand-new cuss words, she is having whispered conversations with the corpse in her head; (15)

Violet's dialogic relationship with the dead girl finally culminates in the conception of Dorcas as her unborn daughter, when she poses the question: "Was she the woman who took the man, or the daughter who fled her womb?" (*JZ* 109) Violet's nightly visits to the mantelpiece, during which "the dark rooms grow darker" (*JZ* 11-12), indicate a haunting that manifests itself in the parental care of a dead girl. Indeed, as the narrator claims, it is Dorcas' spirit who becomes "the only living presence in the house" (*JZ* 11-12) and disturbs their sleep. Morrison's techniques of anthropomorphization further strengthen Dorcas' lifelikeness: Dorcas' picture "sits" (*JZ* 13) in the frame, "star[es] from the mantelpiece" (*JZ* 12), and "wak[es] them up all night long" (*JZ* 13).

In *Death 24x a Second*, Laura Mulvey argues that the medium of photography is marked by a sense of temporal ambiguity that produces a merging of life and death: "[T]he photograph captures the presence of life stilled, the instantaneous nature of human movement and the fragility of human life, it confuses time more thoroughly than, for instance, the presence of a ruin or a landscape in which traces of the past are preserved" (57). In Roland Barthes' *Camera Lucida*, Mulvey's theoretical backup, the essence of a photograph is defined as making present and past intermingle. According to Barthes, "every photograph is a certificate of presence" (*Camera Lucida* 87) and therefore also uncanny because it "adds to it that rather terrible thing which is there in every photograph: the return of the dead" (ibid. 9).[16]

Dorcas' picture is inflicted with the same lifelikeness that Edgar Allan Poe, in his Gothic story "The Oval Portrait" (1850), has once attributed to a painted image of a young girl. Morrison thus repeats the dominant Gothic motif of 'life in death' in that she also depicts

---

16 For a useful and more elaborate discussion of the image and it's relation to the uncanny, see Mladen Dolar's essay "'I shall be with you on your wedding night': Lacan and the Uncanny" published in *Jaques Lacan: Society, Politics, Ideology* by Slavoj Žižek.

Dorcas' representation in the frame as a force "disturbing the neatness and clarity of the real/unreal boundary" (Jervis 14). The photograph of Dorcas, hence, represents the intermediary piece between the external world of the living and the internal world of the dead. However, whereas Poe's painting rather points to the theme of eternal beauty through art, Morrison's photograph functions as an uncanny reminder that we must not forget the damaging effects that slavery has inscribed onto the African American psyche. Dorcas' spiritual presence is not only felt but becomes "a sickness of the house – everywhere and nowhere" (*JZ* 28). Similar to the ghost of Beloved, Dorcas makes her presence felt as the "scary spirit of the unsettled dead" (Mayerfeld Bell 815).[17] At the end of the novel, Morrison refers to Dorcas as "a young ghost with bad skin" (*JZ* 223) and thus confirms that she repeats the absent presence that also characterized the Wild/Beloved character. As Carolyn M. Jones points out, Dorcas continues the symbolism of absent presence that Beloved's ghost initiated in the first part of the trilogy: "Dorcas is the Beloved: the lost and dead parents; the lover who opens up loneliness; and the child that Joe and Violet choose not to have" (482).

"The uncanny," writes John Jervis, "is the presence of the absent and the 'not real'; the implicit presence of disavowed, transgressive forms and locations of personal experience" (35). The picture of Dorcas or, rather, the presence of her restless soul that 'furnishes' the darkness of the living room, comes to represent Violet's uncanny substitute for a child. Getting up every night just to have a look at the face of a motherless girl, Violet not only mourns over the fact that it is too late for her to have children but also, paradoxically, indicates that she is developing a loving relationship with "a rival young enough to be her daughter" (*JZ* 111). Violet conceives of herself as a mother-figure being responsible to 'soothe' the fear of her non-existent and self-proclaimed child. At the same time, however, Violet herself represents a child left in the dark who tries to overcome feelings of fear and loneliness by "sleeping with a doll in her arms" (*JZ* 129). Many would probably read Violet's motherly affection for Dorcas' ghost as another manifestation of craziness. However, it rather signals her growing awareness of the loss that her miscarriages have caused.

---

17 In "The Uncanny," Freud describes the immortal soul as "the first double of the body" (142).

For Violet, the act of placing the photograph onto the mantelpiece suggests her will to confront herself with the cruel parts of her personal history. Thus, she is able to engage in the process of rememory – the most effective strategy to retrieve a stable black female self.

As the point of origin of the characters' madness, the dark apartment functions as the symbolic sphere of the unconscious, the dark place in which repressed memories are located before they suddenly 'return.' Like the dark manhole into which Ellison's Invisible Man retreats, the Trace's apartment signifies the very locus of Violet's psychasthenia[18] or, in other words, a spatialization of Violet's history of family loss and her own inability to "fill the inside nothing" (*JZ* 37). With the dark apartment, Morrison again clearly alludes to a symbolic womb that is empty. It signifies the *un*home, a domestic space marked by the loss of nurturing, protection, and communication.

The chronotopic motif of enclosure is further strengthened through the birdcage in which Violet keeps her birds, "including the parrot that said, 'I love you'" (*JZ* 3). With "wings grown stiff from disuse and dull in the bulb light of an apartment with no view to speak of" (*JZ* 93), the bird in the cage – clearly a symbol of physical bondage and its damaging effects – shares the same fate as Joe and Violet. As a typically urban piece of interior, the birdcage adds another environment of boundaries whose structure is reminiscent of New York's grid, the rigid and restricting division of the cityscape in rectangular blocks, thus signaling the continuation of enforced displacement in African American history. Comparing the rooms in the apartment to "empty birdcages wrapped in cloth" (*JZ* 11), the narrator symbolically hints at the realities of loss, despair, and emptiness the protagonists experience in the city's restrictive environment. When Violet attempts to release the parrot, the animal is unable to find its way back to nature. This spatial alienation serves as a synechdoche for the collective estrangement of American blacks who after the Civil War and after the Great Migration were forced to come to terms with their newly achieved 'freedom' and its spatio-temporal conditions.

---

18 According to Webster's Online Dictionary, *psychasthenia* refers to a neurotic state characterized especially by phobias, obsessions, or compulsions that one knows are irrational. For a more elaborate discussion see Vidler's *The Architectural Uncanny*, 173.

Interestingly, Morrison connects the "lonely mirrors" (*JZ* 13) in the empty birdcage to Dorcas' face in the frame, which is also strangely "glancing back" (ibid) at itself: "An inward face – whatever it sees is its own self. You are there, it says, because I am looking at you" (*JZ* 12). Dorcas' face is described as looking back to itself, thus indicating a mirror moment. Simultaneously, the picture's living presence that 'speaks' to its observers also reveals its role as a mirror, reflecting Violet's own self. In *Will the Parts Hold: Erinnerung und Identität in Toni Morrison's Romanen* Beloved *und* Jazz, Christine Brass and Antje Kley read *Jazz* along the lines of the Lacanian mirror phase, the moment when "the self misrecognizes itself in an ideal reflection" (156). Violet retreats into madness because she constructs herself through the external/ideal image of Dorcas who, in being much whiter and younger than her, meets the standards of beauty Western societies have imposed. Also Joe, when looking at Dorcas' picture, is confronted with his own ideal urban ego he has developed and defined through his obsessive love-affair with the creamy-skinned girl who was "young enough to be that daughter" (*JZ* 108).

The mirror image, which is analogous to Lacan's imaginary order, denotes an illusionary image of wholeness and coherence. However, it is a deceiving image that points to the process of the formation of the ego which involves a crisis of subjectivity or alienation with the self that is archaically tied to the mother figure. Joe, Violet, and Dorcas suffer from a crisis of the self because the ties to their mothers are forever cut. At the same time, it is 'the City' that, according to Brass and Kley, "allow[s] them to identify with the fictional construct of 'who they always believed they were'" (165). In other words, Harlem's cityscape of spectacle and desire clearly works against the formation of a unified black self:

There, in a city, they are not so much new as themselves: their stronger, riskier selves. And in the beginning when they first arrive, and twenty years later when they and the City have grown up, they love that part of themselves so much they forget what loving other people was like – if they ever knew, that is. I don't mean they hate them, no, just that what they start to love is the way a person is in the City; (*JZ* 33)

Violet and Joe fall prey to the spectacle of Harlem, symbolized by their acts of moral ambiguity. They "forget what loving other people was like" (ibid.) only because they fundamentally lack the love and support that is usually provided by social relationships within a family unit.

In Mladen Dolar's study on Lacan and the uncanny, he notes that "[t]he double is the mirror image in which the object a [sic] is included" (70). Most obviously, Lacan's *objet petit a* – the unattainable object of desire – that is contained in Dorcas' picture is, on the one hand, Violet's wish for a daughter, and, on the other hand, Joe's arrival at the trace leading to his (lost) mother. In a conversation with Gloria Naylor, Morrison states that she conceives of black subjectivity as a double or mirror-image, or in her own words, "as though the self were really a *twin* or a thirst or a friend or something that sits right next to you and watches you, which is what I was talking about when I said 'the dead girl'" ("A Conversation" 208). Although Morrison obviously alludes to the ghost of Beloved when talking about 'the dead girl,' it is more than evident that Dorcas acquires the same role in *Jazz*. In both novels, *Beloved* and *Jazz*, Morrison depicts African American identity as fragmented, also because her characters often, as Carolyn M. Jones puts it, "locate the best of the self in an 'other': the beloved" (481). Sethe and Joe's acts of homicide are driven by their desire for love and/or appropriate mothering/fathering, and Dorcas' voluntary death and silence (she does not reveal Joe as her murderer) prove that she, as Morrison explains to Naylor, "loved something other than herself so much [so that she] placed all of the value of her life in something outside herself" ("A Conversation" 207).

Even though the couple's nocturnal visits to Dorcas' picture bring them closer to each other, it is only when Violet returns the photograph to Alice Manfred that the haunting stops and that Joe's sobs, as the narrative voice points out, become "quieter" (*JZ* 197). However, the uncanny manifests itself anew when Violet spots a girl from her porch that "was another true-as-life Dorcas" (*JZ* 197). Looking like "a mirror image of Dorcas" (*JZ* 221), Felice, Dorcas' dark skinned friend, enters the Trace household on a "pure and steady" (*JZ* 195) day, revealing that, on that fatal night, Dorcas bled to death because she "let herself die" (*JZ* 209). Felice, through metaphorically embracing darkness[19] and providing the true story of Dorcas' death, enables Joe to let loose of his sense of guilt and to recover

---

19 The name Felice derives from Latin *felix* which means 'happy.'

emotionally. Unlike Dorcas, Felice is "nobody's [...] toy" (*JZ* 222) and her slow and self-assured movements in the city hint to the fact that she has a stable sense of self. For Violet, Felice fulfills a therapeutic function. As another orphaned girl, Felice can be seen as a more positive and more authentic return of Dorcas, or respectively, the daughter Violet never had. As Jocelyn Chadwick-Joshua claims, Felice provides the necessary space for self-renewal:

> In her three visits to the Trace home, Felice [...] engages Violet in conversations that cause Violet to articulate how she understands herself in relation to the city: its impact on her home, Rome in Vesper County, and her relationship with her husband Joe and the dead girl Dorcas. (176)

By disentangling the problematic and complicated plot Morrison has built up, Felice, thus, becomes the *deus ex machina* that, unexpectedly, paves the way for a happy ending.

At the end of the novel, a domestic space is reestablished that allows for openness and domestic liveliness. Instead of a lifeless apartment, Joe and Violet let music "floa[t] in [...] through the open window" (*JZ* 214). Although the nested apartment's windows do not allow for a direct view outside, it is music that finds its way inside and thus reawakens the domestic space. Instead of an empty birdcage wrapped in cloth, Joe and Violet take their new bird in the cage to the roof "where the wind bl[ows]" (*JZ* 224). Yet, Morrison does not restrict the process of opening-up to the private sphere but transgresses it to the public and even beyond the (invisible) boundaries of Harlem:

> Once in a while [Joe and Violet] take the train all the way to 42nd Street to enjoy what Joe calls the stairway of the lions. Or they idle along 72nd Street to watch men dig holes in the ground for a new building. The deep holes scare Violet, but Joe is fascinated. Both of them think it's a shame. A lot of time, though, they stay home figuring things out, telling each other those little personal stories they like to hear again and again. (*JZ* 223)

Here, Morrison suggests that the process of healing also requires an awareness of history. The new holes in Manhattan's cityscape thus not only symbolize the potential for self-renewal but simultaneously allude to the erosion (or forgetting) of history. It's the "little personal stories" (ibid.) that must be verbalized and passed on in order to counteract a white hegemonic historiography that represses, forgets, or disallows accounts of African American history and culture.

THE UNCANNY VOICE

Most commentaries on Toni Morrison's *Jazz* have identified the narrative voice of the novel as highly ambiguous and, therefore, impossible to pinpoint. Indeed, the narrator reveals herself[20] as an entity that is complex, contradictory and, most importantly, category-defying. As a major source of doubt, the narrative voice does both, confirm and abrogate omniscience, positions herself within and without the text, is at times reliable, at times highly unreliable, and even lends her first-person voice to other characters. The narrator clearly inhabits a narrative space which lies in between categories, a space that allows the narrator to hide and keep her identity secret but at the same time to access the character's most intimate and illicit desires and fears. This ability to establish distance and intimacy alike leads to the assumption that the narrator inhabits a supernatural world, or more specifically, that the narrative voice tells the story from a ghostly point of view. In the following excerpt, the narrator reveals her spectral identity:

I haven't got any muscles, so I can't really be expected to defend myself. But I do know how to take precaution. Mostly it's making sure no one knows all there is to know about me. Second, I watch everything and everyone and try to figure out their plans, their reasonings, long before they do. (*JZ* 8)

The disembodied voice in Morrison's text is not only a metareferential element repeating the haunting presences of Beloved/Wild and Dorcas on the level of *discours* but, more importantly, establishes a connection between traumatic experiences (death) and the potential of narration (oral storytelling) to overcome the return of the repressed. In "Studies on Hysteria," Freud notes that "each individual hysterical symptom immediately and permanently disappeared [...] when the

---

20 Although Morrison does not explicitly reveal the narrator's sex, the gossipy tone of the narrative's voice suggests that the narrator's sex is female.

patient had described that event in the greatest possible detail and had put the affect into words" (57). Hence, the narrator, while telling the story, repeats the 'talking cure' Violet undergoes when consulting Alice Manfred. This implies that the voice is, just like the other characters in the novel, also a victim of her own past.

Chronotopically speaking, the narrator, by transgressing spatial and temporal boundaries, establishes an external interiority, what Lacan has conceptualized as *extimité*. For Lacan, *extimité* (a neologism combining the French terms *exterieur* and *intimité*) fuses the intimate with something foreign and unknown. Obviously, *extimité* then is the Lacanian term for the uncanny. Mladen Dolar, in his study on Lacan, relates the uncanniness inherent in *extimité* to a transgression of boundaries:

All the great philosophical conceptual pairs-essence/appearance, mind/body, subject/object, spirit/matter, etc.—can be seen as just so many transcriptions of the division between interiority and exteriority. Now the dimension of *extimité* blurs this line. It points neither to the interior nor to the exterior, but is located there where the most intimate interiority coincides with the exterior and becomes threatening, provoking horror and anxiety. The extimate is simultaneously the intimate kernel and the foreign body; in a word, it is *unheimlich*. (6)

Morrison's narrative voice establishes "the intimate kernel" (ibid.) through the veil of secrecy and gossip. "Sth, I know that woman" (*JZ* 1), the opening line of the novel, not only indicates an intimate relationship between 'that woman' and the narrator, but also that the story that is to be told should be kept secret. The whisper, indicated by the initial "Sth," also suggests an affectionate, private bond between the narrator and the reader, as the story is revealed to everyone who starts reading the book. In "Unspeakable Things Unspoken," Morrison explains that whispering suggests "that the teller is on the inside, knows something others do not, and is going to be generous with this privileged information" (21).

According to Slavoj Žižek, the extimate voice is uncanny because it "functions as a strange body, which smears the innocent surface of the picture, a ghost-like apparition which can never be pinned to a definite visual object" (1). Also in *Jazz*, the voice is clearly disembodied and, by refusing to reveal her gender or physical features, she cannot be visualized. The extimate nature of Morrison's narrator is further strengthened through the sudden change of narrative modes. In *The Story of Jazz*, Justine Tally reminds us of Morrison's use of 'quasi-direct speech' which, according to Michael Holquist, is "a threshold phenomenon, where authorial and character intentions are combined in a single intentional hybrid" (432).[21] Hence, through 'quasi-direct speech,' the text-internal and text-external levels are confused. In the following passage, an abrupt change from indirect to free indirect speech signals the transition from external to internal focalization, or in other words, the shift of the focus of perception from the narrator to Joe:

The streets he walks are slick and black. In his coat pocket is the forty-five he pawned his rifle for. He had laughed when he handled it, a fat baby gun that would be loud as a cannon. Nothing complex; you'd have to fight your own self to miss it, but he isn't going to miss because he isn't going to aim. Not at that insulted skin. Never. Never hurt the young: nest eggs, roe, fledglings, fry. (JZ 181)

Again, the inside view into Joe's mind reveals images of nature and innocence, i.e., images that he deliberately tries to repress and forget. In contrast, Joe's conscious thoughts, i.e., his obsession and hunt for Dorcas, are explicitly identified in direct speech: "'She will hold out her hand, walk towards me in ugly shoes, but her face is clean and I am proud of her. Her too-tight braids torture her so she unlooses them as she moves toward me. She's so glad I found her'" (JZ 183-184).

Lacan's *extimité*, which finds its structural visualization in the form of the Moebius strip, also positions the center of the subject outside, and more precisely, at the strip's margin. Joe's repressed wish to reunite with his mother manifests itself in the exterior space of the narrator, the space of the 'other.' Joe's subjectivity, which is solely defined through his transient existence or, in other words, through the imaginary trace back to his mother, thus is located in the 'other' or at the margin. The Moebius strip is also a form that defies hierarchies and borders of various kinds. Thus, it becomes a symbol of the margin as such and, more specifically, of the marginalization of African Americans in the political and intellectual spheres. Interestingly, as

---

21 See also Justine Tally, *The Story of Jazz* (89-90).

bell hooks explains in *Yearning: Race, Gender and Cultural Politics*, even if the notion of the margin may suggest a space of danger, risk or deprivation, it also provides a space of openness, new possibilities, and resistance:

> As a radical standpoint, perspective, position, "the politics of location" necessarily calls those of us who would participate in the formation of counter-hegemonic cultural practice to identify the spaces where we begin the process of re-vision. . . . For many of us, that movement requires pushing against oppressive boundaries set by race, sex, and class domination. Initially, then, it is a defiant political gesture. [...] For me this space of radical openness is a margin – a profound edge. Locating oneself there is difficult yet necessary. It is not a "safe" place. One is always at risk. One needs a community of resistance. (149)

In Morrison's *Jazz*, the narrator dwells on this very margin and thus represents a counter-narrative to dominant white hegemonic discourses and thus a "political gesture" (hooks, "Choosing" 153). When Joe and Violet start to appreciate Harlem's community values, e.g., through the family-like bonds they establish with Alice and Felice, they can conceive of New York City as a place that furthers the construction of a more authentic black self.

In *Thirdspace*, Edward Soja reads bell hooks' notion of the margin as a thirdspace[22] – a positive site of cultural resistance and claims that the margin is "a spatiality of inclusion rather than exclusion, a spatiality where radical subjectivities can multiply, connect, and combine in polycentric communities of identity and resistance; where fragmentation is no longer a political weakness but a potential strength" (99). The novel's narrator embodies all the positive features that this marginality generates and, therefore, allows some stories to resurface, some to recur, and some to be kept secret. It is also due to the decenteredness of the narrator that, at times, other voices can claim narrative authority. The heteroglossic variety that results from this

---

22 Edward Soja defines 'thirdspace' as an alternative approach to spatial thinking which fuses 'real and imagined' spaces. Soja exemplifies his notion of thirdspace with the Mexican-American borderland as articulated by Gloria Anzaldua as space of radical openness (129).

marginalization works against monological and unified ideologies that are hierarchal and destructive.

Towards the novel's end, the narrative voice also openly confesses her unreliability that seems to have been generated by the city:

> I thought I knew them [i.e., Joe and Violet] I got so aroused while meddling, while finger-shaping, I overreached and missed the obvious. I was watching the streets, thrilled by the buildings pressing and pressed by stone; so glad to be looking out and in on things I dismissed what went on in heart-pockets closed to me. (*JZ* 220-221)

Here, the voice's unreliability is the result of the holistic perspective from above, a panoptic view that simulates an idea of order. Similar to Joe and Violet, also the narrator has obviously fallen victim to the city's 'thrill' and its illusory and deceiving forces.[23] In Lacanian terms, the Harlem Renaissance city, as depicted by Morrison, symbolizes the Imaginary, the site of imagination and deception where intrinsic alienation results from the formation of a black ego-ideal. Nonetheless, the narrator does not explicitly reveal "the obvious" (ibid.), all that which is untouched by the light of "wasteful street lamps" (*JZ* 34), but leaves it open to the reader's hermeneutic skills. The narrator's unreliability repeats itself in the city's built structure that Morrison depicts as a vast accumulation of different signs whose messages are highly distorting and illusive:

> The City is smart at this: smelling good and looking raunchy, sending secret messages disguised as public signs: this way open here danger to let colored only singlemen on sale woman wanted private room stop dog on premises absolutely no money down fresh chicken free delivery fast. (*JZ* 64)

Like the narrator, the city is an enigma because, as Jocelyn Chadwick-Joshua points out, it has the "ability to mean different things to different people at the same time" (176).

---

23 In "Walking the City," Michel de Certeau argues that the positioning of a subject atop a tower results in the panoptic view which enables a coherent and 'readable' urban text. However, de Certeau goes on arguing that this god-like view can only create a chimera, a fiction (180-181).

Justine Tally reads the phantom voice as a "private investigator-narrator" (*The Story* 41) who hides in the background in order to secretly observe the character's actions. She also notes that the exact descriptions of interiors and actions are part of a strategy that invites the reader to participate in the process of uncovering the ambiguous actions and motives of Joe and Violet (43). However, what is even more appealing about Tally's analysis is that she associates the narrator to Benjamin's modernist concept of the *flâneur*. Indeed, the basic features of the *flâneur*, as an observer and interpreter of city life, can be traced in the narrator's reading of the visual signs of the Harlem cityscape. Yet, upon closer examination, comparing the narrative voice to a *flâneur* is slightly problematic in Morrison's context. First, Benjamin conceives of the *flâneur* as a (white, masculine) walker, and more precisely, a walker who strolls through the arcades for the purpose of being absorbed by the city's consumerist aesthetic.

Morrison's narrator is also absorbed and deceived by the glittering city, but she does not physically participate in the urban text. In other words, the phantom voice is not a walker. As mentioned above, it rather takes on a static and godlike position from which she, for example, overlooks "strips of green grass lining the river" (*JZ* 7) and "church steeples" (ibid.). The narrator's ability to look into the character's lives is rather the result of her supernatural omniscience and omnipresence and not of close observation on the spot. Second, while Benjamin's *flânerie* is driven by the spectacle of consumer goods displayed in shopping windows, the narrative voice of *Jazz* observes the city dwellers out of neighborly curiosity. Her main goal of observation is not to leisurely experience the phantasmagoric effect of commodities, but rather to pass on the events she witnesses and evaluates through the channel of gossip. As the narrative voice admits: "I watched them through windows and doors, took every opportunity [...] to follow them, to gossip about and fill in their lives" (*JZ* 220).

Thus, it is through the motif and tone of gossip that the narrator becomes a transition figure between an objective/external narrator and an almost homodiegetic first-person voice that, at many points, suggests being part of the character's community. What Morrison's narrator does share with the *flâneur* is her ability of being both observer and participant of urban life at the same time. Morrison's narrator may not be physically present, but she is mentally. As the extimate narrative voice provides more and more access to her own interior, she finally reveals her desire to be anthropomorphized and bodily loved:

I envy them [Joe and Violet] their public love. I myself have only known it in secret, shared it in secret and longed, aw longed to show it – to be able to say out loud what they have no need to say at all: *That I have loved only you, surrendered my whole self reckless to you and nobody else. That I want you to love me back and show it to me. That I love the way you hold me, how close you let me be to you. I like your fingers on and on, lifting, turning. I have watched your face for a long time now, and missed your eyes when you want away from me. Talking to you and hearing you answer – that's the kick.*
But I can't say that aloud; I can't tell anyone that I have been waiting for this all my life and that being chosen to wait is the reason I can. If I were able I'd say it. Say make me, remake me. You are free to do it and I am free to let you because look, look. Look where your hands are. Now. (*JZ* 229)

In the passage printed in italics, the narrator expresses her longing for physical affection towards a narratee – most likely the flesh-and-blood reader – to whom she also assigns final authority. The narrator's wish to be 'made' or 'remade' alludes to the establishing of physical contact, a call-and-response relationship between the implied author and the actual reader from which something new can originate. The contact space that the narrator establishes at the very end, therefore, is also the space of epistemological freedom and openness that the individual reader inhabits. Morrison closes her novel by creating a space of ambiguity in which the strict boundaries between author, implied author, narrator and character entirely blur.

The final lines of the book are a metafictional gesture towards the 'talking book' and to the necessity of breaking the veil of silence that has sheathed the brutal history of African Americans. The book's voice, the reader realizes, is Morrison's attempt to draw attention to the importance of (re-)articulating stories too cruel to remember. The foregrounding of the word 'look' in the final line not only suggests the urgency towards an awareness that radically fights forgetting and national amnesia, but also the need to repeat these stories over and over again, so that they will be inscribed into and never erased from American cultural memory.

Needless to say, the ending also draws attention to the act of reading itself. Hence, it is the reader who is granted the power to 'reawake' or render alive these dead (stories). By leaving open many gaps of understanding, Morrison deliberately avoids closure and invites a never-ending 'remake' of the numerous stories told. In an interview with Christina Davis, Morrison points out that in the practice of oral storytelling neat endings and clear solutions are rather avoided: "You don't end a story in the oral tradition – you can have the little message at the end, your little moral, but the ambiguity is deliberate because it doesn't end, it's an ongoing thing and the reader or listener is in it and you have to think" ("An Interview" 232). Irresolution, thus, not only signifies the psychic struggle that Morrison's narrator undergoes, but also the necessity of an ongoing reworking of history and reconsideration of race politics.

The uncanny voice of *Jazz* is a spirit which remains immortal as long as it remembered. Only if contact with the ancestor is maintained, can the psychic wounds heal. Only if the importance of ancestor worship is accepted and understood by a Western (academic) mindset can one effectively read Morrison's 'supernatural' realism. For Morrison, ghosts or ghostly characters have always represented a folkloristic tool to symbolize not only the return of individual repressed traumas experienced but also, as Ellen J. Goldner observes, a radical counter-discourse to Western modes of thought:

> As hauntings preserve the dead amid the living and the past amid the present, they defy the concept of linear time, the bedrock of cause and effect that enables prediction. They thus defy the Western dream of control. In these texts, haunts also defy the Euclidean conception of the world as a uniform space, infusing the space of the abstract grid with signs of the specific history and suffering of slaves, charging the atmosphere with the emotional, moral, and political forces which the project of science claims to disregard, and the project of slavery seeks to disregard. (62)

The narrator of *Jazz* clearly delineates an urban space that pays testimony to African cosmology and Western modernity alike. Morrison's textual and narrative indeterminacy suggests that urban experiences can be manifold, and that the black urban experience is radically different from white modernist conceptions of urban living. This difference, however, is not so much generated by the physical city but rather by the city of the mind that infused an urban black consciousness.

The Harlem of the mind, as Morrison powerfully demonstrates, is a city of uncanny paradox that confuses the borderlines between (racial) spectacle, imaginative possibility, oppression, fear and an unconscious idealization of a rural past. In it, the black American self can be imagined, reborn, shattered, split and, finally, healed.

Conclusion

The uncanny, as an emotion evoking fear and terror, has generated a multiplicity of forms and discourses in various disciplines ever since its first theorizations by Ernst Jentsch and Siegmund Freud. This multiplicity results from an openness that allows the uncanny to be many things at once: an emotional effect, a psychoanalytical symptom, an aesthetic category, a visual chimera, or a literary technique. The fact that Freud's highly influential psychoanalytic study "The Uncanny" (1919) also contains an elaborate literary analysis of Hoffmann's tale "The Sandman" shows that the psychic uncanny stimulates, and has always stimulated, creativity and, in particular, literary production.

Early literary accounts of the uncanny (dating back to the eighteenth century) were characterized through what Mikhail Bakhtin has labeled *Schlosszeit*, a spatio-temporal condition which privileged the return to medieval times and places. Spatially, this return to a bygone past was signaled through enclosed and decaying spaces such as old monasteries or castles. The Gothic classics of Horace Walpole and Ann Radcliffe prove that in Romantic writing inexplicable or threatening forces can clearly be localized within the walls of antiquated spaces. Although in American Gothic fiction, most notably in the works of Poe and Brown, the uncanny continues to emerge through tropes of enclosure or isolation, it is the urban context which provides the dominant spatio-temporal context for 'locked room mysteries' and the emergence of paralyzed and alienated characters.

The dissemination of the uncanny to the urban context also entailed a major shift that concerned the *chronotopoetics* of literary works. With E. A. Poe's "The Man of the Crowd" or Henry James' *The American Scene*, for example, the uncanny could no longer be located in a walled-off space but manifested itself through confrontations with the public 'other' forming the crowd. The uncanny, thus, became inherent in the industrial city's mechanic pulse – a spatio-temporal feature that later was to become one of the key signifiers of high modernism. The threat that was captured in many urban fictions of modernism was primarily related to time rather than space. However, next to the dominance of confusions with temporal categories, as Jo Collins and John Jervis argue, the modern urban experience also signaled an alienation of the subject that was related to space:

> A sense of unease, linked to a loss of continuity with the past and the natural environment, is associated with a range of distinctively modern anxieties which become increasingly codified as neuroses; and some of these, notably disturbances of the spatial sense (claustrophobia, agoraphobia) prove both symptomatically and culturally to have pronounced affiliation with the experience of the uncanny. (4)

The fact that the modern, heterogeneous city threatened the stability of the modern subject also entailed a reemergence of the uncanny in literary discourses. Counteracting aesthetic harmony and realist discourse, the uncanny was more than appropriate to denote the function of modern art which is, first and foremost, concerned with defamiliarizing the familiar and alienating the observer/reader. In the middle and late twentieth century, especially with scholars such as Hélène Cixous and Jacques Derrida, the uncanny disseminated to the field of poststructuralism in order to denote the aesthetics of deconstruction and, more generally, the ambiguity of language itself.

The key problem, as stated in the introduction, centers around the question why postmodern urban novels have never been analyzed along the lines of the uncanny. This question seems even more pertinent when considering the fact that in the 1990s the uncanny experienced a notable remystification in literary and cultural discourses. As a literary effect that defies final closure and captures unrepresentability as such, the uncanny has the potential to point to major anxieties and threats that the era of postmodernity has generated and is still generating – a crucial aspect which conscientious poststructuralist readings tend to neglect.

"To say and not to say at the same time, to leave everything implicit," writes Marcella Goldsmith, "this is the function of the uncanny in art marked by an obscure, solitary silence as significant as words" (96). In the analysis of Morrison's *Jazz*, we have seen that hermeneutical gaps or blank pages powerfully evoke the presence of stories untold or forgotten by a white supremacist discourse. Thus, the subjective uncanny, at the same time, points to a collective uncanny that reveals the repressed history of slavery that still torments and haunts the urban African American subject. Similarly, Auster's *City of Glass* does not close with the solution of the mystery, but leaves us wondering what happened to the abstruse detective case and its detective Quinn. Also Auster is concerned with neglected discourses of socially disadvantaged and underprivileged groups. When Quinn is unconsciously transforming into a homeless, his notes also are becoming less rational and specific. It is also no coincidence that the story establishes a clearly white, middle-class, male perspective of things. Virginia Stillman is presented as the female uncanny 'other' in the story – a strategy that Auster uses in order to point to the dominance of cultural discourses that are exclusivist.

Although the two novels confront us with intellectual uncertainties and acts of ambiguity from the very beginning, they initially present New York as a rather innocent setting which, in fact, turns out to be a deluding and unreliable wilderness of mirrors, so that the familiar turns strangely unfamiliar. The threatening aspect that the city gradually reveals is, in both examples, connected to cryptic forces that make ghosts of the past revisit the present. When Quinn recognizes his dead son in the puppet-like apparition of Peter Stillman Jr., or when Violet has conversations in her head with her husband's dead mistress, these forces are heavily at work. This ongoing process of revisiting the past is also stylistically expressed through the use of intertextuality. The incorporation of earlier texts, in both works, signals that all writers are haunted by writers and stories of the past. These texts are marked by uncanny resemblances to the fictions at hand which make the uncanny returns of previous texts a metafictional element.

Both novels employ a detective plot which also underlines their affiliation to the uncanny. As Maria Tatar argues, "detective stories are [...] the logical heirs to the traditional ghost story" (173-174), because their protagonists are also concerned with unveiling "secret knowledge that envelops an event in an aura of mystery or suspense" (ibid.). The aura of mystery and suspense is also captured in the city's confusing jungle of signs, a heterotopic space that, in both novels, cannot be read or rationalized. All characters analyzed initially do not accept the city's illusoriness but only gradually learn that in New York City things are not what they promise to be. Urban identities are built upon the tropes of homelessness, dislocation, and aberration. However, as soon as the protagonists give up the idea that rational knowledge and logic can provide 'truth' and 'meaning,' and as soon as they accept that temporal and spatial fragmentation is the one and only reliable structuring principle of their lifeworlds, then the psychic wounds can begin to heal, and the ghosts of the past that have been stirred out of their sleep return to their slumber.

Auster's *City of Glass* and Morrison's *Jazz* are both concerned with post-traumatic effects which can only be captured convincingly through discontinuous chronotopes. Therefore, their characters continuously transgress spatial, temporal, and semantic boundaries. Both authors concentrate on surfaces, physical and psychological, but also make clear that these surfaces appear alien and unfamiliar because the characters' perceptions of them are filtered through their unconscious mind. Therefore, it is structural principles such as fragmentation, repetition, multiplication and inversion that mark the presence of the uncanny in these texts. These principles are based on a spatio-temporal model that resists linear temporality and homogenous space. As Gerhard Hoffmann explains, 'chronotopes of the uncanny' are essential for the establishing of uncanny effects in literature:

The primacy of space lies in its ability to represent the uncanny not as a succession of different possibilities within time, but as a side-by-side coexistence of these possibilities. This parallelism must be made visible, audible, and felt in the narrative world through a complex and confusing arrangement of the spatial condition and its secret and hidden contents. (162-163, my translation)[1]

---

1 "Die Erklärung für den Primat des Raums liegt darin, daß das Unheimliche nicht das Nacheinander verschiedener Möglichkeiten in der Zeit, sondern ihr nicht aufhebbares Nebeneinander darstellt. Dieses Nebeneinander muß in der Erlebnissituation des Unheimlichen sichtbar, hörbar oder fühlbar gemacht werden, und zwar durch die Unübersichtlichkeit der räumlichen Verhältnisse und dessen, was sie verbergen." (162-163)

Stadtzeit, unlike *Schlosszeit*, does not allow a clear localization of uncanny forces. The analyses of the chronotopic motives used in this book prove that a focus on time and space, or, more precisely, the (mental) journeys of characters through time and space, provide useful clues to the transformation processes that the uncanny has undergone in history.

The translation of Paul Auster's *City of Glass* into a visual narrative has shown that the urban uncanny also emerges in relatively new literary genres such as graphic novels. The encounter between textuality and visuality, in particular, demonstrates not only that, as Bakhtin famously formulated, "the novel is the expression of a Galilean perception of language, one that denies the absolutism of a single and unitary language" (366) but also that the 'image' constructed through words is the threshold to memory and thus to a subjective reality. Benjamin's dialectical image symbolizes this threshold in which temporal categories defy linear chronology. In terms of spatiality, the graphic adaptation prioritizes space over time, or, the visual over the verbal discourse.

Since the late twentieth century, not only the frames of reference of the uncanny have changed, but also our awareness and conception of it. In our age of postmodernity, we have to accept two things: First, the fact that the uncanny cannot be rationalized because, as Freud and Todorov have shown, any rationalization of the uncanny is limiting and restrictive. Rather, we must conceive of it, as Anneleen Masschelein has pointed out in a 2009 lecture, as an *un*-concept that involves a compound of ideas that are built on the destruction of binary logic. But the uncanny is also an *un*-concept because it relates to all that which is *un*-representable and *un*-conscious. It is a negative 'cast' of the external, displaying all that which is supposed to be hidden. Second, we must subsume the uncanny as part of our postmodern reality, in which real events, such as the terror attacks of 9/11 or the 2011 environmental disaster in Japan seem stranger than fiction, and in which political and economical institutions and the media are granted the power to hide or conceal events from their agenda.

Unfortunately, this study could not allow more space and time for further investigations of the urban uncanny and its relation to gender studies or, more precisely, Freud's discussion of the female as the uncanny other, which would provide another fascinating field of research. Furthermore, the uncanny is more and more being visualized in the field of animated film, such as Guilherme Marcondes' *Tyger* (2006),[2] in which Bunkraku puppetry, cartoon animation, and photographic stills are combined to an artwork of postmodernist pastiche creating highly uncanny and estranging visual effects. As Anneleen Masschelein has rightly suggested, looking at animated films through the lens of the postmodern uncanny would open up a fruitful area for future research.

Also Michael Arznen's book *The Popular Uncanny* (2009) enters a new and fascinating scholarly terrain that concerns the role of the uncanny in advertising and consumer culture. For example, Arnzen discusses "Perfect Petzzz" – stuffed animals that pretend to be alive through mechanical breathing, or "photoshop disasters" – accidents in image editing that reveal the 'fakeness' behind advertising photography.[3] Women's legs too long and slim to be beautiful or accidentally missing limbs strike us as uncanny and make us aware of the omnipresence of phantasmagoric effects that digital culture generates.

This renewed interest in the uncanny is, as we have seen, the result of significant modifications in our perception of (urban) time and space. As materializations of repressed memories and histories, the chronotopes of the uncanny explored in this book provide access to both subjective and collective terrors apparent at the end of the twentieth century while pointing to the fact that the Western (post-)metropolis is not *a priori*, as commonly assumed, a warrant for a better life. At the same time, however, Auster's *City of Glass* and Morrison's *Jazz* exhibit traces of hope and irony so that the city cannot, unlike in many modernist accounts, be viewed only as a destructive and disenchanting force. With the third part of her trilogy, *Paradise*, Morrison tries to imagine a place "where race exists but doesn't matter" (qtd. in Dreifus 1), and New York City, as "the cradle of America's cultural plurality" (Peprník/Sweney 1), has great potential to become such a place.

---

2   The film's title is an intertextual reference to William Blake's famous poem "The Tyger."

3   For more examples of the uncanny in pop culture also visit Michael Arnzen's extensive blog entitled "The Popular Uncanny" which can be accessed via http://www.gorelets.com/uncanny/

Auster and Morrison, at the very end, leave us with the materiality of the text in order to suggest that it is the processes of writing and storytelling that can help us to overcome uncanny experiences. At the same time, however, both authors make us aware that confrontations with the dark spheres of our subjectivity are more than just an exercise in psychoanalysis. They fuel our cultural and literary imaginaries which, in turn, considerably shape our understanding of the world.

Works Cited

Abraham, Nicolas. "Notes on the Phantom: A Complement to Freud's Metapsychology." *Critical Inquiry.* 13.2 (1987). 287-292.

Addison, Joseph. "Pleasures of the Imagination." *Papers from the Spectator.* 419. http://www.mnstate.edu/gracyk/courses/phil%203 06/ Addison_index.htm [16. Mar. 2009].

Adorno, Theodor. *Minima Moralia: Reflections on a Damaged Life.* London/New York: Verso, 2005.

Aguirre, Manuel. *The Closed Space: Horror Literature and Western Symbolism.* Manchester/New York: Manchester UP, 1990.

Atkinson, Paul. "The Graphic Novel as Metafiction." *Studies in Comics.* 1.1. (2010). 107-125.

Augé, Marc. *Non-Places: Introduction to an Anthropology of Supermodernity.* Trans. John Howe. London/New York: Verso, 1995.

Auster, Paul. *City of Glass.* In: *The New York Trilogy.* London/Boston: Faber and Faber, 2004. 1-133.

Auster, Paul. *Ghosts.* In: *The New York Trilogy.* London/Boston: Faber and Faber, 2004. 137-198.

Auster, Paul. *In the Country of Last Things.* New York: Penguin. 1987.

Auster, Paul. *Man in the Dark.* New York: Henry Holt & Co, 2008.

Auster, Paul. *Smoke & Blue in the Face: Two Films.* New York: Miramax Books/Hyperion, 1990.

Auster, Paul. *The Art of Hunger.* Los Angeles: Sun & Moon Press, 1992.

Auster, Paul. *The Invention of Solitude.* New York/London: Penguin, 1988.

Auster, Paul. *The Locked Room.* In: *The New York Trilogy.* London/Boston: Faber and Faber, 2004. 201-314.

Auster, Paul. "Interview with Dominik Kamalzadeh." *Standard*. 25. Okt. 2008. A5.

Auster, Paul. "Interview with Gérard de Cortanze." Trans. Carl-Carsten Springer. *Magazine Littéraire*. 338. (1995). 18-25.

Auster, Paul. "Interview with Larry McCaffery and Sinda Gregory." *The Art of Hunger*. Los Angeles: Sun & Moon Press, 1992. 277-320.

Bachelard, Gaston. *The Poetics of Space*. Trans. Maria Jolas. Boston: Beacon Press, 1969.

Bakhtin, M.M. *The Dialogic Imagination*. Ed. Michael Holquist. Trans. Caryl Emerson and Michael Holquist. Austin/London: U of Texas P, 1981.

Baldwin, James. *Go Tell It On the Mountain*. New York: Laurel-Dell, 1981.

Baldwin, James. "Many Thousands Gone." *Notes of a Native Son*. Boston: Beacon, 1984. 24-45.

Balshaw, Maria. *Looking for Harlem: Urban Aesthetics in African-American Literature*. London/Sterling: Pluto Press, 2000.

Balshaw, Maria. "'Black Was White': Urbanity, Passing and the Spectacle of Harlem." *Journal of American Studies*. 33. (1999). 307-322.

Banfield, Ann. *Unspeakable Sentences: Narration and Representation in the Language of Fiction*. Boston/Melbourne: Routledge, 1982.

Baraka, Amiri. "Return of the Native." *The Oxford Anthology of African-American Poetry*. Ed. Arnold Rampersad. Oxford/New York: Oxford UP, 2006. 59.

Baraka, Amiri. "The Myth of a Negro Literature." *Within the Circle: An Anthology of African American Literary Criticism from the Harlem Renaissance to the Present*. Ed. Angelyn Mitchell. Durham: Duke UP, 1994. 165-171.

Baridon, Michel. "The Gothic Revival and the Theory of Knowledge in the First Phase of the Enlightenment." *Exhibited by Candlelight: Sources and Developments in the Gothic Tradition*. Eds. Valeria Tinkler-Villani and Peter Davidson. DQR Studies in Literature 16. Amsterdam/Atlanta: Rodopi, 1995. 43-56.

Barone, Dennis, ed. "Introduction." *Beyond the Red Notebook: Essays on Paul Auster*. Philadelphia: U of Pennsylvania P, 1995. 1-26.

Barthes, Roland. *Camera Lucida: Reflections on Photography*. Trans. Richard Howard. London: Vintage, 1993.

Barthes, Roland. *The Rustle of Language*. Trans. Richard Howard. Berkley/Los Angeles: U of California P, 1986.
Basu, Paul. "The Labyrinthine Aesthetic in Contemporary Museum Design." *Exhibition Experiment*. Eds. Paul Basu and Sharon Macdonald. London: Blackwell, 2007. 47-70.
Baudelaire, Charles. "On Wine and Hashish." [1851] *Artificial Paradises*. Trans. Stacy Diamond. New York: Citadel Press, 1996. 1-26.
Baudrillard, Jean. *Simulacra and Simulation*. Michigan: U of Michigan P, 1994.
Bauman, Zygmunt. *Life in Fragments: Essays in Postmodern Morality*. Oxford: Blackwell, 1995.
Benjamin, Walter. *Charles Baudelaire: A Lyric Poet in the Era of High Capitalism [1935-1939]*. Trans. Harry Zohn and Quentin Hoare. London: New Left Books, 1973.
Benjamin, Walter. *The Arcades Project*. Cambridge: Harvard UP, 1999.
Benjamin, Walter. "One Way Street." *Reflections: Essays, Aphorisms, Autobiographical Writings*. New York: Schocken, 1986. 61-96.
Benjamin, Walter. "Theses on the Philosophy of History." *Illuminations*. Ed. Hanah Arendt. New York: Schocken Books, 1969. 253-264.
Bennett, Andrew and Nicholas Royle. *An Introduction to Literature, Criticism and Theory*. Harlow: Pearson, 2004.
Bernstein, Susan. "It Walks: The Ambulatory Uncanny." *MLN*. 118.5 (2003). 1111-1139.
Beville, Maria. *Gothic-Postmodernism: Voicing the Terrors of Postmodernity*. Amsterdam/New York: Rodopi, 2009.
Bhabha, Homi. *The Location of Culture*. London/New York: Routledge, 2004.
Bhabha, Homi. "The Hybridity of Culture." Lecture. University of Vienna. 9. Nov. 2007.
Botting, Fred. *Gothic*. The New Critical Idiom. New York: Routledge, 1996.
Brass, Christine and Antje Kley. *"Will the Parts Hold?": Erinnerung und Identität in Toni Morrisons Romanen* Beloved *und* Jazz. Tübingen: Gunter Narr Verlag, 1997.
Brooker, Peter. *New York Fictions: Modernity, Postmodernism, and the New Modern*. London/New York: Longman, 1996.

Brown, Charles Brockden. *Arthur Mervyn, or Memoirs of the Year 1793*. [1800] Project Gutenberg. Ed. Graeme Mackreth. 2006. ibiblio. http://www.gutenberg.org/etext/18508 [24 Feb. 2009].

Brown, Charles Brockden. *Edgar Huntley; or Memoirs of a Sleep-Walker*. [1799] BiblioBazaar, LLC, 2008. http://books.google.at/booksid=pniYn_QMeQC&printsec=frontcover&source=gbs_summary_r&cad=0#PPP1,M1 [17. Feb.2009].

Bruhm, Steven. "The Contemporary Gothic: Why We Need It." *The Cambridge Companion to Gothic Fiction*. Ed. Jerrold E. Hogle. Cambridge: Cambridge UP, 2002. 259-276.

Burgin, Victor. *In/Different Spaces: Place and Memory in Visual Culture*. Berkeley/Los Angeles: U of California P, 1996.

Burke, Edmund. *Philosophical Enquiry into the Origins of our Ideas of the Sublime and Beautiful*. London/New York: Routledge, 2008.

Castle, Terry. *The Female Thermometer: 18th Century Culture and the Invention of the Uncanny*. New York: Oxford UP, 1995.

Chadwick-Joshua, Jocelyn. "Metonomy and Synechdoche: The Rhetoric of the City in Toni Morrison's Jazz." *The City in African-American Literature*. Eds. Yoshinobu Hakutani and Robert Butler. Madison: Fairleigh Dickinson UP, 1995. 168-180.

Cixous, Hélène. "Fiction and Its Phantoms: A Reading of Freud's 'Das Unheimliche." *New Literary History*. 7.3. (1976). 525-548.

Cohen, Samuel S. *After the End of History: American Fictions in the 1990s*. Iowa City: U of Iowa P, 2009.

Collins, Jo and John Jervis, eds. *Uncanny Modernity: Cultural Theories Modern Anxieties*. Hampshire/New York: Palgrave Macmillan, 2008.

Collins, Jo and John Jervis. "Introduction." *Uncanny Modernity: Cultural Theories, Modern Anxieties*. Eds. Joe Collins and John Jervis. Hampshire/New York: Palgrave Macmillan. 2008. 1-9.

Collins, Patricia Hill. "Learning from the Outsider Within: The Social Significance of Black Feminist Thought." *Social Problems*. 33 (1986). 526.

Coughlan, David. "Paul Auster's *City of Glass*: The Graphic Novel." *Modern Fiction Studies*. 52.4. (2006). 832-854.

Crang, Mike and Penny Travlou. "The City and Topologies of Memory." *Environment and Planning D: Society and Space*. 19.2. (2001). 161-177.

Crary, Jonathan. *Techniques of the Observer: On Vision and Modernity in the Nineteenth Century*. Massachusetts: MIT Press, 1992.

Crickenberger, Heather Marcelle. "Passengers: John Dos Passos' Manhattan Transfer." *The Arcades Project Project*. http://www.thelemming.com/lemming/dissertationweb/home/passéngers.html [15. Mar. 2009].

Cutter, Martha J. "The Story Must Go on and on: The Fantastic, Narration, and Intertextuality in Toni Morrison's Beloved and Jazz." *African-American Review*. 34.1. (2000). 61-75.

Dallmann, Antje. *ConspiraCity New York: Großstadtbetrachtungen zwischen Paranoia und Selbstermächtigung*. Heidelberg: Universitätsverlag Winter, 2009.

Davidson, Justin. "The Glass Stampede." *New York Magazine*. 7. Sept. 2008. http://nymag.com/arts/architecture/features/49959/ [28. Jan. 2010.]

De Certeau, Michel. *Heterologies: Discourse on the Other*. Trans. Brian Massumi. Minneapolis: U of Minnesota P, 1986.

De Certeau, Michel. "Walking in the City." *The Cultural Studies Reader*. Ed. Simon During. London/New York: Routledge, 1993. 151-160.

Deleuze, Gilles. *Difference and Repetition*. New York/London: Continuum, 2004.

Derrida, Jacques. "Aphorism Countertime." *Acts of Literature*. Ed. Derek Attridge. London/New York: Routledge, 1992. 414-434.

Derrida, Jacques. Dissemination. Chicago: U of Chicago P, 1981.

Derrida, Jacques. *Of Grammatology*. Trans. Gayatri Chakravorty Spivak. Baltimore/London: The Johns Hopkins UP, 1978.

Derrida, Jacques. *Psyche: Inventions of the Other*. Vol.1. Stanford: Stanford UP, 2007.

De Saussure, Ferdinand. *Course in General Linguistics*. London: Collins, 1974.

Dolar, Mladen. "'I Shall Be with You on Your Wedding-Night:' Lacan and the Uncanny." *October*. 58. (1991). 5-23.

Du Bois, W.E.B. "The Souls of Black Folk." *The Heath Anthology of American Literature*. 3rd Ed. Vol. 2. Eds. Paul Lauter et al. Boston/New York: Houghton Mifflin, 1998. 946-966.

Dos Passos, John. *Manhattan Transfer*. [1925] Boston, Houghton Mifflin Company, 1953.

Eliot, Thomas Sterne. "The Waste Land." Collected Poems: 1909-1962. London: Faber und Faber Limited, 1963. 61-79.

Ellis, Eugenia Victoria. "City of Dreams: Virtual Space/Public Space." *Writing Urbansim*. Eds. Douglas Kelbaug and Kit Krankel McCullough. London/New York: Taylor & Francis, 2008. 372-383.

Ellison, Ralph. *Shadow and Act*. New York: Random House, 1964.

Ellison, Ralph. "Harlem is Nowhere." *The City: American Experience*. Eds. Alan Trachtenberg, Peter Neill, and Peter C. Bunnell. New York: Oxford UP, 1971. 294-299.

Fisher, Rudolph. "The City of Refuge." *The City of Refuge: The Collected Stories by Rudolph Fisher*. Ed. John McCluskey Jr. Columbia: U of Missouri P, 2008. 35-47.

Fisher, Rudolph. "Vestiges: Harlem Sketches." *The New Negro*. Ed. Alain Locke. New York: Antheneum Press, 1970. 57-84.

Fiske, John. *Reading the Popular*. London/New York: Routledge, 2003.

Foucault, Michel. *The Order of Things: An Archeology of Human Sciences*. Milton Park/New York: Routledge, 2002.

Foucault, Michel. "What is an Author?" *Language, Counter-Memory, Practice*. Ed. Donald F. Bouchard. Ithaca, New York: Cornell UP, 1977. 113-139.

Foucault, Michel. "Questions of Geography." *Power/Knowledge: Selected Interviews and Other Writings 1972-1977*. New York: Pantheon, 1980. 63-77.

Foucault, Michel. "Of Other Spaces." *Foucault, Info*. http://foucault.info/documents/heteroTopia/foucault.heteroTopia.en.html [2. Okt. 2009.]

Förster, Kim. "Literarische Landschaften: Über die Repräsentation von (urbanen) Räumen in Paul Auster's *The New York Trilogy*." *Postmodern New York City*. Eds. Günther Lenz und Utz Riese. Heidelberg: Universiätsverlag Winter, 2003. 248-299.

Freud, Sigmund. *The Interpretation of Dreams*. New York: Kessinger Publishing, 2004.

Freud, Sigmund. *The Psychopathology of Everyday Life*. [1901] New York/London: Penguin, 2003.

Freud, Sigmund. "Beyond the Pleasure Principle." *The Standard Edition of the Complete Psychological Works of Sigmund Freud*. London: Hogarth Press, 1955. 3-143.

Freud, Sigmund. "Remembering, Repeating, and Working-Through (Further Recommendations on the Technique of Psycho-Analysis)." *The Standard Edition of the Complete Psychological Works of Sigmund Freud.* London: Hogarth Press, 1958. 145-156.

Freud, Sigmund. "The Uncanny." [1919] *The Uncanny.* New York/London: Penguin, 2003.123-162.

Freud, Sigmund. and Josef Breuer. "Studies on Hysteria." *The Standard Edition of the Complete Psychological Works of Sigmund Freud.* Ed. James Strachey. London: Hogarth Press. 1991. 1-335.

Gates, Henry Louis. *The Signifying Monkey: A Theory of African-American Literary Criticism.* Oxford/New York/Toronto: Oxford UP, 1988.

Gardner, Craig Shaw. *Batman.* New York: Bantam Books, 1989.

Gibson, Donald B. "The Harlem Renaissance City: Its Multi-Illusionary Dimension." *The City in African-American Literature.* Yoshinobu Hakutani and Robert Butler. Madison: Fairleigh Dickinson UP, 1995. 37-49.

Gilloch, Graeme. *Myth and Metropolis: Walter Benjamin and the City.* Cambridge: Polity Press. 1996.

Gilman, Charlotte Perkins. "The Yellow Wallpaper." *The Heath Anthology of American Literature.* Ed. Paul Lauter et.al. Second Edition. Vol. 2, Lexington, MA: Heath, 1994. 800-812.

Goddu, Teresa A. *Gothic America.* New York: Columbia UP, 1997.

Goldner, Ellen J. "Other(ed) Ghosts: Gothicism and the Bonds of Reason in Melville, Chesnutt, and Morrison." *MELUS* 23.1. (1999). 59-83.

Goldsmith, Marcella. *The Future of Art: An Aesthetics of the New and the Sublime.* Albany: State U of New York P, 1999.

Goodin, Analisa Violich. *The Sight of Trauma: Loss, Memory, and Rachel Whiteread's Reversals.* http://sites.cca.edu/currents/sightlines/pdf/08goodin.pdf [12. Aug. 2010].

Gordon, Avery F. *Ghostly Matters: Haunting and the Sociological Imagination.* Minneapolis: U of Minnesota P, 1997.

Grabes, Herbert. *Einführung in die Literatur und Kunst der Moderne und Postmoderne.* Tübingen/Basel: A. Franke, 2004.

Grein, Birgit. *Von Geisterschlössern und Spukhäusern: Das Motiv des Gothic Castle von Horace Walpole to Stephen King.* Wetzlar: Atelier für Graphik und Gestaltung, 1995.

Guyn, William. "Basil Wright's 'Song of Ceylon'." *Documenting the Documentary: Close Readings of Documentary Film and Video.* Detroit: Wayne State UP, 1998.

Hamacher, Werner. "'Now': Walter Benjamin on Historical Time." *Walter Benjamin and History.* Ed. Andrew Benjamin. London/ New York: Continuum, 2005. 38-68.

Hartoonian, Gevork. "What is the Matter with Architectural History?" *Walter Benjamin and History.* Ed. Andrew Benjamin. London/ New York: Continuum, 2005. 182-196.

Harvey, David. *The Condition of Postmodernity: An Enquiry into the Origins of Cultural Change.* Malden/Oxford: Blackwell, 1990.

Hawthorne, Nathaniel. "Rappaccini's Daughter." [1844] *The Heath Anthology of American Literature.* Ed. Paul Lauter et.al. 2nd Ed. Vol. 1, Lexington, MA: Heath, 1994. 2237-2255.

Heinze, Denise. *The Dilemma of 'Double-Consciousness': Toni Morrison's Novels.* Athens: The U of Georgia P, 1993.

Herzogenrath, Bernd. *An Art of Desire: Reading Paul Auster.* Amsterdam/Atlanta. Rodopi, 1999.

Hoffmann, E.T.A. "The Sandman." [1817] *Virginia Commonwealth University. Department of Forgeign Languages.* http://www.fln.vcu.edu/ hoffmann/sand_e.html [16. Jan. 2008].

Hoffmann, Gerhard. *Raum, Situation, erzählte Wirklichkeit: Poetologische und historische Studien zum englischen und amerikanischen Roman.* Stuttgart: Metzlersche Verlagsbuchhandlung, 1978.

Hogle, Jerrold E. "Introduction: The Gothic in Western Culture." *The Cambridge Companion to Gothic Fiction.* Ed. Jerrold E. Hogle. Cambridge: Cambridge UP, 2002. 1-20.

Holland, Sharon Patricia. *Raising the Dead: Readings of Death and (Black) Subjectivity.* Durham/London: Duke UP, 2000.

Holquist, Michael. "Glossary." *The Dialogic Imagination.* By M.M. Bakhtin. Ed. Michael Holquist. Austin/London: U of Texas P, 1981. 423-434.

hooks, bell. *Yearning: Race, Gender and Cultural Politics.* Boston: South End Press, 1990.

hooks, bell. "Choosing the Margin as a Space of Radical Openness." *The Feminist Standpoint Theory Reader.* Ed. Sandra Harding. New York: Routledge, 2004. 153-160.

House, Elizabeth. "Toni Morrison's Ghost: The Beloved Who Is Not Beloved." *Studies in American Fiction*. 18.1. (1990). 17-26.
Hughes, Langston. "Harlem: A Dream Deferred." [1951] *A Raisin in the Sun*. Lorraine Hansberry. New York: Signet, 1994. 3.
Hutcheon, Linda. *A Poetics of Postmodernism: History, Theory, Fiction.* London/New York: Routledge, 1988.
Huxley, Aldous. "Prisons." *Savoy Web*. http://www.savoy.abel.co.uk/HTML/prisons.html [18 Feb. 2009].
Huyssen, Andreas. *Present Pasts: Urban Palimpsests and the Politics of Memory.* Stanford: Stanford UP, 2003.
Huyssen, Andreas. "Modernist Miniatures: Literary Snapshots of Urban Spaces." *PMLA* 122.1. (2007). 27-42.
Huyssen, Andreas. "Nostalgia for Ruins." *Grey Room*. 23 (2006). 7-20.
Ickstadt, Heinz. "Kommunikationsmüll und Sprachcollage: Die Stadt in der amerikanischen Fiktion der Postmoderne." *Die Unwirklichkeit der Städte: Großstadtdarstellungen zwischen Moderne und Postmoderne*. Reinbek bei Hamburg: Rowohlt, 1988. 197-224.
Jay, Martin. "Forcefields: The Uncanny Nineties." *Salmagundi* 108 (1995). 20-29.
Jentsch, Ernst. "On the Psychology of the Uncanny." *Angelaki: A New Journal in Philosophy, Literature, and the Social Sciences*. 2.4 (1996). 7-21.
Jervis, John. "Uncanny Presences." *Uncanny Modernity. Cultural Theories, Modern Anxieties*. Eds. Jo Collins and John Jervis. Palgrave Macmillan, 2008. 10-50.
Jevtic, Iva. "Between Word and Image: Walter Benjamin's Images as a Species of Space." [Data File] http://inter-disciplinary.net/ci/vl/vl2/Jevtic%20paper.pdf [27. Aug. 2010].
Johnson, James Weldon. *Black Manhattan*. [1930] New York: Da Capo, 1991.
Jones, Carolyn M. "Traces and Cracks: Identity and Narrative in Morrison's Jazz." *African-American Review*. 31.3. (1997). 481-495.
Kamio, Mitsuo. "The Locked-In Consciousness: Keats, Coleridge, and De Quincey." *JSL*. 1. (2005). 53-69.
Kennedy, Liam. *Race and Urban Space in Contemporary American Culture*. Edinburgh: Edinburgh UP, 2000.

Kindermann, Wolf. "The Slumber of Reason: Poe's 'The Pit and the Pendulum." *AAA Uni Halle*. www.aaa.uni-halle.de/downloads/slumber%20of%20Reason.pdf [1. March 2007].

Koolhaas, Rem. *Delirious New York: A Retroactive Manifesto for Manhattan*. New York: The Monacelli Press. 1994.

Kristeva, Julia. *The Powers of Horror: An Essay on Abjection*. New York: Columbia UP, 1982.

Kunze, Donald. "The Natural Attitude versus The Uncanny." McGill School of Architecture http://www.arch.mcgill.ca/theory/conference/papers/Kunze_Donald_revised_June6_07.pdf [28. Jan. 2008].

Lacan, Jacques. *The Ethics of Psychoanalysis*. London: Routledge, 1959.

Laurence, Ian, John Thompson and Wendy W. Fok. "An Uncanny Presentation." *Design.WishieWashi*.(2005) http://www.powershow.com/view.php?id=P1245361698sbAfV&t=An+Uncanny+Presentation [31. Feb. 2010].

Lee, Maurice S. "Absolute Poe: His System of Transcendental Racism." *American Literature*. 75.4 (2003). 751-781.

Lehan, Richard. *The City in Literature: An Intellectual and Cultural History*. Berkeley/Los Angeles: U of California P, 1998.

Leiss, William. "Modern Science, Enlightenment, and the Domination of Nature: No Exit?" *Fast Capitalism*. 2.2. http://www.uta.edu/huma/agger/fastcapitalism/2_2/leiss [2. Feb. 2008].

Lewis, Earl. "Connecting Memory, Self, and the Power of Place in African American Urban History." *The New African American Urban History*. Eds. Kenneth W. Goings and Raymond Mohl. London: Sage, 1996. 116-141.

Little, William G. "Nothing to Go On: Paul Auster's *City of Glass*." *Contemporary Literature*. 38.1. (1997). 133-163.

Lloyd-Smith, Allan. *American Gothic Fiction*. New York: Continuum International Publishing Group, 2004.

Locke, Alain. "Foreword." *The New Negro: An Interpretation*. Ed. Alain Locke. New York: Athenaeum, 1968.

Locke, John. *An Essay Concerning Human Understanding*. London: William Tegg & Co, 1838.

Löbbermann, Dorothea. "Weg(be)schreibungen, Ortserkundungen: Transients in der amerikanischen Stadt." *Topographien der Moderne*. Ed. Robert Stockhammer. München: Fink, 2005. 263-285.

Lyotard, Jean-Francois. *The Postmodern Condition: A Report on Knowledge*. Trans. Geoffrey Bennington and Brian Massumi. Minnesota: The U of Minnesota P, 1984.

Madoff, Mark. S. "Inside, Outside, and the Gothic Locked-Room Mystery." *Gothic Fictions: Prohibition/Transgression*. Ed. Kenneth W. Graham. New York: AMS Press, 1999. 49-62.

Malpas, Simon. *The Postmodern*. London/New York: Routledge, 2005.

Marcuse, Peter. "The Grid as City Plan: New York City and Laissez-Faire Planning in the Nineteenth Century." *Planning Perspectives*. 2. (1987). 287-310.

Markoff, John. "Scientists Worry That Machines May Outsmart Men" *New York Times*, 25. July 2009. http://www.nytimes.com/2009/07/26/science/26robot.html?_r=2 [31. Jan. 2010].

Massey, Doreen. "Space-Time and the Politics of Location." *Architecturally Speaking: Practices of Art, Architecture, and the Everyday*. Ed. Alan Read. New York: Routledge, 2000. 49-62.

Matthews, W.H. *Labyrinths and Mazes*. London: Longmans, Green and Co, 2008.

Maxwell, William. "On 'The White City'." *Modern American Poetry*. http://www.english.illinois.edu/maps/poets/m_r/mckay/whitecity.htm [05.Jul.2010].

Mayerfeld Bell, Michael. "The Ghosts of Place." *Theory and Society*. 26.6 (1997). 813-836.

McGrath, Patrick and Bradford Morrow. "Introduction." *The Picador Book of the New Gothic*. Eds. Patrick McGrath and Bradford Morrow. London: Picador, 1992. ix-ixv.

McKay, Claude. "The White City." *Poetry Foundation*. http://poetryfoundation.org/archive/poem.html?id=175760 [08. Jul. 2010].

Merleau-Ponty, Maurice. *Phenomenology of Perception*. London/New York: Routledge, 2004.

Merrill, James. "An Urban Convalescence." *The New Oxford Book of American Verse*. Ed. Richard Ellmann. Oxford: Oxford UP, 1976. 901.

Mighall, Robert. *A Geography of Victorian Gothic Fiction: Mapping History's Nightmares*. Oxford: Oxford UP, 2003.

Miller, J. Hillis. *Ariadne's Thread: Story Lines*. New Haven: Yale UP, 1992.

Mirzoeff, Nicholas. "Ghostwriting: Working Out Visual Culture." *Journal of Visual Culture*. 1.2. (2002). 239-254.

Mogen, David, Scott P. Sanders and Joanne B. Karpinski. "Introduction." *Frontier Gothic: Terror and Wonder at the Frontier in American Literature*. Eds. David Mogen, Scott P. Sanders, and Joanne B. Karpinski. Rutherford/Madison: Fairleigh Dickinson UP, 1993. 13-27.

Mori, Masahiro. "Bukimi No Tani." ["The Uncanny Valley."] Trans. Karl F. Mac Dorman and Takashi Minato. Energy. 7. (1970). 33-35.

Morrison, Toni. "Rootedness: The Ancestor as Foundation." *What Moves at the Margin: Selected Nonfiction*. Ed. Carolin C. Denard. UP of Mississippi, 2008. 56-64.

Morrison, Toni "Talk with Toni Morrison." *Conversations with Toni Morrison*. Ed. Danille Taylor-Guthrie. Jackson: UP of Mississippi, 1994. 43-47.

Morrison, Toni "Unspeakable Things Unspoken: The Afro-American Presence in American Literature." *Michigan Quarterly Review*. 28.1 (1989). 1-34.

Morrison, Toni. "A Conversation: Gloria Naylor and Toni Morrison." *Conversations with Toni Morrison*. Ed. Danille Taylor-Guthrie. Jackson: University Press of Mississippi, 1994. 188-217.

Morrison, Toni. "An Interview with Toni Morrison." [Interview with Christina Davis.] *Conversations with Toni Morrison*. Ed. Danille Taylor-Guthrie. Jackson: UP of Mississippi, 1994. 223-233.

Morrison, Toni. *Beloved*. [1987] London: Vintage, 2005.

Morrison, Toni. *Jazz*. [1992] London: Vintage, 2001.

Morrison, Toni. "Talk with Toni Morrison." [Interview with Mel Watkins.] *Conversations with Toni Morrison*. Ed. Danielle Taylor-Guthrie. Jackson: UP of Mississippi, 1994. 43-47.

Mulvey, Laura. *Death 24x a Second: Stillness and the Moving Image*. London: Reaktion Books, 2006.

Murfin, C. Ross. "Feminist Criticism and Jane Eyre." *Eastern Illinois University*. http://www.ux1.eiu.edu/~rlbeebe/what_is_feminist_criticism.pdf [17. Mar. 2009].

Nietzsche, Friedrich. *Nachlass*. KSA 10: 4[55].

Nora, Pierre. "Between Memory and History: Les Lieux de Mémoire." *Representations*. 26 (1989). 7-24.

Nowlin, Michael. "Toni Morrison's Jazz and the Racial Dreams of the American Writer." *Amerian Literature.* 71.1 (1999). 151-174.

Osofsky, Gilbert. "Harlem Tragedy: An Emerging Slum." *American Urban History.* Ed. Alexander B. Callow, Jr.. New York/Oxford: Oxford UP, 1982. 309-327.

Page, Philip. "Traces of Derrida in Toni Morrison's *Jazz.*" *African American Review.* 29.1 (1995). 55-66.

Palladino, Mariangela. "Sound and Sign in Toni Morrison's *Jazz.*" *University of Strathglyde Glasgow.* http://www.strath.ac.uk/media departments/englishstudies/ecloga/media_135055_en.pdf. [1. June 2010].

Paquet-Deyris, Anne-Marie. "Toni Morrison's *Jazz* and the City." *African American Review.* 35.2 (2001). 219-231.

Pascal, Blaise. *Pensées.* Paris: Gallimard, 1966.

Peprník, Michal and Matthew Sweney, eds. *New York: Cradle of America's Cultural Plurality.* Olomouc: Palacký UP, 2007.

Phillips, James. "Time and Memory in Freud and Heidegger: An Unlikely Congruence." http://www.klinikum.uni-heidelberg.de/fileadmin/zpm/psychatrie/ppp2004/manuskript/phillips.pdf [7. Jan. 2008].

Poe, Edgar Allan. "The Fall of the House of Usher." *The Heath Anthology of American Literature.* Eds. Paul Lauter et.al. 2nd Ed. Vol. 1, Lexington, MA: Heath, 1994. 1461-1474.

Poe, Edgar Allan. "The Man of the Crowd." [1840] *The Harper American Literature.* Eds. Donald McQuade et.al. Vol.1. New York: Harper Collins, 1994. 1600-1605.

Poe, Edgar Allan. "The Pit and the Pendulum." [1842] *The Complete Poems and Stories of Edgar Allan Poe.* Vol. 1, New York: Alfred A. Knopf, 1967. 435-445.

Punter, David. "The Uncanny." *The Routledge Companion to Gothic.* Eds. Catherine Spooner and Emma McEvoy. Oxon/New York: Routledge, 2007. 129-136.

Quéma, Anne. "The Gothic and the Fantastic in the Age of Digital Production." *ESC.* 30.4 (2004). 81-119.

Radcliffe, Ann. *The Castles of Athline and Dunbayne: A Highland Story.* [1789] Build-A-Book. A Celebration of Women Writers. Ed. Jamie Marchant. http://digital.library.upenn.edu [12. Dec. 2008].

Radcliffe, Ann. *The Romance of the Forest*. Ebooks. The University of Adelaide. http://etext.library.adelaide.edu.au/r/radcliffe/ann/forest/ [17. Mar. 2009].

Ramsey, Guthrie P. *Race Music: Black Cultures from Beebop to Hip-Hop*. Berkeley/Los Angeles: U of California P, 2003.

Rank, Otto. *The Double: A Psychoanalytic Study*. Chapel Hill: U of North Carolina P, 1971.

Raskauskiene, Audrone. "The Nightmare World of the Gothic Castle: The Interpretation of the Image of the Castle in Ann Radcliffe's (1764-1823) Fiction." *Literatura*. 2003. http://www.literature. http://www.literature.lt/TXT/E-203/raskauskiene.htm#_edn12 [12. Feb. 2007].

Ricoeur, Paul. *Freud and Philosophy: An Essay on Interpretation*. New Haven: Yale UP, 1970.

Rigney, Barbara Hill. *The Voices of Toni Morrison*. Columbus: Ohio State UP, 1991.

Rogers, Robert. *A Psychoanalytic Study of the Double in Literature*. Detroit: Wayne State UP, 1970.

Rotella, Carlo. *October Cities: The Redevelopment of Urban Literature*. Berkeley/Los Angeles/London: U of California P, 1998.

Royle, Nicolas. *The Uncanny*. Manchester: Manchester UP, 2003.

Rubinstein, Roberta. "Doubling, Intertextuality, and the Postmodern Uncanny: Paul Auster's New York Trilogy." *LIT*. 9 (1998). 245-262.

Ryan, Judylyn S., and Estella C. Májoza. "Jazz. . . On 'The Site of Memory.'" *Studies in the Literary Imagination*. 31.2. (1998). 125-152.

Said, Edward. "Reflections on Exile." *Reflections on Exile and Other Essays*. Ed. Edward Said. Cambridge, MA: Harvard UP, 2000. 173-186.

Savoy, Eric. "The Rise of American Gothic." *The Cambridge Companion to Gothic Fiction*. Ed. Jerrold E. Hogle. Cambridge: Cambridge UP, 2002. 167-188.

Scheerbart, Paul. "Glass Architecture." *Programs and Manifestoes on 20th-Century Architecture*. Ed. Ulrich Conrads. Cambridge: MIT Press, 1970. 32-33.

Schütz, Erhart. "Benjamin's Berlin: Wiedergewinnung des Entfernten." *Schrift, Bilder, Denken: Walter Benjamin und die Künste*. Frankfurt am Main: Suhrkamp, 2003. 32-47.

Scruggs, Charles. *Sweet Home: Invisible Cities in the Afro-American Novel*. Baltimore/London: The Johns Hopkins UP, 1993.

Sennett, Richard. *The Conscience of the Eye: The Design and Social Life of Cities*. New York/London: W.W. Norton, 1992.

Shelley, Mary. *Frankenstein*. [1818] Project Gutenberg. [online]. ftp://ftp.mirrorservice.org/sites/ftp.ibiblio.org/pub/docs/books/gutenberg/8/84/84-h/84-h.htm [30.Aug. 2010].

Simay, Philippe. "Tradition as Injunction: Benjamin and the Critique of Historicisms." *Walter Benjamin and History*. Ed. Andrew Benjamin. London/New York: Continuum, 2005. 137-155.

Simmel, Georg. "The Metropolis and Mental Life." *The City Cultures Reader*. Eds. Malcom Miles, Tim Hall, and Iain Borden. 2nd Ed. Routledge Urban Reader Series. London/New York: Routledge, 2004. 12-19.

Slethaug, Gordon E. *The Play of the Double in Postmodern American Fiction*. Carbondale: Southern Illinois UP, 1993.

Smethurst, Paul. *The Postmodern Chronotope: Reading Space and Time in Contemporary Fiction*. Amsterdam/Atlanta: Rodopi, 2000.

Smith, Hazel. "A Labyrinth of Endless Steps: Fiction Making, Interactive Narrativity, and The Poetics of Space in Paul Auster's City of Glass." *Australasian Journal of American Studies*. 21.2. (2002). 33-51.

Smith-Wright, Geraldine. "In Spite of the Klan: Ghosts in the Fiction of Black Woman Writers." *Haunting the House of Fiction. Feminist Perspectives on Ghost Stories by American Women*. Eds. Lynette Carpenter and Wendy Kolmar. Knoxville: U of Tennessee P, 1991. 142-165.

Soja, Edward. *Thirdspace: Journeys to Los Angeles and Other Real-And-Imagined Places*. Cambridge/Oxford: Blackwell, 1996.

Spiegelman, Art. "Picturing a Glassy-Eyed Private I." Introduction to City of Glass. Adaptation by Paul Karasik and David Mazzucchelli. New York: Picador, 2004. vi-x.

Spurr, David. "The Study of Space in Literature: Some Paradigms." *The Space of English*. Eds. David Spurr and Cornelia Tschichold. Tübingen: Gunter Narr Verlag, 2005. 15-34.

Stave, Shirley Ann. "*Jazz* and *Paradise*: Pivotal Moments in Black History." *The Cambridge Companion to Toni Morrison*. Ed. Justine Tally. Cambridge: Cambridge UP, 2007. 59-74.

Stephanson, Anders. "Regarding Postmodernism: A Conversation with Fredric Jameson." *Diacritics*. 12:3. (1982). 72-91.

Stephart, Katrin. *Gegenwartskonzepte*. Würzburg: Königshausen & Neumann, 2006.

Stein, Joanna S. "The Ambiguous Forest: Marvelous Landscapes in Ovid's *Metamorphoses* and Thomas Malory's *Le Morte Darthur*." Digital Commons Macalester College. 2006. http://digitalcommons.macalester.edu/cgi/viewcontent.cgi?article=1005&context=English_honors [29. Aug. 2010].

Stephens, Paul and Robert Hardwick Weston. "Free Time: Overwork as an Ontological Condition." *Social Text*. 94. 26.1. (2008). 137-164.

Tally, Justine. *The Story of Jazz: Toni Morrison's Dialogic Imagination*. Hamburg: LIT, 2001.

Tally, Justine. *Toni Morrison's Beloved: Origins*. New York/Oxon: Routledge, 2009.

Tatar, Maria. "The Houses of Fiction: Toward a Definition of the Uncanny." *Comparative Literature*. 33.2. (1981). 167-182.

Te Heesen, Antje. "The Notebook: A Paper-Technology." *Making Things Public: Atmospheres of Democracy*. Eds. Bruno Latour and Peter Weibel. Cambridge/London: MIT Press, 2005. 582-589.

Todorov, Tzvetan. *The Fantastic: A Structural Approach to a Literary Genre*. Ithaca: Cornell UP, 1973.

Toth, Jennifer. *The Mole People: Life in the Tunnels beneath New York City*. Chicago: Chicago Review Press, 1993.

Trigg, Dylan. *The Aesthetics of Decay: Nothingness, Nostalgia, and the Absence of Reason*. New York: Peter Lang, 2006.

Trigg, Dylan. "The Uncanny Space of Decay." *Psy-Geo Provflux* 1.1. Crosswalk. http://www.pipsworks.com/crosswalk/prov04/c1dylan.html [2. Apr. 2008].

Turner, Victor. "Liminality and Communitas." *The Ritual Process: Structure and Anti-Structure*. Chicago: Aldine, 1969. 95.

Van der Zee, James, Owen Dodson and Camille Billops. *The Harlem Book of the Dead*. New York: Morgan & Morgan, 1978.

Vidler, Anthony. "New Skins for a New Age: Glass Culture in the Work of Barkov Leibinger." *Barkov Leibinger Reflect*. Ed. Andres Lepik. Stuttgart: Hatje Cantz, 2007. 25-28.

Vidler, Anthony. *The Architectural Uncanny: Essays in the Modern Unhomely*. Cambridge/London: The MIT Press, 1992.

Vidler, Anthony. *Warped Space: Art, Architecture, and Anxiety in Modern Culture*. Cambridge/London: The MIT Press, 2000.

von Hoff, Dagmar and Marianne Leutzinger-Bohleber. "Travestie des Unheimlichen." *Orte des Unheimlichen: Die Faszination verborgenen Grauens in Literatur und Bildender Kunst*. Eds. Klaus Herding and Gerlinde Gehrig. Göttingen: Vandenhoek & Ruprecht, 2006. 95-115.

Walpole, Horace. *The Castle of Otranto*. [1764] New York: Holt, Rinehart and Winston, Inc., 1963.

Waugh, Patricia. *Metafiction: The Theory and Practice of Self-Conscious Fiction*. New York: Methuen, 1984.

Werth, Wolfgang. "Der Literarische Chiffonnier." *As Strange As The World: Annäherungen and das Werk des Erzählers und Filmemacher Paul Auster*. Eds. Andreas Lienkamp, Wolfgang Werth und Christian Berkemeier. Münster/Hamburg: LIT, 2002. 131-146.

Wilcots, Barbara J. "Toni Morrison's Folk Roots." *African American Review*. 26.4. (1992). 691-694.

Wilke, Helmut. *Heterotopia: Studien zur Krisis der Ordnung moderner Gesellschaften*. Frankfurt am Main: Suhrkamp, 2003.

Wolfreys, Julian. "The Urban Uncanny: The City, the Subject, and Ghostly Modernity." *Uncanny Modernity: Cultural Theories, Modern Anxieties*. Eds. Joe Collins and John Jervis. New York: Palgrave Macmillan. 2008. 168-181.

Wright, Richard. *Black Boy*. New York: Harper & Row, 1966.

Zinganel, Michael. *Real Crime: Architektur, Stadt und Verbrechen*. Vienna: Edition Selene, 2003.

Žižek, Slavoj. *Enjoy your Symptom!: Jacques Lacan in Hollywood and Out*. London: Routledge, 2001.

Zukin, Sharon. "Postmodern Urban Landscapes: Mapping Culture and Power." *Modernity and Identity*. Eds. Scott Lash and Jonathan Friedman. Oxford/Cambridge: Blackwell, 1992. 221-224.

Printed by Printforce, United Kingdom